John Ford

Books by Andrew Sinclair

Prohibition: The Era of Excess
The Emancipation of the American Woman
The Available Man: A Biography of Warren Gamaliel Harding
The Last of the Best: The Aristocracy of Europe
Che Guevara
Dylan Thomas: No Man More Magical
Jack: A Biography of Jack London

NOVELS
The Breaking of Bumbo
My Friend Judas
The Project
The Hallelujah Bum
The Raker
Gog
Magog

PLAYS AND SCREENPLAYS
Adventures in the Skin Trade (play)
Under Milk Wood (screenplay)

Andrew Sinclair

JOHN

FORD

London
George Allen & Unwin Ltd.
Boston   Sydney

First published in Great Britain 1979

George Allen Unwin Ltd.
40 Museum Street, London WC1A 1LU

Copyright © 1979 by Andrew Sinclair [Productions] Ltd.

British Library Cataloguing in Publication Data

Sinclair, Andrew

John Ford
1. Ford, John, B. 1895
I. Title
791.43'0233'0924 PN 1993.A3F/
ISBN 0-04-791038-0

Acknowledgments

On February 1, 1978, nearly five years after John Ford had died, John Wayne appeared at the front door of a house on Old Prospector Trail in Palm Desert, California. "My name is John Wayne," he told a nurse. "I came to visit Mary Ford on his birthday." He spent the day sitting by her bed, talking of the days they had known with her husband. "I just came to reminisce," Wayne said. "We don't have many to reminisce with any more."

That is the reason for the writing of this book. Some of the reminiscences need to be captured while there is still time. My debt is to all those people who have recorded their memories of John Ford, either to other writers or to myself. Whenever they talked of him, they kept him alive. He himself wrote very little— a working script has no more than "Why?" or occasionally "What?" scribbled in the margin. He put his messages into his talking pictures, his signs into all of his films. His memorabilia are in his house, where his wife and daughter are generosity itself to visiting pilgrims. What family papers exist are in the possession of his grandson, Daniel Ford, who will hopefully help to create one day a full Ford Archive that will honor the greatness of the man by making the papers accessible to all qualified researchers.

Since John Ford left so few records of his own outside his films, my gratitude goes to all those who have talked about him or written about him. Some of the people who have helped me the most with their words and concern were, in alphabetical order: James Agee, Lindsay Anderson, Eugene Archer, Mark Armistead, Jean-George Auriol, Michael Barkun, John Baxter, James Warner Bellah, Peter Bogdanovich, Ward Bond, Lucille Boston, George Bluestone, the editors of *Cahiers du Cinéma*, Ernest Callenbach, Frank Capra, Harry Carey, Jr., Olive Carey, John Carradine, Merian C. Cooper, William Corson, Vine Deloria, Jr., Mark Donskoi, Joanne Dru, Allan Dwan, Sergei Eisenstein, William K. Everson, Allan Eyles, Stepin Fetchit, Charles Fitzsimmons, Henry Fonda, Barbara and Daniel and Mary and Patrick and Timothy Ford, Robert Emmett Ginna, Jr., Roger Greenspun, Philippe Haudiquet, Howard Hawks, Nicola Hayden, Jim Heneghan, Katharine Hepburn, Winton Hoch, Penelope Houston, Brian Desmond Hurst, Lewis Jacobs, Ben Johnson, Nunnally Johnson, the Lord Killanin, Arthur Knight, Gavin Lambert, Anna Lee, Jay Leyda, Cynthia Lindsay, Milton Luboviski, Joseph McBride, Andrew and Victor McLaglen, Axel Madsen, Louis Marcorelles, Brick Marquard, Lee Marvin, Arthur C. Miller, Jean Mitry, Dudley Nichols, Frank Nugent, Darcy and George and Francis J. O'Brien, Maureen O'Hara, Robert Parrish, Bob Patton, J.A. Place, Cecil Maclean de Prida, Jean-Louis Rieupeyrout, David Robinson, Jean Roy, Robin Rue, Georges Sadoul, Andrew Sarris, Richard

Schickel, Leon Selditz, George Sidney, George Stevens, James Stewart, Woody
Strode, Jack and Patricia Swain, Roger Tailleur, Bob Thomas, Jon Tuska, King
Vidor, James Wade, Raoul Walsh, John Wayne, Orson Welles, Richard Widmark,
Michael Wilmington, Peter Wollen, Mr. and Mrs. Bob Wood, Robin Wood, Hank
Worden, Colin Young, Darryl Zanuck, and Maurice Zolotow.

Without these and many other recorders of John Ford no writer could attempt
to deal with the man, nor without the help of the Institut des Hautes Etudes
Cinématographiques in Paris, the British Film Institute in London, Lincoln Center in New York, and the American Film Institute in Beverly Hills. Truly, this is
a record of other people's work in the service of John Ford. Only the opinions
are my own.

ANDREW SINCLAIR
Los Angeles, 1976–1978

Table of Contents

To Mary Ford
For her grace and courage.

The truth about my life
is nobody's damn business
but my own.
—John Ford

John Ford

1: The Long Voyage Away

I come from a family of peasants. They came here and got an education.
They served this country well. I love America. I am not political.
—John Ford

From Galway and the Western Isles the way led across the ocean to the sunset. From the east and the sunrise, destruction had always come to Ireland—from the Vikings who had burned the great monasteries, from the Norman conquerors and the black troops of Cromwell, and finally from the Victorian landowners and administrators who thought a great hunger was the way to control a greater Irish population. Starving was their remedy for breeding too much.

Among the white crofts and green hills of western Ireland the potato had been a blessing and a curse, feeding the people until there were ten million of them on the whole island. Then the blight came in 1845, followed by the famine. During the next fifty-five years nearly five million men and women sailed across the Atlantic Ocean to a dream of plenty in North America. They felt not only a hunger for food, but for a respectable life in a new world, free from oppression.

In the village of Spiddal in Galway, John A. Feeney was born just after the time of the famine. Feeney was a Connacht name, spelt in Gaelic Ó Fiannaidhe or Ó Fianna, although the Galway Feeneys spelt it Ó Fidhne. The family lived by the estates of the Morrises, later given the title of the Lords Killanin. The Morrises were Irish and Catholic themselves, no invading conquerors from England; one of them was reared in the Feeney family as a foster child; and there were blood connections between the two families. Over the hill in the next village, the Currans lived. They had a daughter called Barbara, but it was a clannish society and the young people did not meet. To walk over the hill was half as far as crossing the Atlantic Ocean.

John was brought up to speak Gaelic and respect the Catholic Church and hate the British governors, who did not allow parochial schools in Galway. There might well be, after all, a link between education and later rebellion. So John remembered stealing out of the cottage at night to learn his lessons in the "hedge schools," where the priests educated the village boys in reading, writing, and the faith. The girls were not educated, since their job was to rule the home and listen to the priests and bear sons for Ireland at home and abroad. When Barbara Curran was sent by her family to America at the age of sixteen with her small sister, neither of them could read or write. Yet they could count and bargain, coming from a land where money was rarer than eggs.

The practice in the Galway villages was to save shilling after shilling until there was enough to send a younger son or daughter to America so that they could become rich there and bring over the rest of their brothers and sisters one by one. The old ones stayed on their little plots and tiny farms, and they planted the traditions and the hatreds in the children. In 1872 at sixteen years of age John himself was sent to Boston after the end of the Civil War. He was packed with the other human cattle belowdecks of one of the new Cunard steamships and was one of the lucky survivors of the long voyage away.

The journey was foul in the wooden stalls and stink of the steerage, and there were no jobs to be found in Boston; but there was a warmer welcome waiting in Portland, Maine, the nearest American port to Galway. To the young immigrant the three hundred and sixty-five islands in Casco Bay seemed as rocky and scattered as the Aran Islands he had left behind. And just beyond the wharves and long brick warehouses of the port, the Irish settlers had built a shanty village at Gorham's Corner. "With Bank, York, Fore and Danforth Streets acting as spokes, it could be likened to the hub of a great wheel painted by a crazy artist, who, in a spirit of mischief, had added Welch's Alley and Dumphy's Lane to give it that individual touch of two badly broken spokes."[1]

There the Irish stayed and worked on the docks or the railroads until the great fire that burned down most of Portland in 1866. Then they began to move up Munjoy Hill into the new clapboard and shingle-sided houses that sheltered under the shadow of the tall old tower known as the Portland Observatory. It stood six stories high on the peak of the hill with its widow's walk for the sailors' wives to look toward the bay and the ocean for a sight of their husbands' ships sailing home.

John A. Feeney soon found himself a job in the gas company, not on the railroads that had made Portland into a prosperous city. Before the end of the century two great stations were built to bring in the winter grain from Canada when the St. Lawrence River was frozen, and also the summer visitors from New York. These two terminals, the Grand Trunk Railroad and the Union Passenger stations, reared their brick spires as the twin cathedrals of Portland's prosperity, standing beside its deepwater bay on the trade routes between Europe and Canada and the Far West. John A. Feeney lived beside these railroads until he married Barbara Curran and settled on Munjoy Hill to raise a good American family near the three spires of the greatest brick cathedral of them all, the Church of the Immaculate Conception. He also meant to rise as the Irish had always risen in Portland, by imitating the Yankees who had arrived before them.

Rum was the secret of success in Maine society. The richer Yankees had made their money at the rum trade with the West Indies before becoming respectable and branching out into commerce and retailing, lumber and banking. The few old Irish settlers from the time of the Revolutionary War had done the same thing before they had acquired property, become respectable "lace curtain" Irish, and forgotten their saloonkeeping past. Now the new waves of Irish immigrants were coming to a place where the upcountry farmers with their cellars full of hard cider would vote against the wicked city saloons. Maine was the first state to enact a prohibition law in the middle of the nineteenth century—a law which was often repealed and often reenacted, but always more broken than observed.

John A. Feeney and his partners set themselves up in one or two saloons and restaurants, where the 3.2 percent legal beer was officially sold and the hard liquor was kept under the bar. The Feeney places in Fore and Center streets were as shuttered and dingy as the other Portland saloons, but that was because the dry laws could put them out of business. This usually happened when a Yankee Republican reformer wanted to rise to political power on a crusade against the demon rum and the Democratic party—very much an Irish preserve based on control of the police force and saloons in the city. "They were all part," one of the old Portlanders remembers, "of the same pack."[2]

The saloon was traditionally the center of politics for the Irish, who brought with them from their ancestral villages a talent for clandestine organization as well as a thirst for liquor. The Irish peasants proved to be brilliant American politicians and bureaucrats, with each city ward and its saloons arranged like an old country village run from its pubs. If the immigrant Irish now rejected the land for the city because the land had already rejected them, they still brought their folkways to the new business of urban living. They made the growing city slums tolerable with a new class of city bosses and ward heelers, who helped the poorer members of the community in return for their votes. "The Irish village was a place of stable, predictable social relations in which almost everyone had a role to play, and in which, on the whole, a person's position was likely to improve with time."[3] Transferred to Portland, this was the essence of Democratic politics.

So it was with John A. Feeney. He bought a house in Center Street and rose to a position of some power and influence in the city. Through his saloons and restaurants down in Gorham's Corner he became a ward politician, and his contacts helped his nephew Joseph Connally rise to be a justice in the state supreme court. He would always meet the young Irish boys arriving off the boats in the harbor. The very next day he would make them apply for citizenship. He needed their votes for his political influence, and in return he would find them jobs working for the city.

The Portland city directories show the Feeneys as part of the rising group of immigrants. In the seventeen years before 1915 the 39 listed working Feeneys increased in number by fifty percent and had left their shanty trades for lace-curtain professions. Half of the Feeneys were manual laborers in 1898, but only a fifth by 1915, while the number of Feeneys who were clerical workers had doubled. Like the rest of the Irish immigrants who had left the dockside slums to more recent arrivals—the Italians and the Jews and the Poles—the Feeneys were changing from manual to white-collar workers, "part and parcel of a very prosperous lower middle-class respectable Irish group in a very class-conscious city."[4]

Munjoy Hill itself was a mix of Irish and Yankees by the turn of the century, before the Italians began to move up from the downtown flats. If the Yankees resented the Irish invasion at first, it was only a matter of religion, Protestant against Catholic as in Ulster, not a matter of language or skin color. To become an American was the reasonable intent of every hard-working Irishman who had made the crossing and meant to stay.

Later, John A. Feeney's youngest son, who was to call himself John Ford, would tell a lot of tall stories about his Irish relations in America. He would say that his father and his four uncles all fought in the Civil War —three for the Union, one for the Confederacy, and one on both sides to get two pensions. In fact only one cousin Feeney is listed among the Union dead in the Portland cemeteries, and only one cousin Connally is known to have fought. John Ford would also say that the family frequently crossed over to Ireland because of the ease of getting on the regular boats sailing between Portland and Galway; but these were only dreams of the old land, to which his father never returned until he was an old man.

To the Irish who settled in Maine, Galway was a fond memory, a voyage of the mind that became more unreal with the passing years for a father and mother of American children. They would speak in Gaelic to be private in front of sons who could hardly understand them.

2: The Signs from the Observatory

I have kept from my childhood a liking for good people, simple people, people who go on doing their job in the middle of cheats and crooks. Sometimes I am blamed for being an idealist. I don't deny it.

—John Ford

John Augustine Feeney was born on February 1, 1895, in a farm house on Cape Elizabeth near Portland. He was the eleventh and last child of the family. The eldest, Mary Feeney, was nearly twenty years older than the new baby, who had three surviving brothers and two sisters. His five other brothers and sisters had died in infancy in that age of large families and poor hygiene when death was a frequent visitor to the cradle. Barbara, the mother of them all, did not go to a hospital to bear her many children. She bore them in the house, and if they survived their first few years and illnesses, they lived in the close, warm, tight Irish circle of those times, almost in a conspiracy of kin and faith against the prying and pressing outer Protestant world of the Cape.

The old wooden farmhouse was built in three joined sections for the expanding family and for the horses in the barn at the end. The surrounding one hundred and ninety acres of their pastures ran down to the river. It was a fine, strong country childhood for the small boy, romping with the animals in the grass or playing in the snow in the long winters. Although his father was rarely back home from his business in the city, he would take the family each year to his sister's summer house on Peak's Island, the nearest of the innumerable islands in Casco Bay, the first stop on the ferry from Custom House Pier. So the small boy grew up between grass and sea, happy as the day was long, waiting for his huge father's stories of swimming across Galway Bay or lifting up boulders on his back or stopping a runaway horse by yanking it to its knees. "I was born on a farm," the boy said later. "We weren't rich or really comfortable or well-to-do . . . I was pinching poverty while I was growing up."[1]

Times were good or bad for the Feeney family, depending on whether the prohibitionists were losing or winning. When the drys were losing, the saloons flourished, but when the dry law was passed again, the saloons went out of business. Before his youngest son was four years old John A. Feeney had to give up the farm; soon he no longer listed his trade in the Portland city directories as a saloonkeeper, but under the camouflage of "laborer." He even started a saloon in Portsmouth, New Hampshire, across the state line, to provide an income when Maine went dry. There the trains would make an unscheduled stop for the thirsty passengers on the way to Portland, where not a drop was to be found.

Out on Peak's Island every summer John A. Feeney would grow his rows of tomatoes and vegetables and flowers. His pride was in his garden, covered by rotting seaweed, the traditional fertilizer of Galway. His children were the spawn of the sea, going everywhere by rowboat or sailboat, swimming in the cold bay water until they were as hardy as otters. There was only one automobile on the whole island, a cab for those who brought over too much baggage on the ferry. It was the healthy strenuous life, beloved by President Theodore Roosevelt. The children would even hustle fifty cents a time for picking up and boiling alive dozens of lobsters for the squeamish Eastern visitors, who liked to eat well but preferred not to kill their own dinner personally.

The traditional Irish respect for the mother was early ingrained in the Feeney family. It was not so much a reverence for a madonna, an unapproachable Mother of God who was also a Virgin. (John Ford in his later films never showed that face in his Irish women, only in a Mexican woman in his overwrought film *The Fugitive*.) An Irish mother was held to be earthy enough, but the queen of her home ground. With a husband almost always out of the house in the city Mrs. Feeney ruled the roost. She was perpetual, the real source of discipline and authority.

Barbara Feeney herself was a small, soft-spoken woman with dark hair, dark eyes and a resolute mouth and chin. Her low voice was a command to her large sons. All her children did what she told them to do. They would hardly leave the house without asking her permission. She never shouted at them or lifted her hand to smack them. She governed through her quiet voice and absolute control of the family purse. She was the matriarch of Irish family pride.

Perhaps because he was the youngest and needed a special protector, John Augustine was the most religious of the four brothers. He seemed to love the drama and mystery of the Catholic Church, its towering buildings and unearthly power: at his confirmation, he took the middle name of Aloysius. He also loved the sea. "Ever since I was about four years old," he said later, "I owned a boat. Some old wreck came up, and we caulked it with tar and everything, and I took that, and as I got old, I got a different boat."[2]

The first surviving photograph of the child shows him in a sailor suit, prophesying a service to come. All the local boys dreamed of escaping to the ocean—the youngest Feeney, early known as "Johnnie," was no exception. He particularly loved the two huge three-masted yachts, one shining black and one shining white, which anchored in the bay every summer. One day he wanted to be as rich as J.P. Morgan and own one of these.

As for his education, his mother feared local bigotry too much to allow her adored youngest son to attend the single-room school by the farmhouse on the Cape. The teacher there seemed to pick on the elder Feeneys, and their playmates baited them for being Catholics and speaking the few words of Gaelic they had picked up from their parents. "We took it on the chin," one of them said. "Kids would run up and see if we had horns."[3] So, because of social conflict and bad times, the Feeney family gave up the farm and moved back to Gorham's Corner, where they bought a house at 48 Danforth Street. But the neighborhood was being flooded by the new immigrants from Europe, so John A. Feeney bought another large house on Monument Street. Unfortunately, he could never make his wife and family move there from the large apartment at 21/23 Sheridan Street on respectable Munjoy Hill, which they rented in 1903. Now little Johnnie Feeney could easily walk to the Emerson Grammar School just above the Eastern Promenade and later to Portland High School downtown past the Catholic cathedral and City Hall, set in the business district and the no man's land of the social conflicts of Maine.

From the top floor of the three-story house on Sheridan Street on the slope of Munjoy Hill, Johnnie Feeney could look out to the wharves and the bay. He could see a crack of blue between the harbor walls and the enclosing islands. If he climbed the hill and the stairs to the widow's walk at the top of the observatory tower, he could circle with his short-sighted stare the whole of his known city world. He could feel himself suspended in midair, as if hovering in one of the new airplanes that had begun to make a buzzing spot in the sky since the brothers Wright had first flown at Kitty Hawk.

Far below in the bay he could see the battle cruisers of Teddy Roosevelt's Great White Fleet when they came with outcurving bows and belching funnels into the harbor. Later he was to tell Cornelius Vanderbilt Whitney that he had spent much of his boyhood on that old wooden tower, gazing out to sea, or else going down to the Portland docks to watch real blue-water sailors.[4] So his passion began for ships and those who sailed in them. To him the era of naval power and ironclad dreadnoughts was a boyish vision from a high eyrie, a dream of battle in a roar of broadsides. He told himself that he would become an admiral and roam the high seas, not knowing that nearly fifty years later he would film from a helicopter the firing of the last broadside from one of the last American battleships, uselessly into Asia.

From the observatory he could feel almost surrounded by the sea with the cove behind him and Casco Bay ahead and only the brick-and-board tongue of Portland running toward the Western Promenade and the interior of the land. He was a lookout in his crow's nest, an Indian scout on a cliff watching the small and vain scurryings of the people beneath. Even the steam and sailing ships in the bay seemed tiny in the distance, the little works of men in the sweep of nature. The beer wagons below pulled by their drayhorses were toys from his height. The ocean and the mainland made human beings and their doings as insignificant as ants in the wilderness. The city itself seemed small in the space of the sea and the vanishing of the continent into the west.

There was the waiting, too. The boy knew that the circular walk behind the railings at the top of the old observatory was meant for sailors' wives, ever hoping that they were not widows now. He was used to the sea partings at the port, the men saying goodbye and not knowing how long their voyages would take, the women waiting daily for the return of the men who never seemed to come. The casting off of the ships in that port, the interminable expectation of their mooring marked the boy as his sensibility grew in the sights from the observatory and the docks.

The very vision of the boy was special. His eyesight was poor and he could merely see a blur without wearing thick spectacles. When he took them off, his view of the world was changed to blocks of color or the distinctions between light and dark. Only the movement of people or animals or machines would make a whisk of reference in his hazy universe. But the act of putting his thick lenses over his eyes would change the boy's perceptions into the definitions of the everyday world. So he could choose either way of sight and direct his eyes from the bright mist of partial blindness into the sharp clarity of normal vision. He would make his disability a special focus on what he wished to see.

There were other signals and images in Portland that informed the growing boy. He retained them, unconsciously storing them in his memory for translation into the visual myths of his later films. There were the two huge railroad stations from which the iron roads and iron horses left for the Far West. There were the fortress of the Armory with its massy defenses, and the bright American flags flying from the military camps and forts on the islands and the headlands. There was the dust of the unpaved streets swirling behind the new horseless fire engines that caused as many fires from their sparks as they put out—and fires were frequent enough, with even city hall burning down and the high school which the boy attended.

Above all, there was the ancient cemetery by the North School where two sea captains who had killed each other were buried side by side, British and American, to show the folly of war. And on the Western Promenade there was the old burying ground with its simple white tombstones leaning and fallen and inscribed with the memory-speaking names of those pioneers who had given up their lives to open the interior, the strong women who had raised their westering children and had died in the process:

MOTHER—FATHER

ARVILLA

ELIZA

HANNAH

PATIENCE

Rest in Peace

Only the restless eyes of the boy would move and look up Horseshoe Curve along the railroad to the White Mountains and the continent waiting to be crossed.

Another sight and sense became second nature to the boy—the sweep and roll of the sea. He would watch it from the wharves and the beaches as the waves swelled and broke and ebbed in their continuity, only to lounge forwards again. The vast rhythm of the ocean was imbued in the Portland boy, who loved messing about in small boats and took with him always a sea hunger, so that his instinct made him fit and edit all of the goings and happenings of mankind into that ceaseless flow and chop and sequence of the sea.

These were some of the escapes and private visions of a strong boy, who felt himself special as all boys do, but did not yet know the reason for it. First he had to get his formal schooling, although the Irish-Americans did not always put a high value on that. So he took the Peak's Island ferry or walked down Munjoy Hill to school. His classmates were the Yankees whose families could not afford to send them to private schools, and the other Irish children, and the recent immigrants from their ghettoes on the flats, Little Italy and Little Jerusalem and Little Poland. There were only twelve black families in the whole of that small conservative city of seventy thousand people, which was no quick melting pot given the general struggle of all to become good Americans at any cost.

In the fistfights at school the Jews would always side with the Irish. They would battle together against the Protestant attack from Bramhall Hill, even in one famous fight on St. Patrick's Day when the Yankee children produced an orange shamrock as a joke. Johnnie Feeney made the football team in Portland High School. He was known as "Bull Feeney" from his low, blind charges forward to block or tackle. With him in the team were mainly Irish boys, three Italians, and one Jew. These were the fighting children, determined to crash their way ahead. The Yankees felt less need to strive.

Johnnie Feeney graduated near the top of his English class and near the bottom of the others, although he did manage to pass Latin because of his love of the Mass. When a classmate asked him later why he had done so much in life with such bad grades in high school, he answered, "When I was in class, I knew how to listen."[5] One of his English teachers particularly fascinated him—Lucien Libby, who taught Chaucer and Shakespeare and who liked to play the country clown, mixing a love of the classics with practical jokes. He would pass nearly every pupil in his class and did not care if his duller students learned anything, mocking his own profession and saying, "Push a hokey-pokey cart and don't be a teacher." Yet this clowning was only a cover for his commitment to learning, and Johnnie Feeney would always revere him as the great instructor of his childhood, later putting some of Libby's wise comedy into the character of the young Abraham Lincoln and his name on the bow of a small boat in *They Were Expendable*.

Two of Johnnie's elder brothers, the silent giant Patrick and the wry, studious Edward, seemed to be settling down in Portland, but the third brother, Francis, had always been restless. He had run away to enlist in the Spanish-American War, and only his father's political influence had taken him out of the army in time to keep him from dying of cholera with the other recruits in Chickamauga camp in Tennessee. Then Francis had run away again, this time with the circus, before leaving that for the stage.

He was a young man of many talents who was bored by the idea of settling for one.

He had taken the name of Frank Ford. By family legend it was the name of the actor he had replaced as an understudy. But in fact Ford was the usual Americanization of Feeney—one of the more famous Irish-Americans of the time was Patrick Ford from Galway, the editor of the New York *Irish World* and a great supporter of Irish independence. If Frank Feeney felt the need to change his acting name from an Irish to an Anglo-Saxon one in order to aid the box office or to protect his family from being associated with strolling players, he was doing what most children of immigrants did to make themselves seem more American.

Frank Ford was lucky in time and place. There had already been a migration from the East to the West Coast by the new motion picture industry. This had started in the penny arcades of the eastern ports with little film clips shown as a novelty. The first significant short movies had come from France, the realism of the Lumières and magic tricks of Méliès. Logically, the movie industry should have grown up in the East, but the weather was fickle, early films needed strong regular lighting, rents were high, and there was all the sun and cheap land in the West that any new business could ask.

The first American story film had been a Western, Edwin S. Porter's *The Great Train Robbery* (1903). Although it had actually been shot for the Edison Company near the Lackawanna tracks in New Jersey, it was a visual dime novel about bandits like the James Brothers plundering the railroad that linked the continent. As trade follows the flag, so movies follow the location. Once Carl Laemmle, based in Chicago, had led the independent film distributors and producers in breaking Edison's attempted monopoly on all film production in America, the audiences of his Western arcade and cinema circuits demanded local themes.

In 1911, Vitagraph began the creation of a new movie capital in the sunny, cheap small town of Hollywood. It was near Mexico, in case the producers and actors and cameras had to disappear south of the border to escape an injunction; Edison was still suing his competitors for patent infringement. Soon afterwards D. W. Griffith set up his Fine Arts studios at the corner of Vermont and Sunset Boulevard. "I hope you'll all behave like ladies and gentlemen," he told his actors and technicians, "now that you've left the four-letter words and the tantrums back in New York." His people all applauded him, then left to raise hell with the locals.[6]

Mack Sennett soon followed Fine Arts with his Keystone Studios. Thomas Ince and Jesse Lasky came fast behind him. Studios sprouted like

barns in clover country. Frank Ford arrived to work as a stuntman and
actor in the early one-reel and two-reel films cranked out continuously
by the infant industry. He rapidly became a serial director and writer and
actor for Carl Laemmle's own production company at Universal Studios.
As a true Irish nepotist, he offered his little brother Johnnie, thirteen
years his junior, some work on the film sets. He could trust his own to
do their damnedest for him.

Movies had first come to Portland in 1908 at the Dreamland on Congress Street. "As a kid," Johnnie Feeney said later, "I was fascinated by
the nickelodeons of that period. Any time I got a nickel or a dime I would
go to the movies."⁷ He would also go to the new Keith's Theater, where
he was a regular visitor to the best vaudeville east of Boston. Out on
Peak's Island he became an usher at the Gem Theater, with its white and
gold foyer and its drop curtain ornamented with anchors and capstans
and fishing nets. The program on stage changed weekly for the summer
visitors, and the young usher developed a gift for mimicry, playing
through all the parts of the actors for his family on weekends. The stage
seemed to be in his blood by the time an opportunity came to change his
life. On screen in the Dreamland he saw Frank Ford starring in a Hollywood serial, and then he was summoned west to aid his brother.

The sacrifice was his higher education. He was good at composition
and grammar and had excelled in English, graduating from high school
in June 1914. He had then been accepted by the University of Maine on
an athletic scholarship. But after a few days on campus Hollywood proved
to be too strong a lure. He took the train across America to work for his
brother as a laborer and third assistant propman. He was excited by the
new medium, determined to excel in what his brother did well. He also
took the name of Ford to identify himself with Frank, and he was soon
called Jack Ford in the easy acceptance of the film set.

Once Frank returned to Maine to make a film with Dorothy Dalton
around Portland. One of Jack Ford's contemporaries remembers Frank
directing his other brother Patrick, who had to push Miss Dalton off the
shore in a punt, then clamber in beside her and row away. He did so, but
he never went to Hollywood like his youngest brother. He preferred
being a fish broker on the Portland docks.

Only one event would have brought Jack Ford back to Portland, and
that was combat. If his new passion was making films, his old passion was
the sea and the navy. He had wanted to enter the Naval Academy at
Annapolis, but he had not been accepted. When Woodrow Wilson took
the United States into the First World War, Jack Ford volunteered for

naval duty. His bad eyesight caused his rejection. Yet he could not accept his disability and would not take no for an answer. He had learned how to operate a camera by this time, and he applied to be a photographer in the new Naval Flying Corps. Aerial surveillance was in its infancy. He could now be a watcher from the winged observatories of the skies.

His patriotic father immediately began pulling strings on behalf of his youngest son. Many senior officials near the Secretary of the Navy happened to come from Portland, and old John A. Feeney knew how to reach them. But the mills of Washington ground so slow that Jack Ford's application to join the Naval Flying Corps was not approved until just before the Armistice of 1918. It was not yet his time to serve.

His niece remembers the effect of the war on Portland, the three forts and training camps in Casco Bay filled with soldiers waiting to be shipped over to France. In the winters the Canadian troops would march through from the railroad station to the port, with the Black Watch filing past to the skirling of the bagpipes, their kilts swinging in the cold wind. When the Black Watch came home, they came back as if in a later John Ford film, stricken in their victory, vainly decimated in the mud of the trenches, a handful of shattered men where once a regiment had marched out gaily to battle.

John Augustine Feeney, now Jack Ford, had not gone to war, but he had seen and heard of those who had gone to war. He had grown up with three passions and had been given one extraordinary opportunity. He loved the sea and Irish Catholicism and the great West of the American continent. He was a tough, ambitious, clever young man at the birth of a new art and industry. He had escaped from the restrictions of a narrow and proud upbringing. "I can't imagine there was much growth in Jack Ford's general outlook," one of his Irish friends said, "until he *left* Portland."[8] If he was shaped by his Irish immigrant heritage, he needed a new and growing culture for his development.

What was valuable to him in his legacy were the signals and pictures of his boyhood, always present in his mind along with the myths and stories of old Ireland and the settling of a new continent. As Portland was a conduit between the United States and the American interior, so Jack Ford was to be a carrier to California of the old ways and faiths whose westering was not yet done, and a carrier to the world at large of the history of a great country whose face was hardly yet seen.

3: Straight Shooting

In the East, they think what I show is false, but I want to show them what happened. That's the way it was. I'm interested by the folklore of the West . . . showing what really happened, almost a documentary.

—John Ford

"How did I get to Hollywood?" Jack Ford was asked later, and he answered, "By train."[1] The rear observation car was the moving platform from which the traveler in 1914 first saw the cities and plains and mountains and deserts of the American continent. Behind the car the twin iron tracks ruled their parallel lines across the grid-pattern fields of the prairies, an enduring monument to the tens of thousands of Irish laborers who had constructed the transcontinental railroad. The farmhouses and water tanks, the halts and the large stations passed by from Chicago to Council Bluffs to Cheyenne to San Francisco. So for the first time Jack Ford viewed his beloved country as a moving picture that took a week to unreel between Maine and California.

The Wild West of cowboy and stagecoach had already been gone for thirty years, and only its legend remained. The last great cattle drives of 300,000 longhorns from Texas to the railhead at Dodge City, Kansas, had taken place in 1885, before barbed wire and blizzards and drought had ended the prosperity of the early ranches and the sheepmen and the homesteaders had fenced in the trails and the plains. The railroads had bound the United States from north to south and east to west like a package in baling wire, and they had driven out the Pony Express and the Concord stagecoach celebrated by the dime novels, the mustang and the covered wagon. The heroes and villains of the continental crossing by the pioneers had become vaudeville artists and showmen— Buffalo Bill Cody had turned the West into a traveling circus, while even Geronimo sold photographs of himself, staring into camera with his rifle, for two bits each to tourists at the St. Louis World's Fair.

The frontier had officially ended a quarter of a century before Jack Ford reached Hollywood. Wyatt Earp was living in Pasadena, an old retired marshal whose bones were frailer than the legend of his killings. Unemployed cowboys were drifting over the Rockies to stand outside the casting offices, "shitkickers" stabbing the dirt with the points of their boots while waiting for work. They would do stunts with horses and steers as in rodeos, performing for the camera eye just as they did for country crowds.

Ever since *The Great Train Robbery* had proved that millions of people would pay to see the bandits of the American badlands, the Western movie had become a staple of the new film industry pushing up in the little studios and dry gulches and wagon cuts near Hollywood. After the Wild West roadshow and the dime novel, the one-reel and two-reel films in the new nickelodeons provided the next stage in the growth of the Western myth. "Every kid is in love with the West, you know," Ford used to say later. "In those days I read novels about the West. And movies came along."[2]

The young Ford "arrived penniless, as the expression goes." He soon found a Nebraska cowboy, Edmund "Hoot" Gibson, to be his roommate in the small town where he had come to work for his brother. Hollywood Boulevard was then called Peppertree Lane because of the great trees that arched over the dusty road and dropped their leaves on the boardwalks in front of the few stores and lunchrooms like the Oasis, where those who were working in the movies would pick up the check for those who were waiting to work, and all expected to make it tomorrow in the boomtown of the new frontier of illusion.

Jack Ford and Hoot Gibson both worked as stuntmen, catching speeding trains on horseback, jumping in the saddle off cliffs, canoeing down rapids, and doing whatever the director asked them to do. As Frank Ford was making serials for "Uncle Carl" Laemmle at Universal Studios, his young brother usually had a job. There was some antagonism between the two brothers. The screenwriter Frank S. Nugent used to tell stories about Jack being blown up by Frank Ford, who once had a cannon ball fired at his kid brother as he was sitting at a desk full of dynamite. In another sequence in Frank's serials Jack had to dive seventy-five feet off the roof of a freightcar rolling over a trestle bridge—Jack spoiled the shot by blessing himself before he jumped. He was also blown out of an automobile speeding along a mined road, and so broke his arm.

The high point of fraternal persecution was reached when Jack was doubling for Frank, wearing a Confederate uniform and "dodging shot and shell on a hell's half-acre battleground. Frank was pitching the powder bombs." He saved the last one for a close shot and bounced it off his young brother's head so that it exploded just below his chin. "That was a close thing," Frank told Jack when his brother woke up in hospital. "Another second and audiences would have realized I was using a double."[3]

Perhaps Frank Ford already recognized in young Jack his replacement and nemesis. If he taught his brother a craft, he also picked on him unmercifully. Yet Jack could also take a risk and play a practical joke. His first year as a prop boy ended in a blaze of glory. In a circus sequence he filled the red fire-buckets with gasoline. When these were used to put out the flaming bigtop, the whole tent exploded into an inferno. It was dangerous and expensive, but excellent cinema. Laemmle did not fire Jack but promoted him to assistant director.

Soon after his rise at Universal another opportunity came to the young Jack in the happy-go-lucky free-for-all of early Hollywood. There was a party on the set for Laemmle, with Jack as the bartender. As a result he slept under the bar and was ready to start work next morning when the director and the main actors were still sleeping off their hangovers. As Laemmle was arriving, the young assistant had to improvise an action sequence to cover up for the absence of the principals—cowboys falling off their horses in squads and the whole false front of the western town burning down, "more like a pogrom than a Western."[4] Laemmle remembered the hurlyburly and the young man shouting orders. So Jack Ford got the job of directing the rising star Harry Carey in *The Soul Herder* in 1917 because Laemmle thought "he yells real loud. He'd make a good director."[5]

Ford always considered this the first of the pictures under his control, although he had already directed himself as a stuntman in two two-reelers as a rough rider and a scrapper. He went on working with Harry Carey in a series of Westerns, developing his own style in concert with his star. He did not escape the influence of D. W. Griffith and *The Birth of a Nation* —Ford later claimed to have been one of the Ku Klux Klansmen charging to the girl's rescue in their white costumes, "the one with the *glasses.*" What with the slipping hood and his poor sight blinding him, he was knocked off his horse by a low branch and woke on the ground to find Griffith offering him a drink from a silver flask and saying, "Are you all right, son?" while several hundred extras watched his downfall.

Later, Ford always gave Griffith the credit for inventing the grammar of the American cinema. "I wouldn't say we stole from him," he told one interviewer. "I'd say we copied from him outright." Both directors used to present their films from the point of view of the ordinary pioneer or soldier, and both used to concentrate on showing the small memorable bits and pieces of war or love or personal character. "D.W. was the only one then," Ford said, "who took the time for little details."[6]

When he himself was winning awards for his films, Ford once had to make a speech, lifted his eyes to heaven, and only said, "Thank you, D.W." It was a fair tribute to the man who changed the early one-reelers into the long feature film in America. "He pushed the business ahead about twenty years," Ford said of him. "Like living in the Dark Ages and suddenly emerging into the light."[7]

Yet as a young director Ford was also adding to Griffith's influence an enormous gusto and enthusiasm and feel for a man in action at his proper work. He showed his star Harry Carey as a cowboy on the range, not as a melodramatic and pasty-faced figurehead like William S. Hart, but as a "sort of a bum, a saddle tramp, instead of a great bold gun-fighting hero."[8]

In this way Ford stitched an Irish realism into the embroidery of the past. However sentimental he may have been, he became a popular artist because of his earthy and comic love of naturalism. The cowboy may have already become in the mass mind the romantic hero described by Walter Prescott Webb, the historian of the Great Plains:

> He lives on horseback as do the Bedouins; he fights on horseback, as did the knights of chivalry; he goes armed with a strange new weapon which he uses ambidextrously and precisely; he swears like a trooper, drinks like a fish, wears clothes like an actor, and fights like a devil. He is gracious to ladies, reserved toward strangers, generous to his friends, and brutal to his enemies. He is a cowboy, a typical Westerner.[9]

Yet Ford's genius lay in making this stereotype into an archetype by showing Harry Carey dirt poor and damn proud in the harsh beauty of his natural setting. In the twenty-six movies Carey did for Ford he usually wore an old blue shirt and vest, patched overalls, and a borrowed cowboy hat. The grandeur lay in his will to survive amid the traps of men and the landscape, the one determined movement of the hero in defiance of the vast display of an indifferent world. Later Ford would admit that he had learned how to make pictures "from Harry Carey mostly. He was actually my tutor."[10]

According to his roommate Hoot Gibson, Jack Ford was "a natural. Only twenty-one, and already close to a genius. He'd make up bits off the cuff, shoot them on the wing as he went along, then afterwards scribble them into the script." He relied on his instinct for form and his talent for observing and mimicry. His temper, though, was already fearsome. "He was worse Irish than me," Gibson recalled.[11] Ford once broke a piano stool on his head because Gibson played "Dardanella" on a player piano morning, noon, and night; but he did help his friend's career by making him double for Harry Carey as a stuntman and then play second lead to the star in Ford's first five-reel feature in 1917, *Straight Shooting.*

The plot of the film was taken from a true western theme, the range war between the ranchers and the farmers. Ford's sympathy lay with those who planted the land like the Irish did. As the outlaw hero, Harry Carey switches sides to become the champion of the tillers of the soil. The plot is mawkish, but the iconography and rhythm of Ford's later films are already nascent. His view from the observatory and the railroad car is shown by two horse guards standing on each side of a cutting—the symbol of the divided range—while below them the outlaws strike and ride to their hideout, the only free men in this war of property rights.

Ford also uses other characteristic devices—door frames to lessen the size of the screen and to pick out an approaching figure, broad comic sequences when the hero and villain get drunk together and become incapable of shooting it out, and moments of pathos, when Harry Carey holds his elbow or his horse's tail to show his sense of loss, and again when Molly Malone hugs her dead brother's dinner plate to her breast in her grief. The climactic gun battle in the western street between Carey and Vester Pegg is a blueprint for that encounter, with its reaction shots of the frightened onlookers and with matching shots of hero and villain advancing toward each other in quickening tempo until the final shot of both together as they fire and the villain falls. If Ford did not invent the shoot-out, he filmed it in a classic way, from the eye level of a witness or the rare, special view of a sentinel or a spy.

There were no easy tricks in the Westerns of that time. Ford would tell of hiring old lawmen like Pardner Jones who would actually shoot the glass out of an actor's hand with his rifle if the script called for it. "They would suggest a lot of things," he said. "We were a very close group."[12] In those days the gap between reality and illusion was small. There simply was no time to rehearse or falsify when the shooting schedule for each reel was three days at the most. For that people's cinema of early Hollywood, the rough and ready was the rule.

If the film was not being shot on the Universal back lot, Ford would ride out with the stars and the cowboys and the technicians to the location and work from dawn to sundown, camping out and spending the night in a sleeping bag. He could not even see what they had shot because the daily rushes were shown in negative. The film technicians and actors did all they could in the time they had for the money they were given— thirty-five to seventy-five dollars a week in the case of Ford. Later he would say that he would not have gone into the film business if he had not been hungry. What he did not say was that his urge to emulate and surpass his elder brother Frank drove him to do better.

But then the Irishman and the westerner have a gift for hiding their motives and exaggerating their exploits. Half the pleasure in a frontier story is in debunking and the other half is in boasting. Ford would always obscure the fact that he cared about making movies and deny that he was an artist. He would protest that he liked stuntmen and money. So he protected his art by disclaiming it and preferred to be a man among men as long as he could command them.

By 1920 Ford had directed twenty-nine features for Universal, all but three of them Westerns, in less than four years. They had the usual flaming titles of the flapper era, such as *The Phantom Riders, Wild Women,* and *Hell Bent.* None of the prints of these features seem to survive. Such reviews as there were of them spoke of Ford's knack "for getting all outdoors into the scenes" and of his gift for action sequences.[13] The plots of only two of the films bear analysis, Bret Harte's story *The Outcasts of Poker Flat* and *Marked Men,* originally called *The Three Godfathers,* which Harry Carey had already made three years before with another director.

The Harte story was Ford's first literary film. It was self-conscious, opening and concluding with Carey reading Harte's story out of a book. If it was the first Ford film to be praised by serious critics, it was not his favorite among his early efforts. That was *Marked Men,* a film about a trio of desperados who break jail, commit a robbery, come upon a dying mother and her baby in the Mojave Desert, and all die but one in an attempt to save the child. In its mixture of male comradeship and hostility and reverence for motherhood and struggle against thirst and barren land, Ford found many of his obsessive themes were united. It also told again in Western terms the story of the three Magi who came to the Christ Child at Bethlehem.

Later, Ford himself was perceptive and humorous about his early Westerns. He liked the fact that Harry Carey and Hoot Gibson and Tom Mix were real men of the West who usually did their own stunts. But he admitted that they made a mistake in making heroes out of vicious and brutal bandits like Billy the Kid. Many of the sheriffs, however, who brought law and order to the West were reformed outlaws like Wyatt Earp. Their past reputations helped them to instil respect without having to draw their guns. Their stare was enough to keep the peace. And, according to Ford, they were lucky in their technology. The Colt revolver was most inaccurate in most hands. Pardner Jones told Ford that if Wild Bill Hickock had been given a six-shooter and put with Jones in a barn, he would not have even hit the walls with a single shot.

Ford also saw the true value of the simplicity of his early Westerns. Because they were silent films, dependent entirely on their action, shot in one take, spontaneous and unrehearsed, the cowboy stars like Harry Carey could play naturally in a style that only became "modern" after another forty years. The horse wranglers in these improvised Westerns gave a more realistic performance than the theatrical *jeunes premières* in the studio melodramas. Ford always found it remarkable that the first film critics used to prefer those who overacted as if they were on stage to those who did what they knew how to do in front of the camera.[14]

At the birth of the film industry Jack Ford had become an experienced director by the age of twenty-five. He worked most of the time and learned on the job. He built up a team of actors and technicians under studio contract, led by Harry Carey. He formed habits of work that served him well all his life—a speed and economy of shooting, a loyalty to his friends that never spared their shortcomings, a willingness to try anything physically to get a good shot, a dislike of shooting in a studio if he could get it into a natural setting, and the assurance that is given by knowing a craft so well that personal obsessions and myths can slip into it as easily as bullets into the chamber of a Colt revolver.

4:   Directed by John Ford

I like fresh air, the wide open spaces, the mountains, the desert. . . . Sex,
obscenity and degeneration don't interest me.
—John Ford

Making movies was not yet socially acceptable in Los Angeles. Hollywood
itself was still isolated from the city and Beverly Hills by orange groves
and market gardens leased to Japanese immigrants. Actors and film technicians were not encouraged as tenants. As Stepin Fetchit said, in those
days "Hollywood was more segregated than Georgia under the skin."[1]
Some signs outside the lodging-houses read: DOGS AND MOVIE ACTORS NOT
ALLOWED, giving film people second billing to animals. The old Protestant
land-grant families of Pasadena, the Catholic Angelenos such as the Do-
minguez and Sepulveda families, the newly-rich oil barons like the Dohe-
nys and the Chandlers, and the California-born settlers did not welcome
the sudden incursion of Jewish garment manufacturers become movie
producers, of western stuntmen and eastern actors and star-struck ste-
nographers from the prairies looking for glamor. Private clubs and land-
lords tried to exclude the new film colony, which rapidly developed its
own camaraderie and outrageous taste in defiance of convention.

Social life in early Hollywood depended on Miss Mira Hershey and the
old-fashioned Hollywood Hotel. Only handsome, attentive young men
and the new film stars were allowed to stay in the hotel—the Talmadge
sisters and Mary Pickford, Mary Miles Minter and Shirley Mason and
Buster Keaton. Miss Hershey would sit on the hotel porch with the stars'
parents and acknowledge the homage of the passers-by in the street. The
dance on Thursday nights at the hotel was the social occasion of the week.
There Jack Ford met Mary McBryde Smith on St. Patrick's Day in 1920;
he married her three months later.

His wife was a Scots-Irish Presbyterian from North Carolina, a beautiful dark-haired young woman with a slender body and large brown eyes. She was proud of her connections and ancestors. Through the Roper family she was related to Sir Thomas More, and her kinship to a Catholic martyr did something to make her mother-in-law Barbara Feeney forgive her son for marrying a heretic who had to be converted to the true faith.

As a girl, Mary McBryde Smith had been trained as a nurse through the influence of her uncle, Surgeon General Rupert Blue. She had then spent nine months at Annapolis because another uncle was Victor Blue, an admiral and Chief of Naval Operations. There she had been courted by many of the future officers in the United States Navy, who were training at the Naval Academy. She had become interested in mental illness before she had gone out to Los Angeles to look after a sick aunt. A cut above the Feeneys in background and connections, Mary Ford was to prove the catalyst and the inspiration for Ford's other career as a secret intelligence agent and a combat naval officer.

"The navy was Jack's heart and soul," Mary Ford always said. "He was never the least bit in awe of them, that's why he did so well." In her recollection he was wearing a naval uniform when she met him in her nurse's uniform. Very possibly, he had already joined the Naval Reserve as a result of his previous application to become a cameraman in the navy's new aerial reconnaissance arm. If he had done this, he may have been asked to go underground for security reasons. He was certainly better as an agent for the navy in his film director's clothes than in a sailor suit.

Initially, however, the newly married Fords had to find a house. They chose to buy a small gray home at 6860 Odin Street on the side of the hill, the back of which later became the Hollywood Bowl. The house was stone-built in the English style with leaded windows. "Every time Jack made a picture," Mary Ford remembered, "we'd knock out a wall and build another room. Every dream we had was in it." The music from concerts would float over the four acres of their wild garden, where Jack would give his famous Sunday parties for his Hollywood friends.

At first the young and sheltered Mary Ford found Hollywood society outrageous. "It was bad, bad taste—I wasn't used to that stuff." Prohibition had made drinking a compulsive show of defiance, while the high salaries of the stars at a time of low taxes had encouraged their flamboyance and wastefulness. Mary remembered her husband's friends as the most beautiful and generous people in the world, who had not even graduated from high school. "People dressed to the teeth to go out. Such bad taste, but such fun—no weeping and wailing for tomorrow." Not until the talkies came would a film star need to have an educated voice.

As a wedding present the director Allan Dwan gave the Fords a keg of bonded whiskey, which was a treasure trove in that first year of Prohibition. On Sundays, after the Fords had been to early mass at the little Church of the Blessed Sacrament on Cherokee, the cowboys would come to drink at the gray house on the hill—Harry Carey and Hoot Gibson, Buck Jones and the great Tom Mix, who became a special friend of the family. Mix always drank too much of what he called "loganberry juice," shot up ceilings and chandeliers with his pistols, and lavished his money on his women and his friends. Once he gave the wife he was thinking of leaving a pearl-handled revolver wrapped in a check for $125,000; but to his friends, he gave all he had. "We had more fun with Tom's money," Mary Ford remembered, "than anyone in the history of the world."

Mix only went out to the Ford parties because they had their own little clique. Ford liked the stuntmen and the cowboys. "Get a bunch of cowboys," he once said, "and they're very tractable, very easy to work with, very easy to live with."[2] He also liked the flying aces and the sailors and the comics. W. C. Fields came once, protesting at the fifty-three steps leading up to the front entrance to the house. So he was sent to drive round the crooked back way. "I won't break a leg," he complained. "I'll just break my neck."

The heavyweight champion of the world and conqueror of John L. Sullivan, "Gentleman Jim" Corbett, actually made a film with Jack Ford in 1920 called *The Prince of Avenue A.* By the time Ford's two children were born, a son, Patrick, in 1921 and a daughter, Barbara, late the following year, their proud father would line them up to shake Corbett's hand with the words, "You'll be able to say that you shook the hand of the hand that shook the world."

Escaping from his religious wife at Pasadena, Wyatt Earp would sneak in to drink with Ford's cowboys. Ford would later claim that he heard the details of *My Darling Clementine* straight from Earp's mouth. "He told me the story of the fight at the O.K. Corral. And that was exactly the way it was done, except that Doc Holliday was not killed."[3] So Ford himself was just in time to become an ear-witness of one of the classic showdowns of the Old West.

Occasionally the studio chiefs came to the Fords' house on Sundays, particularly Irving Thalberg, who had stood up with them at their wedding. To Mary Ford the friendship between the Catholics and the Jews in Hollywood was a natural thing—both groups had a strong sense of family, both were generous to a fault, and both stood united against old

American Protestant condescension and exclusion. "The Irish and the Jews got along together," she said. "They gave first and investigated later. If we got in a hole, they helped us out. If they got in a hole, we helped them."

Yet in early Hollywood most films still reflected the prevailing mass American taste, not the taste or the origins of many of the film producers and film-makers. If history was treated, it was not done in the style of *The Birth of a Nation,* but as *Graustark,* with Norma Talmadge playing the beautiful Princess Yetive, or Douglas Fairbanks playing Robin Hood with a gay quickstep among his merry men. The usual staple short features emphasized American rural humor, the badmen of the West, or morality plays about the false glitter of the cities. Their habitual plots showed country innocents confounding wicked urban materialism. The small town was still pictured as the source of merit and wisdom, while the city was the cesspit of decadence and evil. Virtue washed well in the swimming-hole and drowned in the marble bathtub.

Jack Ford followed the taste of the times by leaving Universal to make two comedies for the Fox Film Corporation, *Just Pals* and *The Big Punch,* starring Buck Jones. The slouching Jones's cracker-barrel philosophy and sloth as he played a loafer in the first film reminded Jack of his favorite high-school teacher, Lucien Libby. *Just Pals* combined relaxed humor—just *watching* others work made Buck Jones tired—with Ford's talent for action sequences in a pleasant blend of small-town fun and western derring-do. *The Big Punch* was more melodramatic, but again in tune with the temper of the American people, who in 1920 had elected a small-town Ohio President to bloviate in the White House and restore normalcy after the First World War. In that second melodrama Buck Jones was framed and had to break out of jail to become a Salvation Army officer and convert a jeering small town to goodness.

After these two exercises in American morality and folk humor Ford returned to Universal to make five more Westerns, three with Harry Carey and two with Hoot Gibson—his elder brother Frank even played under his direction in *Action.* Except for some good night and seasonal photography in his last Carey film for Universal, *Desperate Trails,* Ford seems to have felt trapped in cranking out short Westerns for Laemmle and Thalberg, who did not even renew Carey's contract with the studio. He bequeathed the deadpan comic Hoot Gibson to Universal as their new cowboy star, also a tradition of shooting action sequences without any rehearsal—they cost less and looked spontaneous.

Ford now signed a long term contract with William Fox. He began by making a melodrama with Shirley Mason called *Jackie* about a Russian refugee who wanted to become a great dancer. Then Ford mysteriously disappeared, leaving his Hollywood contract and his new family for six months in pursuit of Irish freedom.

In the summer of 1921 the Sinn Fein and the Irish Republican Army were fighting the British Army and the paramilitary Black and Tans. Jack Ford ignored the fact that his wife was nursing his baby son. Trusting to his neighbors to feed his family in his absence, he took the train to Maine to see his parents. He told them he must go to Galway and help in Ireland's final struggle for independence. His father and mother supported his decision. He took the boat to Galway and tried to contact his cousins, the Thorntons. Their family house had been burned down by the Black and Tans as a reprisal while one of their boys was fighting for independence in the hills.[4]

Ford himself could not join the Sinn Fein or the Irish Republican Army. From the moment he arrived in Ireland for the first time he was a marked man, large and American and suspicious. British spies followed him wherever he went, and his baggage was searched at his hotel. He could not be arrested, as he carried an American passport and the British authorities did not want an international incident featuring a Hollywood director —it is the American passport which saves the substitute condemned prisoner in the last episode of a later Ford film trilogy, *The Rising of the Moon.*

When Ford returned to his ancestral village in Galway, he was as conspicuous as John Wayne would be in *The Quiet Man* (wickedly named Sean Thornton). Ford was almost an expected figure in the eyes of Spiddal—the alien and wealthy American come home to search for nostalgic roots that he had never known except by hearsay. Ford met some of his Feeney relations in their small whitewashed cottages in the green fields. He soaked in their sense of past injustice and present struggle. Then he traveled on to Dublin and saw something of the fighting there. Forty-three years later, while staying at the Shelburne Hotel and preparing *Young Cassidy,* he could identify the room in which two British intelligence officers had been assassinated and say, "That's where *we* killed them."[5] He wanted it known that he was on the rebel side.

Most likely, Ford was not allowed to pick up a gun in Ireland. His identification with the freedom fighters made him refer to himself as one of them. In fact they may have sent him back to America to get what they most needed, money to continue the struggle. Also the Irish Free State was granted a form of independence in 1922 by the British government, and Ford found his Irish friends falling into a fratricidal war between the hard-line Irish Republican Army which Ford supported and those politicians like Michael Collins who had accepted the partition of Ireland into the Free State and Northern Ireland for the sake of peace.

Ford returned home to find a pile of debts, a career in a state of suspense, and an angry wife, tired of being deserted. She had even had to hide their car to keep it from being repossessed. She raged at her husband, who had expected his wife to wait while he went to war, then she resigned herself to his taciturnity. "I never asked him about it," she said later. "It was a sore subject, very secret, and I didn't know the difference between the IRA and my ABC."

Certainly, Ford became an occasional contributor and collector of IRA funds during its continuing fight against British control of Northern Ireland. Yet he hardly ever hinted at his role. He showed a full Irish penchant for secrecy and clandestine operation. He may have gone to Ireland to report on the war there for American naval intelligence as well as to help in the struggle himself. But outside tall stories of his exploits told in Spiddal bars he himself spoke to no witness of what he had exactly done or was doing for the freedom of Ireland. Conspiracy was a habit with him.

Cash for his own needs was Ford's immediate necessity. He returned to directing melodramas and rural comedies for Fox: *Little Miss Smiles* with Shirley Mason (actually a ghetto story about a Jewish family in New York); *The Village Blacksmith;* the classic Prohibition tearjerker, *The Face on the Barroom Floor;* and *Three Jumps Ahead,* Ford's first film with Tom Mix. In 1923 he made *Cameo Kirby* with John Gilbert, a remake of a previous Cecil B. De Mille version and of his own *Hitchin' Posts.* Although the natural beauty of the shots of the American South in *Cameo Kirby* is extraordinary—the tall waving grasses in a horseback chase and a gun duel, the belching fire and smoke of the stacks of the massed paddlewheel riverboats in a race on the Mississippi—Ford only achieved a wooden performance from his leading man, whose good looks might have been carved onto his set face. Yet at least Ford found the picture good enough to make his credit title "Directed by John Ford" instead of the usual "Jack."

Two other minor pictures for Fox followed, *Hoodman Blind* and *North of Hudson Bay,* with Tom Mix dismounted and staggering through the white northern wastes in snowshoes, looking out of place in a murder story as bleak as any of Jack London's Alaskan tales. Then changes in Hollywood renewed Ford's options. The success at the box office of *The Birth of a Nation* had already begun the process of replacing the slaphappy two-reelers by an occasional long epic feature, which demanded careful planning and an increased investment. So the structure of film-making began to solidify, threatening the free-wheeling pioneer directors like Ford. Hollywood was becoming an industry rather than an anarchy, a matter of accountants at their books rather than young men shooting off the cuff.

F. Scott Fitzgerald, beginning as a screenwriter in Hollywood, noticed the change. To him the world cracked up in 1922 or thereabouts. Before that there had been the liberated era of the flappers and the flowing booze. Now there was a more serious purpose and worse drink, supplied by organized crime. Allan Dwan and Raoul Walsh and other contemporaries of Ford noticed that the camaraderie of the early days was giving way to a hierarchy in Hollywood, with the big stars like Douglas Fairbanks, Mary Pickford, and Gloria Swanson forming an aristocracy along with the big studio producers like Zukor, Lasky, and Mayer. Then there came another class of working directors and actors who excluded in their turn the minor technicians and extras. Society with its gradations had come to Hollywood, and people paid only for their own meals now in the Oasis.

Scandal also played its part in the new respectability of Hollywood. There was the sordid Arbuckle affair with the death of Virginia Rappe after a wild party. Then there was the peculiar murder of the director William Desmond Taylor. Mary Ford was a friend of the girl involved in the murder, Mabel Normand, Mack Sennett's star. According to her, Taylor was trying to cure Miss Normand of dope addiction. He was killed by her dope suppliers, who did not want to lose one of their best customers. "I went out to the hospital to see her a week before the murder," Mary Ford said. "She weighed about fifty pounds—a cute little thing. There was a lot of dirt in those days."

In 1922 the owners of the studios reacted to the scandals by setting up the Hays office to check scripts and by setting out a production code of morality. Public excesses by stars and directors were discouraged for fear of shocking the nation and lowering the take at the box office. Righteousness became a part of Hollywood, which began to lose its aspect of a frontier town and take on a new guise as a suburb with a tourist front in Hollywood Boulevard. "It grew so fast you wouldn't believe how rapidly it changed," Mary Ford declared. By 1925 the peppertrees were no longer an arbor over the sidewalks. They were all cut down because the tourists were slipping on their fallen berries. "You couldn't even get a telephone for a year—they ran out of copper wire." Tens of thousands of migrants poured into Hollywood to look for work there, and hundreds of thousands came to stare at the windows of the stars in their new palaces off Sunset Boulevard.

Studio economics also dictated a change. The small independent studios were being forced to close by the large ones, which treated movies like a product on an assembly line for the new national cinema chains. As Lillian Gish said, movies stopped being fun after *The Birth of a Nation* because the major epic film became the hope of instant fortune in Hollywood. In 1923 James Cruze's large-scale production of *The Covered Wagon* made millions at the box office out of the spectacle of the American pioneer experience. So William Fox asked John Ford to make a rival epic about the building of the American railroads to California. It was to be called *The Iron Horse.*

Ford was the right director for the job. He had been brought up in Portland on the romance of the great railroads opening up the heartland of America. He had traveled three times across the continent and had watched from observation cars the iron rails bisecting and defining the beauties of nature. He knew that immigrant Irish laborers had built the Union Pacific and had helped to link the east and west coasts of their mighty adopted country. Without the railroads Ford perceived there would have been no United States, no need to fight a Civil War to preserve the supremacy of the industrial North in the Union. His adolescent dreams, his love of the taming of the wilderness by the hard work of men and his Irish and American patriotism all combined to give him an understanding of the theme.

In another way Ford was the best director for the project after D. W. Griffith. He had learned to handle the production of a film like an admiral or a general. Since his marriage he had begun to take pride in his wife's southern ancestry and to read about the Confederate generals, particularly about Robert E. Lee with his intuitive feel for command and his devolution of responsibility to trusted lieutenants. Ford had to set up a vast military operation to make *The Iron Horse* from a camp in the Nevada Desert. He needed a hundred cooks alone to feed the five thousand extras who played the Irish and Chinese railroad builders, a complete regiment of U.S. Cavalry, and the eight hundred Pawnee and Sioux and Cheyenne Indians who turned up to fight in their original war paint and regalia.

Physically Ford lived through the building of the railroad as if he had been one of the pioneers. The Central Pacific line lent him its ancient locomotive *Jupiter* and the Union Pacific lent him *Old 116,* a twin engine that had helped to construct the original track. Ford and his men actually built three new miles of line and three shack towns that became instant ghost towns with their going. They survived continual blizzards, which were written into the shooting script, and a temperature often twenty degrees below zero. For the first time Ford ignored recall messages from his producer at the studio, refusing to wrap up shooting and return. He had been sent to complete a major feature, and he would do it.

Living was rough. Ford put the women in the railroad cars and worked himself from a private car hired from the Ringling Brothers. The other men had to make their homes on the sets. Later, in a Sonora desert sequence, a production man approached one of the two cameramen, George Schneiderman, to ask where the hotel was. "You're standing on it," Schneiderman replied. Ford drove himself and his people as if he were making a railroad as well as a picture.

Ford's vision of American history is shown in the opening sequence, in which Abraham Lincoln takes time off from directing the Civil War to talk to the railroad planners about a great nation pushing forward the "inevitable path to the West." With the father of the nation supporting Manifest Destiny, the building of the railroad to link the United States can be presented as a mission of strong men and iron machines against the resistance of the wilderness and the Indian tribes standing in their way.

Ford's dialectic is already apparent in *The Iron Horse.* He praises the progress of the pioneers, yet he understands their inevitable conflict with the threatened Indians, led by Chief Big Tree. Although Ford had not yet adopted his later subtle approach to that conflict, he does make his villain a white man masquerading as an Indian. In the attack of the braves on the train, the monster is the iron machine which the courage of the painted warriors halts in its tracks.

Indeed, Ford often uses the Indians as creations of pioneer terror and imagination. He introduces them as a succession of stealthy feet or as moving shadows on the sides of the railroad cars. They are portrayed as savages, but only to the eye of the new westerners. For they are the genuine tribesmen of the plains in the battle sequences, fighting fiercely against their dispossession. Ford had laid the actual tracks of the railroad so he could mount his heavy cameras on trolley cars and move with the splendid charges of the finest contemporary light cavalry and guerrilla fighters in the world. These mobile shots combined with the use of many cameras and dynamic editing have recorded fluid and hectic battle scenes as a fit remembrance of the Plains Indians and their magnificent resistance.

If the plot of *The Iron Horse* is melodramatic, with its hero George O'Brien somewhat vapid and exaggerated, Ford achieved a final grandeur with the driving of the last spike in the link between the Atlantic and Pacific coasts, the meeting of the two locomotives to open the track, and the concluding shot of Abraham Lincoln with the caption, "His truth is marching on." He also showed compassion in his most human shots of a boy kneeling by his father's grave in communion with the spirit of the dead, of an Irish corporal offering some chewing tobacco to a Chinese laborer, and of a small dog licking the chest of its dead Indian master. Such details were to be a characteristic in Ford's work, as was his view from his observatory of a group of mounted Indians as small as ships on the far horizon in the vast sea of the desert. In one particular backtracking shot where a railroad man on a handcar sees his brother falling to his death from a telegraph pole, Ford showed his genius in his portrayal of the insignificance of one human life measured against the large historical view. Somewhere between the heroic myth of the past and our common humanity lay Ford's own vision, most true when it contrasted both the effort and pettiness of men's work against the scale of nature.

Ford's gamble on completing *The Iron Horse* paid off; otherwise it might have ruined his career as spectacularly as *Greed* ruined von Stroheim's. Ford's epic cost $280,000 to make, a small fortune at the time, but it grossed more than $3,000,000 at the box office. When it opened Grauman's new Egyptian Theater on Hollywood Boulevard, a group of Indian warriors wearing complete war regalia were brought down from Wyoming. They were carried from the railroad station on blaring fire engines to camp in the forecourt of the theater and attract the crowds.

Ford himself refused to attend the opening night. He disliked the ballyhoo of selling the films he made. William Fox, the head of the studio, took Mary Ford to the première, and they were mobbed as if they had been royalty. Fox also invited Ford's parents to the New York première, where her daughter-in-law saw Barbara Feeney walk into the foyer "like Queen Victoria" in pride of the achievement of her youngest son. It was a great deal, after all, for a young Irish-American to do before he was thirty years old.

5: Old Worlds, New Ways

I am a man of the silent cinema. That's when pictures and not words had to tell the story . . . Sound wasn't the revolution most people imagine it was.

—John Ford

The success of *The Iron Horse* did not lead to Ford's making more epics. He was never to make so big a picture again. He had to work out his Fox contract for ten long years. He became even more professional, although his reputation stood still until after the coming of sound to the cinema. His technique was so expert that he survived the change into talking pictures, and he used sound to increase the realism of his films. For the silent movie had always seemed a little artificial, more like a book with its breaks for title cards. It had encouraged great mimes, but human society was finally not a Trappist monastery. To make believe that film actors were showing a slice of life, the talkies had to encourage great mumblers.

As well as directing contract films for Fox, Ford spent the Coolidge and Hoover years in bringing up his family in Odin Street and making a fair amount of money. He was a night person who went to bed reluctantly and rose even more unwillingly. If he was making a film, he refused to go out at all. If he was not, he would often drink heavily in the evenings with his male friends, waiting for the next picture.

Ford always loved rituals on the set of his own movies, from the playing of mood music on an accordion to formal practical jokes, hallowed by repetition. But his wife had to practice the first of these rituals upon him to rouse him in the mornings. She would open the bedroom windows noisily, then put "The Battle Hymn of the Republic" on the gramophone. A full chorus would chant the patriotic words, *Mine eyes have seen the glory of the coming of the Lord.* If Ford still refused to move on the crashing sound of *the grapes of wrath are stored,* his wife would change records to army bugle calls sounding reveille to taps and finally to hillbilly music, which usually sent him swearing out of bed.

Ford was always a family man who loved his home and his cronies. He had little to do with the mob of young actresses who tried to involve him personally in their careers. Mary Ford remembered "a lot of contention" from the actresses, particularly Madeleine Carroll, but she refused to listen to any Hollywood gossip during their marriage. "Believe nothing you hear," she always said, "and only half of what you see." On the only occasion that she threatened to leave her husband, he started the car and stood on the horn to hurry her departure. She did not try that tactic again.

Although he was slowly settling for a more respectable and wealthy way of life, Ford enjoyed looking filthy on the film set, particularly on location. There he could hardly be distinguished from a tramp with his worn boots, baggy pants, random jacket, bristling stubble, and weathered cap. On one treasured occasion he walked into the Rolls-Royce showroom on Wilshire Boulevard in his dirty work clothes and began kicking the tires of the newest luxury model. The salesman rushed over to find this tall bum bouncing on the leather seats. When he complained, Ford hammered the woodwork, said the car seemed solid, and had his business manager send over a certified check for more than twenty thousand dollars in the next ten minutes. He had the Rolls-Royce delivered to his home for Christmas. On the back seat lay a mink coat and a message for Mary, *This ought to shut you up for twenty years.* And he did not, according to her, give her another Christmas present for twenty years. He was a man of his word.

As he had stopped making cowboy pictures, Ford began to change the circle of his friends. If he never actually formed the Irish stock company which he was later accused of featuring in his films, he did choose a group of boon companions for his boozing and card-playing. He hardly ever drank during the making of a movie. Liquor was banned on set; but when the shooting was over, he would call for his bottles and his friends.

He did not go in for the regular heavy drinking of the other Hollywood Irish like Raoul Walsh or Errol Flynn after his rise to fame. He stuck to his own gang, where he was boss and had no competition from great names. "Nobody's as clannish as the Irish," his wife said. "Jack would say nobody helped him since the day he was born." But he thrived on a sense of group loyalty and conspiracy, refusing to say that his cronies helped each other, only that they were friends.

His test of friendship was usually to inflict humiliation. If a man could survive a series of degrading practical jokes, Ford would reckon he had the fiber to be a comrade. What Frank Ford had put him through on the set as a young stuntman he made other ambitious young men undergo. The process was like a hazing at West Point or an initiation ceremony in a fraternity. It was also a technique to show the director's dominance on set and keep the tension high. "He always had his patsy for the day or the week," one of his editors said. "He'd plan on it, although he'd never pick on anyone who was integral."[1]

One of his great friends and future stars, John Wayne, went through the process. Then called "Duke" Morrison, he started as a prop boy in Ford's *Mother Machree* of 1928, a sentimental Irish-American vehicle for Belle Bennett, who gave up her son so that he could be brought up better in other mothering arms. Wayne's job was to herd geese and lesser fowl into place on Mother Machree's plot of land. The geese were no performers, Ford became annoyed, and Wayne saw everybody was intimidated. "They were all scared shitless of him, all except me and the geese."[2]

Ford had to vent his frustration on somebody, so the next day Wayne became the patsy. Ford had discovered that his prop boy was a football player, so Wayne was made to get down in a four-point stance. Ford then kicked out his arms from under him and stuck his nose in the mud. "It wasn't the sod of old Ireland," Wayne said later, "and it really hurt."[3] So Wayne challenged Ford to a football scrimmage, then knocked him over with a foul kick in the chest. This riposte made Ford respect the young man. If he liked making other people eat dirt, he also liked it when they stood up to him. Later he confessed that he had tried to get Wayne's goat a million times but had only succeeded on a few occasions.

One of those occasions was during his next film, *Four Sons*. Although Ford only recalled Wayne's blundering into a dramatic scene while he was raking leaves, Wayne insisted that Ford had arranged the whole thing, then humiliated him like the king's buffoon. Martial music was played and Wayne was ceremoniously marched up to a character actor who just happened to be Archduke Leopold of Austria. An Iron Cross was pinned on Wayne's chest, then he was bent over so that Ford could kick him in the ass. Everybody roared with laughter and Wayne nearly walked off the film set forever. "I was never so God-damned embarrassed in my life," he said later. "My God, it was awful."[4]

So Ford ruled his set by the scapegoat principle of baiting and humiliating one of his people. Those who survived the blast of his terrible camaraderie began to form his group of regular actors and technicians. Wayne was one—he was edited out as a condemned prisoner in *Hangman's House* but appeared as a spectator in an Irish horse race in that film, breaking down a picket fence in his excitement. Victor McLaglen was another Ford regular, who first appeared in *The Fighting Heart* in 1925 and was starring for Ford in *Strong Boy* and *The Black Watch* within four years. J. Farrell McDonald also acted character roles for Ford before starring in *Riley the Cop,* while George O'Brien regularly played the lead in Ford pictures after *The Iron Horse,* most notably in two navy features, *The Blue Eagle* and *Seas Beneath.* Another of Ford's close friends, Ward Bond, also came into his life; Bond had been on the USC team with Wayne, and played the part of a football player with him in *Salute* in 1929, a film which showed the sports rivalry between the army and navy. It was mostly shot on location at Annapolis, which had refused Ford as a student because of his poor vision and now turned everything over to him to arrange as he saw fit.

Ford declared later that he could not choose the scripts he made for Fox. "They were thrown at you," he said, "and you did the best you could with them."[5] Yet his preferences did influence the material he was given. Of the twenty-two features made for Fox in seven years after *The Iron Horse,* five dealt with the United States Navy and four with Ireland or Irish heroes. There was also a concentration on horse racing and prizefighting, from *Kentucky Pride* and *The Shamrock Handicap* to *The Fighting Heart* and *Hangman's House*—something of a halfway house with its shadowy prophecies of *The Informer* and comic rural touches of *The Quiet Man.* Westerns were falling out of favor with the public because of a glut of second-rate pictures, so Ford was told to turn to the new urban action themes, making one cop and one gangster film in that period. He also made a convict comedy called *Up The River* in 1930, memorable only as the film debut of two obscure actors, Spencer Tracy and Humphrey Bogart.

Professionally Ford was marking time. In those last seven years at Fox, he only made two major films, his Western, *Three Bad Men,* and *Four Sons.* Shot at Jackson Hole, Wyoming, and in the Mojave Desert, *Three Bad Men* was set in the Dakota land rush of 1877 after the defeat of the Sioux tribes. It was intended to be an epic featuring the Western stars Tom Mix, Buck Jones, and George O'Brien, but the first two dropped out and O'Brien ended as the good Irish immigrant farmer and hero. The three outlaws were played in the manner of Harry Carey's role in *Straight Shooting* as men whose life outside society gave them the honor to stand up against human greed and envy. They became matchmakers for O'Brien and his girl, and they ended by dying in the land rush to save the new farming family which they had brought together.

Ford had a natural and popular sympathy with the lawless because of his admiration for the rebel heroes of the fight for Irish independence, as well as the folk heroes of the American West. He even grafted onto the story of the *Three Bad Men* a Catholic sense of self-sacrifice and redemption, with his unholy trinity being accepted into grace by the supreme gift of their lives, their ghosts riding away into the sunset, all holding out their arms as if Ford were showing Christ and the two thieves crucified on horseback.

Such strong symbolism is new to Ford's pictures and demonstrates his increasing awareness of the myth and the message implicit in his work. Yet the religious element hardly obtrudes above his overpowering feeling for history. Some of the first titles read, "Thousands of emigrants come to seek the reality of their dreams in America" and "Westward the course of empire takes its way." The most memorable shot in the film is one superb Fordian sign from his overview—a tree falling to a pioneer's ax on a small part of the screen, then the iris opening out to show a vast and virgin hinterland even greater than the vision of the interior he had seen looking west from the Portland Observatory.

The strength of *Three Bad Men* lies in Ford's sense of the mixed courage and greed of the settling of the West. There are unforgettable shots of the three outlaws watching the line of covered wagons first rolling along the rim of the wilderness, then the furious building of such early mining towns as Custer, then the actual land rush to the Black Hills, in which Ford again shows the grandeur of the huge arc of wagons on the salt flat before cutting from the pell-mell dash of their start to little comic details —a newspaper printing on board a helter-skelter wagon, a cheap family bicycle broken beneath the rush, and a baby forgotten and just snatched from under the rolling wagon wheels in the headlong scramble for wealth.

Ford was always proud of his work on this film. "We used over two hundred vehicles—stages, Conestoga wagons, buggies, broughams, every blasted vehicle there was—and hundreds of men riding horses, all waiting for the signal to cross over riding like hell."[6] Ford used several extras who had been in the original rush, Duke Lee and others, and thus he could organize and actually relive another climacteric in Western lore. He loved authenticity because it made him a part of the making of American history. He was a practical man who saw his job as showing the mass of the American people the truth of what he recreated about their past.

He succeeded with the land-rush sequence. As one trade journal declared, its production value surpassed even *The Covered Wagon* with its array of prairie schooners.

Yet the box office signaled that the day of the epic Western had eclipsed. *Three Bad Men* did not repeat the success of *The Iron Horse.* This was achieved by Ford's sentimental Germanic drama, *Four Sons,* the one subject Ford chose for himself at Fox. He now displayed the influence of Murnau rather than Griffith or Flaherty, using misty German expressionism rather than earthy American or Irish realism. He even used the same village set that Murnau had used in *Sunrise* the year before, and he spent some time in the Tyrol shooting background sequences, his first trip to the European continent. Over there, the scenes of decadence in Weimar Berlin quite shocked Mary Ford, who fell ill, although her husband was amused to see the feudal aristocracy ruined and barons acting as gigolos to pay the rent.

The plot of *Four Sons* deals with a Bavarian mother, played by Margaret Mann, who loses three sons in the fighting in the First World War, then joins her last surviving son and his family in the United States. It is played for sentiment and strains for its effects. The ex-Kaiser of Germany particularly liked the scene where an American soldier watches one of the four sons dying and asking for his mother. The title reads, "Oh, dem guys have got mothers too!"

As always when he dealt with a culture that he did not understand well, Ford's direction was uneasy. His shawled German women looked like Irish widows who happened to find themselves in the Black Forest on the way to Tipperary. Yet as in his later masterpiece *How Green Was My Valley,* in which Ford was to use a Welsh mining village that obviously got no nearer to Ebbw Vale than the Hollywood hills, he could make his audience ignore artificiality through his understanding of a mother's emotion and his feeling for the tragedy of unnecessary death. Ford's grasp of the common human heart could always redeem his occasional lapses into theatrical and overwrought images, backed by choirs of voices singing lush thematic conclusions.

At the close of the Twenties two catastrophes reached Hollywood together, the Great Crash and the coming of sound. The financial collapse of Wall Street ruined many of the stars and producers. "We were lucky in '29," Mary Ford said. "A Jewish friend and stockbroker flew from New York to tip us off. Everyone else went broke but we came out on top." Ford also survived the second catastrophe, the coming of sound, largely by ignoring it. "He thinks sound and the spoken word is sort of an added thing that sometimes is an advantage," James Stewart said of working with Ford, "but most of the time is a damned bother."[7]

Ford himself was more specific on sound pictures. He learned to accept the advantages of their realism, which helped him as long as the dialogue was "crisp and cryptic." As he was to admit, "They're much easier to make than silent pictures, [which] were very hard work, very difficult to get a point over. You had to move a camera round so much."[8]

At first Ford was fired by his studio with the other silent directors. All their contracts were bought up and stage directors from New York were imported because they were meant to understand the proper speaking of words. Mary Ford remembered the voice coaches coming from the East to teach the silent stars how to enunciate, but they often failed and many of Ford's friends found their careers at an end. Some stars like Garbo had natural voices for new medium; most did not.

Soon, however, Fox and the other studios had to rehire Ford and the old silent directors at an increased salary under new contracts because the theater directors did not know how to make a film. "It was a comedy situation," Ford later told Peter Bogdanovich. "They threw these guys onto the set to make sound pictures—we had schedules of three or four weeks in those days—and after *eight* weeks, these fellows had about a half reel of picture, and the stuff was terrible."[9] So Ford just came back on set and told the actors to say what they were already saying in silent movies, when they spoke their dialogue for the lip readers in the audience.

His first short sound film, *Napoleon's Barber,* was about the French emperor stopping for a shave on the way to Waterloo. Ford made his despised sound technicians record Josephine's coach rolling across a bridge, and it worked despite their protests—"the sound of the horses and the wheels—perfect." *Photoplay* did not agree about the film, finding it all very crude and unreal, with the characters seeming to speak from their vest pockets.[10]

Ford was not out of trouble yet. In his first important film about the British Empire, *The Black Watch,* in 1929, he was only allowed to direct the action sequences, while a theater director, Lumsden Hare, "staged" the long wooden dialogue sequences between Victor McLaglen and Myrna Loy, playing the beautiful Yasmani in brown-face. Ford performed prodigies of back lighting and artifice to simulate some form of reality in the studio sequences of the shell-torn Flanders battlefield and the caves of the Khyber Pass. The film displayed Ford's growing mastery over formal studio productions and some weakening in his dislike of the British army. Yet, even so, he was dealing with a Highland regiment, imperial mercenaries uselessly sacrificing their lives for a distant Crown, just as the Canadian Black Watch had done in 1917, passing through Portland on their way to decimation in the real world war.

In 1930 Ford made his first film with one of his better screenwriters, the part-Irish Dudley Nichols, who had never written a scenario before, but who agreed with Ford to spare the dialogue, not spoil the film. Their first collaboration was called *Men Without Women* and dealt with Ford's growing obsession, the changing methods of naval warfare. In the film fourteen men were trapped in a submarine, and one had to sacrifice himself so that the others might live. It was the first undersea picture shot with a real submarine, and Ford remembered it as very effective for those days. The rescue scenes were filmed in a storm, and the stars did their own dangerous stunts in the raging seas after Ford had casually shamed them into action with the words, "Let's go ahead and do it—what the hell —it's not going to hurt the submarine."[11]

John Wayne also did stunts for Ford during the storm sequence, and he learned how Ford could wrench a performance from a mediocre actor. Wayne watched the director try everything, "but hit him with a club. He played music, pleaded with him, got down on his knees, did everything. Finally he got the scene and he says, 'Christ, now if he gets an Academy Award, I'll cut my throat.' "[12]

Dudley Nichols remembered Ford at the time as a big shambling man with a corrugated face and fading red hair and a temper to match. He used to chew the stems of his pipes to pieces and his danger signal was the moment when he began using his teeth on the corner of his dirty handkerchiefs, which were actually handmade for him in Dublin. He gave Nichols full freedom to ignore the crippling constrictions demanded by the sound department. "You write it," he said, "and I'll get it on film." He did a tracking shot along a street by spacing out boom operators like human telegraph poles to hang their microphones over the heads of the passing actors. He also invented a glass box to put over the camera so that it could record the diving of the submarine. "It is old hat now," Nichols wrote to Lindsay Anderson twenty years later. "Not then."[13]

The trouble with seeing Ford's old features again is that he invented in his fifty years as a director more of the grammar and imagery of film than even D.W. Griffith. He was so often copied that his innovations became the clichés of a host of lesser directors. What Ford proposed, his imitators disposed into the stock shots of ten thousand Westerns and war films. The irony is that to a modern audience the inventor of so many of the elements of cinema can seem sometimes like the copycat of his inferiors.

Ford made a gangster comedy with Nichols called *Born Reckless,* then another good naval picture about a Q-ship, one of the clandestine submarine hunters of the First World War. In *Seas Beneath* the nautical details and battle sequences were admirable, but Ford was forced to accept a leading actress, Marion Lessing, who could neither act nor speak German as she professed to do. One Ford stock character made an appearance for the first time as Mugs O'Flaherty, the boastful, truculent Irishman whom Ford based on his bar companions and his own father. Frank Ford also played for his young brother again, a bit part as a trawler captain, slipping down the Hollywood scale faster than a stuntman doing a nose dive.

Ford's navy pictures were made for fun and propaganda. They were the actual evidence of his playful sense of conspiracy. For he had begun to lead a double life since the middle of the Twenties, and perhaps as early as his secretive expedition to Ireland in 1921. He lived both as a film-maker and as a navy spy. His boyish dream of being both D.W. Griffith and John Paul Jones, a great director and a pirate sort of an admiral, began to grow closer to reality. He was also competitive; he wanted to show his wife, with her family of admirals, that he too could wear gold braid on his white cap.

From her months at Annapolis Mary Ford knew personally most of the admirals on the West Coast. They were flattered by her film connections and came to visit the gray house on the hill in Odin Street. She remembered sailors from the submarine base mixing up pure "torpedo juice." Two drops of it flavored with a few juniper berries and ginger ale passed as gin at the Sunday afternoon parties. The local epidemic of friends dying from bad booze at the end of the Twenties, when greedy bootleggers were mixing ethyl alcohol with their fake Scotch, made the Fords taper off on real beer. But as long as they had their navy sources, they could still serve hard liquor from time to time.

One afternoon Mary Ford remembered two admirals coming to call, Scofield and Richardson, both in the high command of the Pacific Fleet. Her husband was drinking with a friend of his, a deep-sea diver who had served with Admiral Byrd. He came down in his shorts, pleased at the visit of the top brass, and brought along the scared diver, whom he had told to answer all questions with the one word, "Tomatoes." When asked by the admirals what he had done for Byrd, the diver would only say,

"Tomatoes." No other word did he utter until the admirals had gone. He knew how to take direction.

Outside of good stories Ford never told his wife what he was doing for the navy. He was recruited to work for intelligence by two influential admirals in California. The first was Rear Admiral Sims, who was an enthusiast for naval aviation and aircraft carriers. He believed that the future of the fleet depended on its air arm. He brought Ford together with Lieutenant Commander Frank "Spig" Wead, a crippled navy air ace who became a screenwriter for Ford and the subject of one of his best military films, *The Wings of Eagles*. Ford later claimed to have first met Wead as a young deck officer on the battleship *Mississippi* in the period after 1920, when Ford had put aside his reserve naval uniform and had gone underground.

More influential in Ford's life was Captain Ellis Zacharias, who was to become the commander of the 11th Naval District in San Diego. Zacharias spoke Japanese, as did his wife, and he was concerned with the rise of Japanese power in the Pacific. An expert in psychological warfare, he ran a semi-official intelligence unit, using the local naval reserve officers to collect information on Japanese and German influence in Mexico and the Far East. He passed on his information to J. Edgar Hoover, his close friend, and to Vice Admiral T.S. Wilkinson, one of the chiefs of naval intelligence and later a friend of John Ford.

Ford's patriotism and taciturnity and cover as a film director made him immediately useful to Ellis Zacharias. He again joined the naval reserve and rose rapidly to the rank of Lieutenant-Commander. His intelligence activities were unpaid and performed largely on his own initiative because American military intelligence between the two world wars was unauthorized by Congress and largely run by a small subculture of army and navy officers, deeply worried about their country's lack of security and unpreparedness for war. Particularly important in this subculture were Wilkinson and Zacharias, Dudley Wright Knox, and General Ralph van Deman, who set up his own private counterespionage group in San Diego.

Ford may have volunteered a report on the Irish struggle for independence upon his return to Hollywood in 1922, and he always kept in touch with the Irish Republican Army in its continuing struggle against the English in Ulster. On occasional trips to Mexico he certainly reported on the activities of Japanese agents there. When he filmed *Salute* at Annapolis in 1929, he met the leaders of naval intelligence and was given a mission in the Pacific. He disguised his recruitment as a spy with charac-

teristic lightness, saying, "The Admirals' daughters were all in the picture
—you know, ten bucks a day—and we had a lot of fun."[14] He also showed
his lack of bigotry by insisting that the black star Stepin Fetchit stay in
the guest house for distinguished visitors, with the unknown John Wayne
serving as his dresser.

Behind his cover as a fun-loving film director, Ford left the United
States at the end of filming *Salute* for a voyage round the Pacific. He took
George O'Brien with him, officially to research and film Shanghai sequences for the submarine film *Men Without Women,* secretly to report on
harbor access and defenses to naval intelligence. Mary Ford thought she
was going with him on a holiday trip with their family, but when she
arrived at the dock, she was told that she must go alone for a long vacation
to Honolulu. So she went with the two children to the easy welcome of
Hawaii while her husband traveled on a freighter with George O'Brien
to Bali and the Dutch East Indies, then to Singapore, Hong Kong, and
Shanghai. The two men would only confess to enjoying themselves in
these "down to the waist places" and shooting some film stock for *Men
Without Women.*

Ford soon went on another Pacific trip for the navy. His wife and family
found themselves staying in the Philippines for six months in 1931 as the
guests of the military commander there. Ford himself often disappeared
on air-reconnaisance missions with his cameras. Officially again he was
preparing footage for *Air Mail,* the story of the early days of that service.
The script was written for him by Spig Wead from his own experience.
Wead later became a house guest of the Ford family and finally was to
die in Ford's arms.

Ford's public film career and clandestine surveillance for the navy were
becoming enmeshed. Propaganda joined entertainment in his early military service. He was receiving an unusual amount of cooperation from the
navy, which wanted to present its ships and sailors and aircraft in the best
possible light in Ford's films in order to win recruits and funds from
Congress. Concerned over his country's security and wanting to forward
his career in the naval reserve as well as in Hollywood, Ford became
known by producers as a director who could get great production value
from the Pacific fleet for no cost. The double face of John Ford suited
both the admirals and the film accountants.

Ford could also use his Hollywood facilities for editing and processing
the intelligence footage he brought back officially as stock film for his
commercial movies. His cutting editor, Leon Selditz, categorically states
that Ford was working for military intelligence on his two Pacific trips and

thereafter. "He was a perfect underground agent," Selditz says, "with a magnificent eye and an incredible memory."[15]

By the time of the Great Depression Ford had finished his period of preparation. In Hollywood he was known as one of the more professional directors to survive the coming of sound, and by 1931 he could afford to terminate his exclusive contract with Fox and choose his material more carefully. William Fox himself had been ruined the year before and was losing control of his studio to Darryl Zanuck. Without antagonizing the new Fox management Ford accepted Sam Goldwyn's offer to direct Sinclair Lewis's novel *Arrowsmith,* starring Ronald Colman and Helen Hayes. His reputation now exceeded mastery and approached art, even if he denied it, pretending always that he was just a hard-nosed director who did a script if he liked it. As his wife said, "He could be a bastard, but he needed that reputation to command the set and the studios."

He was also committed to naval intelligence and propaganda as the power of the Japanese and the Fascists in Europe grew. He had already recreated the western pioneer experience of the nineteenth century. Now he was ready to examine the social conscience of America during the long presidency of Franklin Delano Roosevelt, when the traditional assumptions of small-town morality were to be shaken by mass unemployment, increasing bigotry, and the threat of foreign wars.

6: Half-Genius, Half-Irish

Ford cannot be pinned down or analyzed. He is pure Ford—which means pure great. John is half-tyrant, half-revolutionary; half-saint, half-satan; half-possible, half-impossible; half-genius, half-Irish—but **all** *director and* **all** *American.*

—Frank Capra

The Irish-Americans produced two artists of genius in the first hundred years of their mass emigration to the United States—John Ford and Eugene O'Neill. Their talents usually flourished in political or religious organization. Yet Ford used these Irish techniques to enhance his genius as a film director. In movies, as in war, half the battle is won before the shooting starts: it is a matter of getting the right people to the right place at the right time.

After directing more than seventy features in fifteen years in Hollywood, Ford knew most of the actors and technicians who could work well with him. Unable to tolerate "movie mothers" on set, he would only work with three large families, the Watsons and the Johnsons and the Parrishes. Between them they could fill a schoolroom with their seventeen children—yet only three mothers needed to appear to discipline their broods. For crowd scenes on location, Ford preferred to use the people who lived there, particularly the Navajo Indians in his Westerns. For character parts he depended on stuntmen and players who would do exactly what he asked without question, put up with bad conditions on location, provide some entertainment in the evenings, and pass his endurance test by practical joke. Through his series of films these Ford regulars included the stuntman Yakima Canutt, the cameramen George Schneiderman and Joe August, and the actors Ward Bond, John Carradine, Andy Devine, Ben Johnson, John Qualen, and Woody Strode. They seemed to appear around every Ford campfire in or out of shot.

49

As production assistants Ford remembered what his brother Frank had done for him and employed his own. His chief aide-de-camp was his brother-in-law, Wingate Smith, who had been a colonel in the army and who ran a tight film regiment with quiet efficiency. Ford's other chief assistant was his elder brother Edward, who also advised him on historical research and was a stickler for period detail. To distinguish himself, Edward changed his name from Feeney to O'Fearna, which his other Ford brothers considered "neither fish, flesh nor Gaelic."[1]

Frank Ford clashed too often with his young brother who had superseded him as a director, so he was only given character roles. In *Judge Priest* he was finally repaid for exploding the bomb under Jack's nose when his kid brother had worked as his stuntman. Frank found himself sitting in a wheelbarrow, secretly attached to a bolting carriage. When he limped back from the ride, sick from swallowing his chewing tobacco, Jack said, "That was for the grenade!" as though he had been waiting for his revenge for nineteen years. Irish reprisal is a slow business.

Like his ward-heeler father and his wife's naval relations, John Ford had the political and military gifts for authority. He could attract and hold men's loyalty. He defended those who worked for him, but he expected them to drop their private lives and alternative careers at his beck and call, even if they had to risk their marriages or take a lower salary. "He'd just say a picture was starting," one of his editors remembers. "We would all drop in. It was a handshake deal. As good as your word is, his word was twice as good."[2] A Ford regular might work for less, but he worked often.

Harry Carey's son Dobie recollects Ford's inscrutability and silent stare as two of the tricks of his command. When he arrived for an interview, Carey would find Ford sitting behind his desk, glaring at him through his green-tinted glasses without saying a word, "the sort of Svengali thing he could do." To break the silence, Carey would feel forced to say something stupid. Then Ford would put him down and refuse to tell Carey what part he was meant to play. "If Ford was going to hire you, he'd say, 'Let your hair grow longer,' and that was that. He'd know what he needed you for, and you'd find out on the set."[3]

If any of his chosen actors or technicians had the temerity to refuse to work for him because of other film or family commitments, Ford would drop them from the stock company for a decade, then would hire them again as if nothing had happened. This happened to one of his oldest friends, the original Harry Carey. The cowboy star had found Ford too Irish and clannish, so Ford had forgotten to employ him for fifteen years.

Then the elder Carey was suddenly asked to play the commandant in *The Prisoner of Shark Island*. If Ford was an Irishman who could never forget, he was also an Irishman who always remembered.

Like any good commander, Ford knew how to keep his men on their toes. He drove himself incessantly, and he drove them. He deliberately created a tension on set, either ridiculing a chosen patsy until antagonism bristled in the air or defusing the hostility he had created with a joke or a word of encouragement. "You couldn't get mad at him," one of his regulars declares. "He would turn it so quickly, a bad time into a good time just like that."[4]

Ridicule, after all, is an old Irish weapon to test the quality of a man. If there is a cruelty in it, there is also a purpose. Although Ford's persecution of some character actors persuaded them that he was sadistic, making them repeatedly cut themselves on stones or fall off horses, those who survived the treatment like Victor McLaglen and John Wayne always praised their director for making them angry enough to act well. Ford believed in provoking a good performance as well as eliciting it. He was ruthless only in getting what he wanted on screen; for, like any political or military leader, he wanted solely to be judged by the final victory. If the battle was won, who cared about what happened on the way there?

Ford helped to keep the loyalty of his men by taking care of their camp as if it were another production sequence. He knew that morale depended on relaxation after a long hard day's work in the sun or the cold. Film talk was banned, songs were sung and mood music played, usually by Danny Borzage on his accordion. Irish and folk tunes were the favorites, especially "Red River Valley." Games were encouraged from dominoes to poker. And practical jokes were interminably played, chiefly on the burly Ward Bond, who was the most opinionated and reactionary of men, Ford's favorite friend and victim.

This group sense and loyalty gave Ford what he wanted as a commander—total obedience mixed with personal responsibility. He knew how to delegate responsibility, as an examination of the camerawork or editing of many of his films demonstrates. He would trust a straightforward lighting cameraman like George Schneiderman to achieve a clear shot or even suggest a set-up, while he would allow the expressionist Karl Freund to make *Air Mail* look as if it were filmed in permanent mist.

As for his editors, he would expect them to know the way he shot a sequence—indeed, he often shot it only one way, without any cover shots to provide an alternative for cutting. Frequently, he would abandon a film after completing photography and never go to the cutting room. He often would not view the rushes of the daily takes, and would have enough confidence in his editors to be sure they would put together the film he wanted. He could not, however, stop the producers or the studio bosses from hacking out a final version, even though he was careful to leave them no alternative takes to use.

Ford never liked producers before he met one of his own sort in Merian C. Cooper. "A producer's function has always seemed to me to be a casual one," he said to Frank Nugent, another of his screenwriters. "Pictures should be the result of a writer and a director getting together with the producer merely standing by in a fatherly, benevolent way to chide them if they spend too much money."[5]

This point of view was a fond illusion. Ford could insist that producers stay off the set while he was actually shooting. His bad treatment of them was legendary. When one producer told him he was behind schedule, he tore ten pages from the script and said, "Now we are three days ahead of schedule." To teach that producer a lesson, he never shot the missing sequences.

On another occasion the associate producer of *The Informer* came on set to say that the rushes of the previous day's shooting were great. Ford then declared that there must be something wrong with the scenes if the front office liked them, so he reshot them for the next two days at an additional cost of $25,000 on the budget. The intruder should have remembered what Ford had done to him when he had dared to appear on set for the first day of shooting. Then Ford had seized his chin, turned his face into profile, and declared to the assembled technicians and cast, "This is an associate producer. Take a good look at him, because you will not see him again on the set . . ."[6]

Ford would not tolerate anyone who tried to interfere with his total control during principal photography. To him finance was the producer's only role during shooting, and to show his contempt of money, he would not even carry it. He would leave his bills for his friends to pick up, and they would have to be repaid by his business manager.

To those who dared to say how they thought a scene should be done, Ford's reaction was immediate. When one actress tried to tell him how to play her part, he assured her that he was paid to direct and asked, "Honey, what do they pay you for?" When an assistant cameraman said he reckoned a shot would look good from a neighboring hilltop, Ford agreed and made him manhandle all the camera gear up there. And when Bob Parrish declared that he wanted to be a director instead of a cutting assistant, Ford stood for minutes with his large Mitchell viewfinder to his eye, then swung it around sharply, opening up a bloody wound on Parrish's forehead. "After you've been at it for a few years," he told Parrish kindly, "you'll discover that your aim will improve and you can knock off two or three associate producers a week. With your eyes closed. That's the end of the first lesson."[7]

So Ford achieved total command and the fidelity of his people. "He was not so much tyrannical," Dobie Carey says. "He made me feel reverent." Ford was taciturn, only explaining what was absolutely necessary, so that everyone hung on his least word. He created tension and then exploded it, never explaining his motives, any more than a priest or an admiral would. He took full responsibility, keeping the producers and the studio from intervening. Once he had chosen his group he allowed them initiative, but never forgave any negligence or incompetence. Through his mastery of the medium and refusal to explain his art he knew how to create an atmosphere of complete dependence and trust in him. Yet strategy and organization won only half of his battle, for much of his genius lay in his pictorial sense, in his understanding of pacing and playing his scenes, in his special view from his private tower, and in his scenes of the rhythm of human life set against his instinct for the seasons of nature and the tides of the sea.

His political talents and his understanding of popular taste were Irish as well. When he had begun making features in Hollywood, the two-reelers had been a people's theater, dealing with mass fantasies like the dime-novel bandits of the West or with common problems like finding a job, a mother's death, or the loss of a child. If these early films were crude, they had a direct appeal to the mass mind and to the human heart. Ford never lost that contact. He kept his comedy broad and slapstick, his emotions strong and clear. He never forgot his first experiences of birth and love and death, his mother's memories of her children lost in infancy, the weddings of the Feeney sisters, and the final cemetery on the Western Promenade at Portland with the tumbling pioneer graves looking westward toward the hope of the free land of the interior.

While directing *Arrowsmith* in 1931 Ford was given the chance to probe into the phenomenon of American social success. The story deals with an idealistic young doctor who refuses to become a colonialist nabob like his colleagues, but insists on continuing his medical research. When an epidemic breaks out, he is forced to choose between the life of his wife and the discovery of his serum—and he chooses the greater good, leaving his wife to die. Ford's direction is as crisp and structured as the hierarchies of behavior which he examines, leading up to a final speech by Ronald Colman about integrity, the hallmark of the coming message films of the Thirties. Yet somehow Helen Hayes steals the picture, fiercely sucking in cigarette smoke to soothe her nerves, hiding her turmoil behind a social mask as inscrutable as a surgeon's.

After *Arrowsmith* Ford directed *Air Mail,* from a story by Spig Wead, who was also to write *Ceiling Zero* for Howard Hawks. Wead's scenarios for both directors were much the same, but Ford's view of flying was different. While Hawks looked at the men in the cockpit from eye level, flying with them from their point of view, Ford stayed in his observatory, showing the pilots and airplanes lost in space, battling the clouds and the elements as if encountering a stormy sea or a twister on the Great Plains.

A French critic has recently stressed the importance of *Air Mail* as the first of Ford's films with his mark printed firmly upon its whole shape. The film shows "a new world, a world of adventure and risk. After the conquest of the West, the conquest of the sky."[8] Two closed groups of pilots live in their little societies, one at Desert Airport, one at Pacific Airport. Ford contrasts the warm, tight pilots' messes with the immensities of raging space outside, the laconic talk of the men set against the burning death of one of their friends who crashes in a fog, the scale of nature opposed to the detail of the everyday.

Into these small groups Pat O'Brien flies, looping the loop, into a closed society in a state of shock. An old Indian observes the airplane bucking into the airport like a bronco. "Aviator, drunk" is his only comment. The Indian preserves his dignity and his place on the ground, while the pilot shows off to prove his manhood and his mastery of the mechanical saddles of the air. So the Old West gives way to the new, the Pony Express to the aerial cowboy, the centaur to Pegasus. Yet Ford's heroes are hardly demigods but small figures battling against space and season and time.

Ford followed *Air Mail* with a run-of-the-mill vehicle for Wallace Beery called *Flesh,* the story of a German wrestler exploited by a group of American gangsters. He then made *Pilgrimage,* one of his greater box office successes in the manner of *Four Sons.* It deals with the journey to France of a group of American mothers to visit the graves of their boys, killed in the First World War.

In this film Ford transcends a mawkish opening to use again the signs from the observatory of his childhood—the scenes of parting in the homes as the men sail away, the widow's walk of women waiting vainly for the return of their loved ones, the stoical grief of a mother at the loss of her child, the ship of bereaved women sailing over the ocean toward the graves of their slain warrior sons, and finally the massed tombstones drawn up in their regiments of duty, standing in their proud ranks to meet the mothers' tears—all this grief lightened and made real by Lucille Laverne's country comedy with her corncob pipe.

So Ford reached 1933 and the entrance of Franklin Roosevelt to the White House and the trough of the Great Depression. It was also the year of a financial crisis and an actual earthquake in Hollywood. When the California banks were forced to close for almost a month, the studio bosses took the opportunity to force pay cuts on most of their employees, who were also informed, "No salaries until banks reopen." Invoking the "national emergency" clauses in the new legislation, Universal Studios suspended all contracts while the film czars met to decide whether to shut up shop altogether.

This economic cataclysm was followed by a real earthquake. Frank Capra was in the crowd that watched the tall tower of the Hollywood Athletic Club "swaying and cracking like a film set in a high wind." He took refuge in the steamroom inside, where he discovered a lone naked figure with a black patch over one eye reading a newspaper. It was his idol, John Ford. When Capra stuttered something about the earthquake, Ford kept his good eye to the newsprint and asked, "What earthquake?" When Capra then tried to tell him about the pay cut, Ford went on reading and said, "That's all a lot of horseshit."[9] Capra then left Ford to his newspaper.

It did appear that Ford was reluctant to involve himself in the Hollywood war between the studio bosses and the new craft guilds, which were girding up for a fight in the tight economic market of the Thirties. In fact, Ford was working behind the scenes to help set up the guilds to protect the livelihood of film actors and technicians. He was traditionally a Democrat and a supporter of Franklin Roosevelt's populism, while his wife helped the Assistance League to find jobs and money for those film people thrown out of work. He hated the producers' policy of hiring their own inexperienced relatives and firing the old-time professionals. But he hated even more the political infighting and squabbling committees. Guilds were for bettering working conditions, and that was all.

"He was so apolitical," one of his editors said of Ford. "He would never commit himself. But when it came down to the balls of it, he made a stand. You'd never think he'd do it—he spoke so infrequently. But when it was a matter of integrity or a person's job was involved, he was the first guy there."[10]

Financially Ford was doing well. He had preserved his money in the Great Crash, he was earning over one hundred thousand dollars a picture, and prices were falling. He could afford to indulge his childhood dream, advance his status, and further his naval career. He bought a white two-masted sailing yacht, which he called *The Araner,* after the people who lived in the western isles off Galway. If the ketch was not as big as the black Morgan boat that used to summer in Casco Bay, it was still large enough to impress any visiting admiral or the Hollywood stars and producers who vied for moorings off the coves of Catalina Island across the channel from Santa Monica.

Discrimination by religion and origin still operated in Los Angeles. The old Protestant families and the land-rich would not accept the Jewish film bosses, who retaliated by forming their own golf and yacht clubs to the exclusion of Gentiles. In a gesture of defiance Ford founded the Emerald Bay Yacht Club of Catalina Island for himself and his cronies. Its infamous slogan was "No Jews and no dues"—Ford's riposte as a film technician and a Gentile, and thus excluded from some of the smart yacht clubs of the mainland. Yet he himself was to resign from one of his clubs because of the blackballing of a Jewish army officer.

He was not a bigoted man personally, although many of his Irish cronies were. Leon Selditz, one of his regular editors for more than a decade, is adamant on this point. "Being Jewish and not a big drinker, I always felt uncomfortable with his stock company, which felt reverse discrimination from the Jewish bosses in Hollywood. But Jack was never discriminatory about me or anything. He had a great relationship with every sort of person—with Harry Cohn of Columbia, Woody Strode, the black actor, and the Navajos. He had a penchant for Negroes and Indians —it was his great feeling for liberty."

The black star Stepin Fetchit agreed with this opinion, finding Ford wholly unprejudiced and "one of the greatest men who ever lived." Lee Marvin, one of Ford's few stars who was a liberal and a Democrat, concurred. "The real regulars, they were hard-assed boys. And they said things about Jews and blacks. Whether they really meant it or not, they acted it out, because they thought that's what Ford liked, whereas in reality Ford was probably the most liberal man I ever met. Yet he didn't act it. He'd act it out in films for you. But you never knew where he stood with you. He was just waiting for you to disclose yourself."[11]

If Ford was sometimes thought to be a bigot, it was because he presented in his films the bigotry he found in the world, in order to create a moral direction or a social dialectic or comic relief. "People think I am a racist," he told one French critic, "but in Arizona and New Mexico, there were lots of Southerners, so it's not surprising I show in my films characters who do have racist feelings."[12] He always tried to counterpoint the good and the bad in his ethnic or social groups, showing heroes and villains and clowns in brown and black and white, in Indian tribal costume or United States Cavalry uniform or pioneer dress. He ridiculed those who mistook his amiable insults for racial slurs. To be called a limey or a mick by John Ford was to be accepted as a working member of his freemasonry of the casual jibe.

For the next twenty-five years Mary Ford spent half her life on *The Araner* with her two children, Patrick and Barbara. "It was terribly expensive," she said, "but it was our life, and we had it—and Jack had his relaxation." The boat was a comfortable ketch with room enough for all. It had two fireplaces and bathrooms, red carpets, a four-poster marriage bed, and a dressing room for Mary Ford. Her husband took over the teak deckhouse as his special area. There he would sit between movies, playing cards and drinking with his special friends like John Wayne and Ward Bond and Grant Withers. Sometimes they played "honeymoon bridge," because, as Ford said, "we're trying to screw each other." At other times they played Ford's version of poker—high low, jack and the game. Ford had the roof of the deck-house raised so that Wayne would not bump his head on it. The trouble was, Wayne was the only regular player who could outbluff the captain himself.

While the games went on Dudley Nichols used to toil at his screenplays in a forward cabin. On one occasion he brought a complete scenario to Ford in the middle of a long poker session. "Be careful with it," Nichols said, "I don't have a copy." "You bet," Ford replied. According to Ward Bond, Ford then leafed through the script, weighed it in one hand, and pitched it through an open porthole into the ocean.[13] There were too many pages in the script, which meant that there was too much dialogue. Nichols returned to his work and made it shorter.

The next major film Nichols wrote for Ford was *The Lost Patrol.* Ford had a great deal of trouble with other screenwriters on the scenario and called in Nichols ten days before shooting was due to start. The two men returned to Philip MacDonald's World War I story *Patrol* and started again from scratch. After eight very long days Nichols had written a new script which Ford began to shoot at once, scoring a great critical success. In movie-making as in art, pressure could produce grace.

In *The Lost Patrol* Ford again particularly examines three men among a dozen straying and dying in a desert—a situation which fascinated him from *Marked Men* to *Three Godfathers*. "It was a character study," he said of the film, "you got to know the life story of each of the men. We shot it at Yuma in two weeks."[14] The differences in this version were that the calvary patrol was British, the desert was Mesopotamian, and Boris Karloff played his only role for Ford as a religious fanatic. Victor McLaglen starred as his usual boastful, swaggering sergeant and ended as the last survivor, staring mutely at the sun-bright swords that marked the graves of his dead comrades, unable to tell the relieving column how they had died.

The power of the film lies in the mystery of their deaths. Unseen Arabs kill the men one by one. The shrinking group vainly scouts for the hidden enemy. Scared and sweating, the soldiers look from their private observatories at the invisible face of death itself. When some Arabs finally appear and McLaglen mows them down with a burst from his machine-gun, he laughs uncontrollably in the release of violent revenge, repaying body for body the stealthy murder of all his comrades.

The austerity of *The Lost Patrol,* which concentrated on how men approach dying rather than the bloody convulsions of interminable battle scenes, won Ford critical acclaim and his composer Max Steiner an Oscar for the score. In fact Lindsay Anderson is correct to criticize Steiner for his blatant and imitative music, which destroys the brooding silence and menace of the dunes that trap the doomed men.[15] Yet in the Thirties a composer had to turn out a score to cover the whole length of a feature. In these new days of the talking picture, producers were scared of any gap in the sound which might remind an audience of the silent era. While Steiner's full-throated music might suit *King Kong,* it deafened *The Lost Patrol.* If Ford had had more silence in his talking pictures, he might have achieved the stoic grace of the Finnish masterpiece *The Unknown Soldier,* about the slow death of a platoon on the Russian front.

Ford made two other inconsiderable films in 1934 and 1935, interspersed with a trilogy starring the cowboy comic Will Rogers. *The World Moves On* was the saga of a Louisiana dynasty, spanning a hundred years —one critic wrote that it was rather like the mating of *Showboat* with *The House of Rothschild.*[16] Madeleine Carroll, who was after Ford as much as the leading role, played the lead with Franchot Tone, but Ford seemed uninterested in drawing a good performance out of these polished actors. He had resisted directing the picture, but he was being paid well and he was under contract. "I argued and fought, and that was how I got the reputation of being a tough guy—which I'm not," he said later. "I can fight like hell, but I always lost."[17] Even Ford could not defeat the studio system, although he once turned down a film from Irving Thalberg because Thalberg kept him waiting for an hour outside his office. Ford walked away, leaving Thalberg a note:

> Dear Irving,
>   I'd save my money. See you later.
>   Jack[18]

As in *Four Sons,* there is a message in *The World Moves On* about the uselessness of the sacrifice of soldiers in foreign wars. The sequences in no man's land in Flanders are so horrific that Howard Hawks borrowed footage from them for *The Road to Glory.* Yet the creeping barrage of words that bombard the ear make this film the probable source of a Ford legend. He used to tell of his revenge on a producer who refused to cut any dialogue in a lengthy script. Ford filmed every word, then left the footage with the producer to edit his own feature from all the talk. Also Lumsden Hare was acting for Ford in the role of a British baronet, and Ford enjoyed letting the co-director who had spoiled *The Black Watch* with long talking sequences now spoil *The World Moves On* with an interminable volley of cultured words.

His other minor picture of this period, *The Whole Town's Talking,* was a gangster vehicle for Edward G. Robinson and Jean Arthur. Ford shot the film as a burlesque of the genre, aided by dialogue from Robert Riskin, who usually injected humor into Capra's comedies. Robinson played a double-headed part, showing both his lovable and his criminal face, as a clerk and as a gangster. It was all good broad fun, but hardly Ford at his most definitive.

His trilogy with Will Rogers, however, was very much a part of his vision of America. The three films, *Doctor Bull* and *Judge Priest* and *Steamboat Round the Bend,* might easily have been mere scene-shifting behind the famous Rogers folksy performance. Ford, indeed, had to give Rogers his head, making a virtue out of his star's bumbling and unpolished delivery. He told Rogers that no writer could write for him, so that the cowboy humorist would have to get the sense of a scene and play it in his own words. This Rogers did, turning out three vintage character studies for Ford, whose contribution was to scale down Rogers's performance by the clever use of camera lenses and to set him in credible rural backgrounds, so even the idiosyn-

cratic actor seemed to sprout from a social context, a place, and a
time.

The Rogers trilogy has a leisured nostalgia and a populism that is still
appealing. The films illuminate Ford's gift for recreating the lost past of
most Americans' dreams—that rural Golden Age they had rarely had but
usually remembered having. In *Doctor Bull* Rogers is the outrageous general practitioner who copes with his patients' little illnesses, then combats
an epidemic with the same rambling assurance. If there is a conflict, it lies
in Rogers's folk wisdom set against the test tubes of his modern rival. The
film, however, in one critic's words, "is little more than the sum of its
digressions," with its leisurely pacing more suitable to Kentucky than
Connecticut.[19] Ford seemed to prefer the small-town dream of the South
and West to his own boyhood memories of Maine, as though his nostalgia
had migrated with his craft.

Rogers also plays the title role in *Judge Priest,* set in a small Kentucky town of the 1890's that is unable to forget the Civil War. The
film is anecdotal and drenched in sentiment. It is Ford's tribute to the
memory of D.W. Griffith as much as to the Old South—in the climactic court scene Henry B. Walthall echoes his role in *The Birth of a Nation* and saves an accused man by recalling in flashback his brave
deeds in the Confederate army. Stepin Fetchit gives a vintage performance thicker than molasses. It is an ironic and illuminating burlesque on the blackface minstrel tradition, although the worried producers cut out a scene of Rogers saving Fetchit from a lynching.
Ford's triumph again was to fix Rogers's performance firmly into a
rich historical myth, so that he sits in his crumpled white suit as com-
fortably as a watermelon in its patch.

Steamboat Round the Bend was Rogers's last film before his death and
Ford's best American comedy. Underrated by most critics, it debunks
history and deflates sectarian religion as lethally as Herman Melville's
The Confidence Man, while it commemorates the repeal of the hypocrisy
of Prohibition in a blaze of belching fire from the smokestacks of a
paddlewheel steamer.

The first line of the film is spoken by the huge white-robed New
Moses on the stern of a steamboat. He damns the demon rum with
the shout, "Repent, ye sinners!" Moving about among the crowd is
Will Rogers as a patent medicine salesman, selling his cure-all Pocahontas Remedy as readily as Melville's confidence man sold his Samaritan Pain Dissuader. The medicine is mere moonshine and puts
the spirits back in the sinners. With his profits Rogers buys a histori-

cal waxworks show which he installs in an old steamboat to cruise along the Mississippi. For Ford as for Melville

> "here reigned the dashing and all-fusing spirit of the West, whose type is the Mississippi itself, which, uniting the streams of the most distant and opposite zones, pours them along, helter-skelter, in one cosmopolitan and confident tide."[20]

So Ford sets the scene for a comedy about Victorian morality, with the flow of the mighty river and Will Rogers mocking history and sectarian quarrels and righteousness. As a riverboat showman, Rogers knows his audience and changes the identity of his historical waxworks. He makes the Virgin Queen become Pocahontas. He has never heard of King George III, so he calls him George Washington. Ulysses S. Grant loses his cigar and is transformed into Robert E. Lee. Stepin Fetchit falls into a stuffed whale's mouth and speaks as Jonah. Great men are ludicrous and interchangeable—what is certain is that they have made many poor soldiers and sailors die. Yet, finally, the authority of the waxworks can quell a mob who have come to burn the boat because shows are downright immoral.

The ambiguities of history and virtue are further shown in the melodramatic plot. Rogers's innocent nephew is condemned to be hanged for a murder that he has not committed. He is married in jail to a "swamp girl" not good enough for him, and he is saved at the scaffold by the testimony of the New Moses, who has been called to witness by a baptism in the Mississippi at the end of Will Rogers's rope. Social and religious hierarchies and vanities are mocked, while the heroes of progress are the iron horses of the paddle-steamers, belching out their pillars of smoke and fire in a race downriver based in part on Ford's previous film *Cameo Kirby*.

Rogers's old boat wins the race, fueled by his bottles of Pocahontas Remedy which make his smokestacks flare like jet engines and explosively push his craft on its way. The waxworks are consigned to the flames, Fetchit himself is nearly thrown into a lynching oven, the New Moses feeds the fires with moonshine in a hilarious holocaust of past pretensions. The moral is Will Rogers's dictum to his nephew's girl as she steers the boat as slowly as a mud turtle. "Lord's much broader-minded than you think he is."

Soon after completing shooting on *Steamboat Round the Bend* Rogers decided to go to Alaska with the pioneer aviator Wiley Post, who wore a black patch over one eye like a pirate. Ford's yacht *The Araner* was docked at Santa Monica, so he gave a farewell party for Rogers and Post. He wanted to make another film with Rogers in Hawaii where *The Araner* was sailing, and he pressed Rogers to take the boat with him and Ward Bond and his crew. In a cryptic adieu Rogers said, "You keep your duck and go on the water, I'll take my eagle and fly."

He took his one-eyed eagle and flew north and crashed in the nose-heavy airplane into the Walakpa Lagoon near Point Barrow in Alaska. Both he and Wiley Post were killed. He used to call Mary Ford "the lion tamer," and she needed all her strength to assuage her husband's grief and horror at the manner of his friend's death. "We had a terrible time with Jack," she remembered. "He went all to pieces. He was superstitious, and those last words of Will's kept going through his ears—'You keep your duck and go on the water . . .' "[21]

So one of the figures in Ford's nostalgic recreation of America was killed on a pioneer flight to America's last frontier. There was nothing to do but sail back to Hollywood and go to work. A few years previously Ford had begun occasionally to wear a black patch over one eye like Wiley Post. There was an embarrassment in this because Raoul Walsh had also worn a black patch ever since a jackrabbit had jumped through the windshield of a location car while he was playing the Cisco Kid in one of the first outdoor sound features, *In Old Arizona.* After an operation to remove one eyeball Walsh had returned with his new patch to a party of his old Hollywood friends. There Ford had told him that no one would believe he had not been stabbed in the eye while looking through a keyhole. And then Ford had added, "That black patch will get more dames than you ever had before."

Walsh was not so sure. When he looked at himself in the mirror, he thought he was Black Bart, the stage-robber. "If I ever decided to become a bandit," he wrote later, "I would only need half a mask."[22] When Ford took up his own black patch, Walsh had his revenge. He suggested to his rival director that he also had his bad eye plucked out. "Jack turned white," Walsh said.[23]

John Ford had been born short-sighted. The weak eyes of his boyhood had grown weaker by 1935—"the Klieg eyes" of those who had worked for decades in the blinding glare of the studio lamps which burned retinas more cruelly than the noon sun. He had long worn tinted glasses against the glare and also to conceal his sensitive expression. "If he had shown his kindly eyes," his daughter says, "they would have walked over him on the set."[24] His new black patch was a good disguise, turning his hooded stare into a pirate's inquisition. Like Admiral Nelson at Copenhagen, Ford learned the art of putting his viewfinder to his blind eye, or of reading a page in the script by lifting up his patch. If he did not want to do anything, he could show it clearly enough.

In fact he seemed to take a perverse pleasure in choosing two careers, film director and naval intelligence officer, which normally demanded an eagle eye. It was as if he saw his opportunity in his disability. One of his veteran cameramen, Arthur C. Miller, noted that Ford would hardly communicate with him at all, perhaps only fifty words a day, because he would only work with technicians who sensed what he wanted. "He knew nothing of lighting," Miller said. "He never once looked in the camera when we worked together. You see, the man had bad eyes, as long as I knew him, but he was a man whose veins ran with the business."[25] His occasional use of a viewfinder seemed theatrical, a ruse to persuade people that his vision was better than it was.

It remains the chief irony in Ford's life that he could hardly see. Yet his Irish pride and native genius turned this embarrassment into an original approach to the cinema. His blurred vision did not allow for the meticulous placing of people in artificial spaces, but demanded the broad sweep of movement across the shadings and masses of nature. Only with his spectacles on did he choose the extended two shot, in which two characters could meet and talk with that intimate ease that was Ford's trademark with his friends and in his films. His insight compensated for his lack of sight.

In his next film and first acknowledged masterpiece, *The Informer*, Ford decided to use the stumbling uncertainty of his blurred natural vision to suggest the moral confusion of his hero. Against a great deal of resistance from RKO, then headed by the Irish-American Joe Kennedy, Ford had managed to win studio assent to the filming of his distant cousin Liam O'Flaherty's novel, which would star Victor McLaglen. The subject was dear to Ford's heart, set as it was in Dublin in 1922, when he had observed the victory of the Sinn Fein and the shifting allegiances of the Irish patriots and their attacks on the British and on each other. For the screenplay he went to Dudley Nichols, who had worked with Lamar Trotti on the second and third features of the Will Rogers trilogy.

It was a new experience for Nichols. He was called in to meet the composer, Steiner, the art director, Van Nest Polglase, and the camera-man, Joe August, before he wrote the script. The style was set in advance of the screenplay—a foggy German expressionist world where the swirls of mist would hide the falsity of the painted studio drops and would wreathe and drift with the moods of the Informer himself, Gypo Nolan. This cinematic vision would also serve as Ford's own impression of the complexity and treachery of Irish politics, as well as the natural fog of his view of the world.

To show the fraility of men's loyalty, Ford wanted to put aside a clear view of right and wrong for the shifting haze of moral ambiguity. What he saw with his own weak eyes would show Gypo Nolan's mental confusion. Until Camus wrote *The Fall*, about a man trapped in the infernal mists and canals of Amsterdam, Ford's foggy Dublin would remain the obscure definitive labyrinth of the uneasy moral choices of man.

According to Nichols, the key to *The Informer* was its stylized symbolism. "I brought to the script, and Ford brought to the direction of this film, everything I had learned and all that he knew. Never since have I been able to work so freely or experimentally."[26] Joe Kennedy sold the studio while Ford was in the middle of shooting the film, but because it was a low budget picture the new chiefs allowed Ford to complete his work without any interference in a large neglected stage on the lot.

He provoked an extraordinary and puzzled performance from Victor McLaglen. By Hollywood tradition he kept McLaglen drunk or suffering from a hangover for three weeks to capture the groping confusion of Gypo Nolan on screen—a story Ford fiercely denounced as libelous. He was also said to have printed rehearsal and rejected takes to catch his star's mistakes. When McLaglen won an Oscar for his performance, he bitterly denied that Ford had tricked it out of him. Yet he was never to play so well again. The fact was that Ford ruthlessly bullied, badgered, and bamboozled his actors into showing him what he wanted to record.

Although *The Informer* was internationally recognized as an instant classic, the apogee of the American sound film to date, and one of the ten best films ever made, it was hailed more as homage than experiment. The swirling fogs of the camerawork had drifted from the early German studios; the exaggerated chiaroscuro derived from *Warning Shadows* (whose director, Arthur Robison, had actually made a silent version of *The Informer*); the strong religious symbolism of the Judas figure recalled all the Passion Plays ever performed. Ford seemed to have blessed Hollywood with the holy water of Europe. Thus, as time passed, film critics tended to consider the picture imitative and overwrought, ignoring its nightmarish coherence and engulfing ambivalence.

For the foggy and shadowy Dublin of *The Informer* is the groping projection of Gypo Nolan's mind. We see the studio Irish city through a lens darkly and then Nolan suddenly face to face, only to lose him again on his drunken stumble through the obscurity of his desires. He is an Aristotelian tragic hero, whose moral character is revealed by what he chooses or avoids. At first he is excluded from his group loyalty for refusing to murder a political victim for the Irish rebel cause. Then, starving in a city of night and soup kitchens, he dreams of love and escape to America, sailing on a liner he sees in a poster reflected in window glass, tempting him with the message: *10 pounds to America: Information Within.* The twenty pounds of his Judas money for betraying a comrade to the British army tinkles on the music track and gleams on the table top and slips through his fingers in greed and lust and shame and conscience, until he is mortally wounded by his avenging friends and finally shriven by his confession to the Mother Ireland figure in a Catholic church.

Forgive us, O Lord, he seems to say to us, *for we know not what we do.*

Ford knew what he was doing. The most haunting moments of the film are indelible in the vocabulary of the cinema: the wanted poster blowing after Gypo Nolan and pursuing him like the tip-tap of the cane of the blind man who witnessed the betrayal; the woman lifting her shawl and changing herself from madonna to whore; the death of the betrayed gunman, his fingernails scratching on the windowsill; the boy street-singer chanting, "The minstrel boy to the war is gone/In the ranks of death you'll find him," then turning to throw away the policemen's tip; the disgust on the British officers' faces as they pay Nolan his blood money, throwing it on the table and pushing it across with a cane. Max Steiner's music counterpoints its lure for Nolan, but the only words spoken as the informer picks it up are the British officer's dismissal, "Show him out the back way."

For such economy John Wayne always praised Ford as the best editor in the business. In the original script, for instance, Nichols had written a long "thirty pieces of silver" sequence, which Ford finally directed in the mime of eloquent disdain. He had made the scene unnecessary by putting a prologue on the work, permissible in the film vocabulary of the Thirties. It set the moral before the audience saw the images of the film, thus adding to their sense of Nolan's tragedy.

> Then the Judas repented himself—and cast down the thirty pieces of silver—and departed.

So Ford condemned Nolan to his inexorable fate, but the subtlety of his condemnation was to show Nolan's uncertain treachery, to understand the warped choices put before a poor man in bad times. Ford presented the old gnostic riddle of Saint Judas, called by God to betray Jesus in order to make the Crucifixion possible. Thus Nolan is received into grace by his confession beneath the Cross. In *The Informer* Ford is the arbiter who speaks in Randall Jarrell's dread lines from "For an Emigrant":

> *Forgive. Forgive? Forgive no one.*
> *Understand and blame.*

7: An Inner Vision

Ford had the true eye of the film-maker. His sight was not very good,
but he had the surprising power of an inner vision.

—Dudley Nichols

In a film director's life a combined critical and commercial success is usually something of a catastrophe. It persuades the lucky man that he can do it again and again, though the gap between art and the box office is wider than between beauty and the beast.

The Informer had cost little to make, soon earned back its budget, and won a host of awards. Ford himself won both an Academy Award and the New York Film Critics Award, while Oscars were also voted to Victor McLaglen, Dudley Nichols, and Max Steiner for the score. This broad sweep by such a European-style picture prophesied Billy Wilder's later remark to his cameraman on *Sunset Boulevard:* "Keep it out of focus. I want to win the foreign-picture award."

By 1936 the continuing slump had led to a consolidation of the studio system in Hollywood. Five major studios and three minor ones now dominated the industry. They were determined to survive by strict cost accounting, and by trying to clip the wings of such independent directors as Ford in an effort to produce nothing but certain box-office successes. They were also trying to lower everybody's salary except the studio executives'.

This ruthless new economic policy led to a labor war with King Vidor leading the Directors' Guild in its fight against the studios. Part of the strategy of the various guilds was to wreck the promotional value of the Academy Awards, because Oscars helped a film at the box office. Frank Capra was asked to become president of the embattled Motion Picture Academy, and he persuaded D. W. Griffith to attend the awards dinner that year and to accept a special small statue for his pioneering work in the cinema. Ford himself would not appear in person to accept his first Oscar. He hated all political infighting and all ceremony, outside the navy. He did, however, accept the award by proxy, while Dudley Nichols refused it because of his support of a boycott by the Writers' Guild.[1]

Such success encouraged Ford and Nichols to work on two more pictures at RKO studios on the subject of Celtic resistance to the British Crown. The first of these was *Mary of Scotland,* which Nichols adapted for the screen from a verse play by Maxwell Anderson. This costume drama begins with Mary, the new Queen of Scotland, appearing out of the fog on a ship, bringing her from widowhood and exile in France in a hopeless effort to keep her country independent of Queen Elizabeth I of England. She is, in her way, the royal counterpart of the Informer in her preordained doom, although her weakness is her love for Bothwell, played by Fredric March, and her trial takes place in a high court in front of five looming judges and an empty throne, on which the rival queen's symbols of dominion rest—crown and scepter and orb.[2]

Mary is also the doomed Catholic heroine, loving and frail, matched against the sexual frustration and vengeance of the virgin Protestant queen. Here Ford stresses his historical mythology beyond the call of fact. Mary plays the role of the religious martyr, faced with fanaticism and the cruel oppression of the law. In her fate at the hands of Queen Elizabeth we are made to see the ancient battle between Rome and Geneva, the Pope and Calvin, the unending clash between grace and predestination.

In the opening sequences of *Mary of Scotland* Ford informs us that the struggles of human life are temporal and irrelevant to the eternal, for both rival queens now lie buried side by side in Westminster Abbey—in the same way as the rival sea captains in the ancient burial ground of Ford's boyhood. They are twin visions which Ford has called forth on screen to replay the dialectic of doom and choice, destiny and bravery, power and the human heart. History is only a setting for social and individual conflict, which is the same in the sixteenth as in the twentieth century. Although that conflict is perpetual, since it lies in human nature, time resolves all with God above all.

Mary's redemption and victory lead her to the scaffold. She will survive and triumph through her son, who will succeed her barren rival on the English throne. Like the Informer, she goes to her death dwarfed by the signs of the cross—in this case, between two rows of linked stakes on either side of the scaffold steps, which pen her wholly within the symbol of her crucifixion and her ascension to grace. Unlike the Informer, she is killed for refusing to cooperate with intriguing heretic power, yet she is victorious in death—a mother alone against a spinster with an army. Ford's Irish conditioning is fully displayed on the screen, showing the strength of martyrdom and motherhood in outlasting the mailed fist and a Herodian law.

His good fortune was to have Katharine Hepburn to play Mary for him. There was such a strong feeling between director and star that they could never work together again. But this passion infused her performance as a madonna and as a Magdalene, making her transcend her material. She is shown as a prisoner within her heavy gowns and beneath the ornate ceilings and stone walls of her castles, yet she plays most humanly with her confidant Rizzio and her lover Bothwell, who passes on the Stuart sword of succession to her small son. Both of these adored figures die in a prophecy of her own death, Rizzio running from room to room before drawing a bedspread over his face to hide the deadly daggers from his spent eyes, Bothwell expiring in an alien cell during a windstorm as he dreams of his lost love, Mary. Again they represent Ford's vision of the two crucified thieves, who must die before Mary herself replays the role of Christ the Martyr on her own scaffold.

Yet finally the restrictions of the studio production limit Ford's genius for setting his characters in space and nature and time. He can only film the shadow play of human conflict, not an organic struggle rooted in the earth. He tried, even with Fredric March, to redeem the heaviness of the sets and the material with his usual broad strokes of humor. "I was playing Bothwell," March recalled, "and I didn't seem to be getting there, so I asked Ford. 'It's a comedy,' he said about the tragedy. 'Play him for comedy.' "[3]

Little of that comedy reached the screen, and Ford's striving for a human touch was condemned by the unreality of the sets and of the dialogue adapted from a play in verse.

Mary of Scotland was followed by another of Ford's and Nichols's commercial failures about Celtic resistance. They had to fight to film their chosen subject, Sean O'Casey's *The Plough and the Stars.* Ford was trying to defend his new and hard-won independence. "They've got to turn over picture-making into the hands that know it," he told an interviewer in 1936. "Combination of author and director running the works: that's the ideal."[4] Yet though he fought the censors and the financiers at every point to do the O'Casey play, and though he managed to import the Abbey Players from Dublin to act the supporting roles, he lost over his star casting. Barbara Stanwyck was imposed upon his picture like a *grande dame* in an Irish bog, crying for help in her American voice as she struggled in the domestic interludes inserted in the script.

These compromises ruined the film. There were three separate stories that did not unite in the mystery of a trinity. The first story dealt with Barbara Stanwyck's attempts to stop her husband from joining the Irish rebels in the attempted coup of 1916, the second was a separate play about the complexities and failings of Irish character during the Easter Rising, and the third was Ford's own praise of the heroism of the rebel martyrs, doomed in their self-sacrifice.

Ford knew the film did not work and had a quarrel with the studio chiefs after they sent out an assistant director to shoot additional love scenes between Barbara Stanwyck and her husband before their marriage. "Completely ruined the damn thing," Ford commented later. "Destroyed the whole story—which is about a man and his wife."[5] Yet the film was flawed in concept and execution, with the Abbey Players mismatching their performances with Hollywood stars like Stanwyck. The final result looked both authentic and contrived, extremely Irish and American with no hyphen to hold them together.

For the time being this was the last of Ford's trilogy of Celtic protest, begun with *The Informer.* The second and third of his artistic films in this vein with Nichols flopped badly at the box office. His heart and tradition might still lie with resistance to the British Empire, but his emotional commitment was not helping his career or paying his bills at home. Ford was always a professional before he was an artist, just as he was an American patriot before he was an Irish rebel.

It was true that he had again visited his Aunt Margaret in Spiddal in Galway. She lived in a two-room cottage with an iron kettle hanging over the fire in the hearth—a background he would use for Noel Purcell's cottage in *The Rising of the Moon.* He had again met his Thornton cousins, who had fought against the Black and Tans during his first visit to Galway and who were still active in the Irish Republican Army. He was still providing occasional funds for the underground war against the British in Ulster, and he had returned to Hollywood with the emotional strength to make him push ahead with his Celtic trilogy in the unsympathetic studio system. Yet at the last he put his job and his country first, and the Irish cause was secondary to his vision of America, both as a film director and as a naval officer.

His dual role in the intelligence service became more pronounced after he had acquired *The Araner.* The influence of Japanese and German agents in Mexico and California was growing. One of Ford's later military comrades in the Second World War, the burly and aggressive Carl Eifler, had been a prohibition agent on the Mexican border in the early Thirties. He had submitted a secret report on Japanese spying in Baja California and along the frontier. He had also informed on a proposed German-Mexican defense pact—the visiting battlecruiser *Karlsbad* was even sighted flying the Mexican flag. Despite this report the American authorities allowed the Japanese to bring their shrimpboats into San Pedro and Long Beach harbors to transfer their catches to Japanese freighters. Although diplomatic action diverted Mexico from a Japanese or German alliance, American security was threatened in southern California itself.[6]

In this situation Ford combined relaxation with counterintelligence. Briefed by Zacharias in the Eleventh Naval District at San Diego, he would cruise the coastline down to Baja California and Acapulco on the watch for Japanese shrimp fleets commanded by disguised officers from their navy. Usually it was an all-male trip with John Wayne and Ward Bond and other close friends with closed mouths, rather more effective than Hemingway's private campaign against U-boats in the Caribbean.

Mary Ford was briefed and gathered intelligence on two occasions. Once she got aboard a Japanese shrimpboat to make a distress telephone call, only to find in the fishing captain's cabin a photograph of the man in full naval officer's uniform. Another time she came dripping out of the sea near San Diego harbor and asked to change her clothes at a house rented by visiting Japanese businessmen; it was full of cameras and surveillance equipment. On that same voyage she was alone on watch on the deck of *The Araner* when a German battle-cruiser came alongside, then vanished.[7]

The Araner played a hidden role in counterintelligence during the prewar years that is only suggested by Ford's first official commendation from the Commandant of the Eleventh Naval District. By 1939 Ford had already risen to be a Lieutenant Commander in the naval reserve, and he was praised for his initiative in securing valuable material, contained in an intelligence report on Baja California and the Gulf. "Your efforts to obtain this information, voluntarily and at your own expense," the commandant's letter to him ran, "are considered very commendable."[8]

Ford also sailed *The Araner* frequently to Hawaii. He was very much master of his yacht, even insisting that all the crew stay aboard when a hurricane struck *The Araner* at anchor off Honolulu. He and his family were always welcomed by the Hawaiians in those relaxed and unspoiled years between the wars. He maintained his cover as a film director and mere visitor because the American navy was widely unpopular at the time as a result of a local murder case. He did not want to present himself to the Hawaiians as one of the feared "blue suits," although he secretly continued to help the fleet air arm develop its reconnaissance facilities from Pearl Harbor. He spent so much time there with *The Araner* that one of the islands near its approaches became known as Ford's Island—the shellfish there were very good.

He would wait on his ketch off Hawaii for his next film assignment. A cable would arrive from his new studio employers, Darryl Zanuck or Sam Goldwyn, and he would fly or sail home for the picture they had arranged for him to direct. There was no question of his independence after the commercial failure of his Celtic trilogy. His new chief screenwriter, Nunnally Johnson, was clear on that point. At Twentieth Century-Fox with Zanuck, Ford did not initiate a production—he only had the right of veto over a screenplay which a Fox producer might bring to him.

This dependence on the studio system was made easier by Ford's trust in Darryl Zanuck as a superb editor. They had an agreement. "As soon as I finished a picture," Ford said, "he would cut it. The last night or the next day, when all the film was okayed, I would leave and get on my boat and go to Honolulu or someplace." Ford hated to sit in a cutting or projection room, and he would only occasionally see the final print of one of his films. He had shot it so that it could only be cut in one way, unless an integral part was dropped or additional scenes added. Ford was so expert that he would know exactly what he had recorded without looking at it. "When they cut one of my pictures," he said, "it always came right down to the length, the full length. If a scene was dropped, the picture was too short."[9]

In a remarkable memorandum written in June, 1937, David O. Selznick made Ford's position in the studio system very clear. He had been discussing a Ford project with one of his previous producers, Merian C. Cooper. Selznick's verdict was this:

> We must select the story and sell it to John Ford, instead of having Ford select some uncommercial pet of his that we would be making only because of Ford's enthusiasm. I do not think we can make any picture because of any director's enthusiasm . . . I see no justification for making any story just because it is liked by a man who, I am willing to concede, is one of the greatest directors in the world, but whose record commercially is far from good . . .[10]

Under this system Ford began to make a miscellany of films again in which his master's voice was always evident, his total control absent. During the shooting of the first of these Nunnally Johnson told of Zanuck himself coming on set to rage at Ford, who had allowed his star to play in a false Southern drawl. Ford threatened to walk off the movie; Zanuck yelled back that nobody ever threatened him in his own studio. Ford was silent and went over to talk to the star. Days later the subject of the quarrel came up in Johnson's presence. "Oh," Ford said casually, "Darryl and I had a little talk, and after that there was no more trouble." He looked at Johnson, who nodded his assent.[11] So Ford kept the legend of his invincibility on set, but actually acquiesced in the fact of the power of the studio boss.

The film was *The Prisoner of Shark Island,* written by Johnson, on the subject of the victimization of the doctor who had treated John Wilkes Booth after his assassination of Abraham Lincoln. The feature opens with a series of set pieces on the end of the Civil War, as stylized as Will Rogers's historical waxworks show in *Steamboat Round the Bend.* Abraham Lincoln moves to his doom as an all-wise, all-forgiving figurehead, an inexorable martyr to his duty and his country like Mary of Scotland. He is more heroic than homespun, more sainted than real. In Frank McGlynn's playing of the aging President there seems to be no foretaste of Henry Fonda's *Young Mr. Lincoln,* except for a moment when McGlynn asks a band celebrating Lee's surrender to play "Dixie." By that one word he tries to heal simply the wounds of a civil war.

The story then switches to the persecution of Dr. Samuel Mudd, whose compassion for Booth leads him to become an American Dreyfus, accused of conspiracy in the death of the President and imprisoned on Shark Island. In that concentration camp, guarded by black soldiers under the command of the aged Harry Carey, Ford's ambivalence towards southern history is shown. The black soldiers are bullies when faced with the noble defiance of their victim, and they are cowards when stricken by an epidemic of yellow fever.

Yet in his strong conclusion Ford redraws his holy picture of the noble, defeated, suffering South oppressed by bayonets and scalawags. The mutiny of the black soldiers has a revolutionary thrust, while the return of the white doctor and his black neighbor to their families has an embracing compassion. Ford did not shrink from showing the conflicts and bigotry of history, yet he would always suggest a solution—that human beings should survive until bad times changed for the better. Even his caricatures and sadists, such as John Carradine's role as the evil jailer, Sergeant Rankin, are capable of redemption—he leads in demanding to sign the doctor's petition for a pardon. No man, Ford suggests, is as black or white as he is portrayed or painted.

This was one of many contemporary films, such as Fritz Lang's *Fury,* which protested against the rising tide of bigotry and lynch law in the American thirties. The Ku Klux Klan in fact tried to recruit new members in Ford's home city of Portland. They attracted many Protestants from the Western Promenade and the smart suburbs of Cape Elizabeth. But the Catholics and the Jews felt threatened by the organization, and they rallied around the few black families in the city. They boycotted stores owned by new Klan members and put them out of business. So Irish boycott fought Southern bigotry in Portland. There, as in the films of John Ford, the sympathy of the immigrant enclaves lay with the victim or the small group threatened by the majority or the injustice of the law.

Ford's next picture for Zanuck seemed a total apostasy. It was a Kipling tale, *Wee Willie Winkie,* sentimentalizing British rule in India and starring the egregious tot, Shirley Temple. Ford could not do much with the standard cute Temple performance except to shoot the film from a child's eye view and emphasize the role of Victor McLaglen as the tough sergeant with the soft heart who taught Miss Temple to drill with a toy rifle for God, for Empire, and for the gross receipts. "He loved Shirley and Shirley loved him," Ford reminisced later about McLaglen, "and pretty soon this grew into a big part."[12] The sergeant's death did provide the only memorable sequence in the movie. It was shot under rainclouds streaked with sunlight, which made an awesome backdrop to the ritual of military funeral.

Sam Goldwyn switched Ford from bathos to apocalypse. Ford had long wanted a Polynesian subject, and he was given one in *The Hurricane.* The reason for its making was its spectacular climax, which was co-directed by the catastrophe expert James Basevi—he had already created a holocaust *In Old Chicago,* shocked *San Francisco* into rubble, and ravaged *The Good Earth* of China with swarms of locusts. His wind and water effects in the studio drenched the stars with driving torrents of deluge. Ford put a second camera on stage in case a roof or a sarong blew off—particularly off Dorothy Lamour, who was to make that single piece of wrapped cloth her symbol on the road.

Lamour played the romantic lead of Marama like a kewpie doll in a Honolulu tourist shop, although her lover Terangi was played by Jon Hall, actually part-Tahitian and a neighbor of the Ford family. Ford gave Hall his chance and he took it competently, although the performances of Raymond Massey and Mary Astor as the French island governor and his wife were marvels of civilized nuance compared with Hall's sweet primitivism. The script repeated Ford's preoccupation with the conflict between the heart and the head, the outlaw forced into an irreconcilable struggle with the symbol of authority without hope of resolution short of death or cataclysm.

Over and over again Massey refuses his wife's emotional pleas to release the noble savage Hall, who is like a bird that must die in a cage. "I am not the representative of a well-meaning point of view," he says. He represents the law, not justice. Even if Hall is a political prisoner, he chooses to prolong his sentence by continual attempts to escape to rejoin his wife and child. Massey cannot permit Hall to subvert the principle of government. He must recapture the outlaw, who has become a myth on the islands because of his demand for freedom and his defiance, which ends with his killing a persecuting guard on his last escape. "Murder and anarchy," Massey insists, "will leave no legend behind."

Only the mass murder and anarchy of a wrathful heaven in the blast of the hurricane could allow Massey to accept Hall's breaking of the law. The noble savage has saved the governor's wife by taking her out of the doomed, wave-battered Catholic church and lashing her to a floating tree with his own family. This symbolic act, proving that the pagan gods of the wind and the sea can be more powerful than the Christian God of the land, has been prefigured in Hall's wedding ceremony, which began with stiff Catholicism and ended with the bride stripped of her civilized white gown and abandoned to the rhythms of the drums and the ancient rituals. Thomas Mitchell, rehearsing his role as the drunken doctor before perfecting it in *Stagecoach,* has already prophesied that civilization won't look pretty in a high wind, and Massey himself has admitted that a sense of honor in the South Seas is about as useful "as a silk hat in a hurricane." So in the last shots of film Massey turns a blind eye through his telescope to Hall's escape from human injustice, acknowledging that the elements are stronger than governments, and that mercy is the true gift of God.

Yet the impact of *The Hurricane* did not lie so much in the acting as in the storm. Ford hated to use doubles and liked humiliating actors, with the result that the elegant Massey and Astor were half-drowned by fire hoses and blown nearly to tatters. In the studio storm Ford directed the Hawaiian extras to climb coconut trees to save themselves from the artificial waves—a survival technique they would actually use later when a real hurricane and tidal wave destroyed Hilo.

Ford followed this apocalyptic film by working with Basevi again on a blizzard sequence in Goldwyn's *The Adventures of Marco Polo,* then by making two more films for Zanuck. The first of them completed his undistinguished Indian imperial trilogy, which had marched off with *The*

Black Watch, survived Shirley Temple, and snickered to an end in *Four Men and a Prayer,* an absurd melodrama of four sons avenging their officer father's death at the hands of gunrunners. Ford kept his tongue in his cheek and his eye on his paycheck. "I just didn't like the story, or anything else about it," he said later, "so it was a job of work. I kidded them slightly."[13] It sounds as if he had personally stuffed plums in the mouths of his leading British actors, who included C. Aubrey Smith, George Sanders, and David Niven. The imperial might of Britain turns out to be more of a giggle than a threat.

Ford's second film for Zanuck in 1938 was *Submarine Patrol,* a routine story of a hard-driving captain licking a broken-down ship and demoralized crew into shape in the First World War. As a boy Ford had seen the old freighters in Portland docks which were adapted to hunt U-boats in the Atlantic. Taken from a novel called *The Splinter Fleet,* the film was a tribute by Ford to the navy and another acknowledgment of his double life. He personally knew the admiral who had been in charge of the ramshackle submarine-chasers, and he used his navy contacts to get his usual cooperation on the docks and on the high seas.

Ford seemed to take a personal pleasure in presenting the scruffy underdogs of the service. As one orderly in the script declares to the hero, *"We're* in the Navy. *You're* going into the Splinter Fleet." Ford enjoyed making his own love of old clothes into a statement about the shabby look of some of the brave. His ragtag sailors negotiate a minefield and destroy a U-boat from their makeshift craft. The film, however, seems more like disguised propaganda for naval preparedness against the threat of foreign submarines than a personal statement by Ford—but then, his vision was as much from the bridge of an American ship as through a viewfinder or a camera lens.

So, as the war clouds gathered over Europe and the Far East, with the Fascists triumphant in the Spanish Civil War and the Japanese armies overrunning China, John Ford finished his two decades of preparation for the two careers in his life. He was the most professional director in Hollywood and a Lieutenant Commander in the Naval Reserve. He was always ready to go on set or to war. He was a spy on human society and alien infiltration. What he discerned with his poor sight he tested against the eagle eye of his inner vision.

He had set out in his Celtic trilogy much of his view of history: his sympathy for the victim, the martyr, the rebel, the outlaw, the human heart trapped in the toils and judgments of authority. Yet he had learned to submit his passion for liberty to the dictates of the studio system and the admirals. He was aware of the paradox of power, which gives command only to those who can receive it. He knew of the necessity of obedience in society and in the navy. If he was the boss on set and on *The Araner,* he obeyed in the studio and in the service. As he acted out his double role, he stayed true to his inner vision of the lone soul living through the purgatory of his allotted place, and time, and government.

8: Stagecoach: The Burial and Resurrection of the West

*You can't do that to that rough-riding son of a bitch . . . He was more
loyal to his country and his friends than any man who ever lived.*

—John Ford over the corpse of Tom Mix

In 1939 the Old West died for John Ford with Tom Mix, and he recreated
it in his own myth and image in *Stagecoach*. In that burial and resurrection
Ford translated his personal loss into a global myth. He turned the
Western into the most popular and enduring American legend. If the
freewheeling West of his youth was dead with his friend, the rolling coach
of his imagination preserved its folklore and illusions forever.

Tom Mix died as he had lived, flamboyant and on the trail. At the time
that he crashed at high speed in his Cord roadster in Arizona while trying
to avoid some highway workers, he was wearing diamonds in his belt-
buckle, fancy cowman's boots with a white Stetson, and he was carrying
$7500 in his pocket. The Cord overturned and broke his neck cleanly, just
as if a bronco had bucked him off. John Ford immediately left with his
wife for the mortuary in Phoenix. "He was superstitious," she said, "and
he didn't like anyone to die and owe him a debt."

When the Fords arrived, they found the corpse of Tom Mix laid out
in a tuxedo. "You can't do that to that rough-riding son of a bitch," Ford
said. So he redressed the corpse in a Stetson hat and covered the body
with an American flag and kept vigil. One of the mourners complained,
saying that Mix had been a deserter in the Spanish-American War. "The
flag stays," Ford replied. "He was more loyal to his country and his
friends than any man who ever lived." Through his intelligence contacts
Ford got the War Department to agree that Mix should be officially
buried with his coffin wrapped in the American flag. His cowboy friend
had actually only deserted to go and fight as a soldier of fortune in the
Boer War, once things had quieted down in Cuba.[1]

So Ford showed his own fierce loyalty to a comrade and to the memory of a larger, lawless West, which had once had far more room for its swashbucklers and free spirits. He returned to Hollywood, set on making a Western for the first time in thirteen years. He had bought a short story, "Stage to Lordsburg," and had worked on a script with Dudley Nichols. The story had overtones of Maupassant's "Boule de Suif," a savage attack on social hypocrisy in which a prostitute during the Franco-Prussian war of 1870 gives herself to an enemy officer in return for a safe conduct for a coachload of bourgeois passengers who despise her for her act of self-sacrifice.

In point of fact the Nichols script of *Stagecoach* had more to do with religious mysticism, Hollywood tradition, and the myth of the outlaw than it had to do with European class divisions. The prostitute in *Stagecoach* is called Dallas, golden-haired and golden-hearted with no gold in the bank. Her act of self-sacrifice is an act of surrogate motherhood—she stays up through the night at a halt on the weary journey to help the virtuous officer's wife have a baby girl. Sex is only her commodity offscreen, and marriage is her goal with the outlaw, the Ringo Kid, who has been wrongly condemned by society for a crime he did not commit. Together they oppose ostracism at the dinner table at Dry Fork. "Well," the outlaw says to Dallas, "I guess you can't break out of prison and into society in the same week."

There is a third outsider in the coach, Doc Boone, the prototype of the drunken doctor, fallen into disrepute because of his love of the bottle. At the beginning of the film he takes the arm of Dallas in front of the ladies of the Law and Order League. "We have been struck down by a foul disease called social prejudice," he says. "Come, be a proud, glorified dreg like me." These words suggest that true pride and glory come from individual defiance of the conventions of a misguided society—the town which casts them out is called Tonto, meaning "stupid." The leader of the righteous ladies is married to the villain on the coach, a banker absconding with the funds of his depositors and talking of the need for lower taxes and more troops. He plays a caricature of hypocrisy as his wife plays a comedy of bigotry.

The other passengers on the stagecoach were also to become the stock characters of later Westerns—the gentlemanly southern gambler, hiding his good family name; the seeming reverend who turns out to be a whiskey salesman; the stern, kindly, and courageous sheriff riding beside a buffoon of a driver, who can control his six-in-hand but not his mouth. Their journey from the stupidity of social judgment on their Coach of

Fools is through the purgatory of Monument Valley and Apache attack to a heavenly goal called Lordsburg.

On the way there they will meet their fate or redemption. The three outcasts are saved by love or generosity after helping at the birth of the baby. The seeming clergyman and the gambler fall to the Indians, the banker is arrested, the Ringo Kid is avenged on his accusers for his brother's death, and the sheriff lets him go free with Dallas to spare them the dubious "blessings of civilization."

Ford loved his scenario. Before shooting began he announced with glee that there was not a single respectable character in the cast. In fact the officer's wife is respectable, although she forfeits her honor by her shabby treatment of the generous Dallas. Ford's admiration for the outcast and for the victim of society had also become respectable during the Great Depression, when tens of millions were jobless and put outside the pale through no fault of their own. Poverty was no shame then, bankers were considered crooks with vaults, and human decency was the best hope of group survival. So Ford's *Stagecoach* also somehow represented within its small wooden walls on wheels the whole bandwagon of the Roosevelt years, rolling towards some resolution in the future Lordsburg of prosperity and social justice.

The Apaches typify the wild forces of nature and nemesis—yet they are less terrifying than human hypocrisy. "There are worse things than A- paches," Dallas says, staring back at the glares of the ladies of the Law and Order League. The Apaches stand in the landscape as if they were mere bleak bluffs of sandstone in Monument Valley, then whirling clouds of dust on their pursuing horses. They are as quick and beautiful as the attack of the elements, and even their savagery in the killing of a family of settlers is shown in a posed martyrdom, with their woman victim kneeling like a penitent at the altar of misunderstanding.

Ford specifically used his Indians as natural avengers. The opening titles set them in history without prejudice to their struggle for independence. Ford's statement about them informed his audience of their hopeless war against the new vehicles, which allowed the white immigrants to dispossess them:

> Until the Iron Horse came, the Stagecoach was the only means of travel on the untamed American frontier. Braving all dangers, these Concord coaches—the "streamliners" of their day—spanned on schedule wild, desolate stretches of desert and mountainland in the Southwest, where in 1885 the savage struggle of the Indians to oust the white invader was drawing

to a close. At the time no name struck more terror into the hearts of
travelers than that of GERONIMO—leader of those Apaches who preferred
death rather than submit to the white man's will.[2]

In this statement Ford praised the remorseless wheels of change that
had brought him and previous pioneers across the wilderness, yet he
admitted that the white people were the invaders and the Apaches brave
and terrible in their struggle for independence. Himself an Irish rebel at
heart, he could only admire Geronimo's long guerrilla war. Geronimo
himself appears briefly in *Stagecoach,* played by Chief White Horse, dominant on a sandstone cliff. He directs the attack on the coach as part of his
battle plan, but he does not join in it. He is the general of his people's
struggle for liberty, not a stuntman taking a fall for the entertainment of
a cinema audience.

Ford has been criticized for the last-minute charge of the Seventh
Cavalry to save the stagecoach by a slaughter of the attacking Indians. To
some modern critics, it smacks of racism as much as the gallop of the Ku
Klux Klan in *The Birth of a Nation.* Yet this is a false interpretation.
Historically, the U.S. cavalrymen did defeat the warrior tribes of the
Plains Indians, and mythologically, their intervention is like classical gods
from a machine, arriving in the nick of time to save the stagecoach from
the Furies.

They are a dramatic device, put by Ford in a historical context and
made human. Their massacre of the Apaches is glorified by no words at
all, only by the sound of the bugler blowing the charge and the images
of troopers at the gallop with sabers drawn and their flag held high. They
are no nobler than Geronimo and his braves, high on their monumental
sandstone bluff. In fact they seem alien to the very landscape from which
the Apaches seem to grow.

The landscape is truly part of Ford's technique in translating the
Western into legend. *Stagecoach* was mostly filmed in Monument Valley in Arizona—an ancient salt seabed surrounded by eroded crimson
and scarlet buttes and bluffs, the gigantic sculptures of time and
weather which make the efforts of mankind appear irrelevant and
vain. By setting the wheels of transport and the uniforms of an official
army against these prehistoric masses, Ford reduces the image of
human progress to a few insects crawling beneath the indifferent
stone faces of the ages.

The Apaches, however, are never presented as intruders upon the
majesty of the landscape, but as its true inhabitants, painted like the rocks

and the desert and the eagles and the wildcats, a part of the scale and ferocity and liberty of the place. They are as large as their own land or vanish within it. When once their scouts are seen on the rim of the crevasse through which the stagecoach passes as into the entrance to hell, they seem a distant warning to the eye of the intruder upon their space, like the danger signal a ship might fly in the vast expanse of the ocean.

Ford helped the dignity of the Indian peoples in fact as well as in the cinema. John Wayne, who played the Ringo Kid in his first major screen role, claimed to have discovered Monument Valley as a location for *Stagecoach,* but Ford took the credit for it and Ford was boss.[3] Whoever had the eye to find it, Ford's one good eye made it into the Valhalla of the Western film, and the Navajos into the guardian Indians of screen legend.

They had not been doing well before his coming in the winter of 1938, when there was a snowfall in the Valley. The Depression had hit the tribe more than in most places. The proprietor of the trading post nearby on the reservation, Harry Goulding, said he would have fainted if any of the Navajos had put a dollar on the counter.[4] They were pawning the last of their turquoise and silver jewelry when Ford arrived to spend two hundred thousand dollars while shooting *Stagecoach* there after Goulding had brought to Hollywood some pictures of the location. He transformed the local economy and made a legend of himself, leaving the Navajos "fat and sassy."

He was chosen as an honorary chief with the name of Natani Nez or Tall Soldier. He used to complain that he should have been called Tall Sailor, but he had to accept his name, as the inland Navajos had no word for seafarers. Superstitious as he was, he enjoyed working with Indian medicine men. He claimed that one of the Navajo shamans called Big Fat would get him the weather he wanted—thunderclouds cost one bottle of whiskey and a snowfall cost two bottles. He used the two Bradley brothers as his Navajo lieutenants on twelve pictures, controlling the large Indian crowd scenes under his command. He even spoke a few sentences of Navajo, enough to give the impression that he knew the language if the words could be gotten out of him.

So he aided his Indian group and won their loyalty, just as he had done with his usual company of actors and technicians. John Wayne had worked for him as a prop boy and stuntman and bit player on a string of movies before leaving Ford to star in minor Western fillers. He had remained Ford's friend and drinking companion, and he could not believe it when Ford finally offered him the part of the Ringo Kid and imposed his choice on the studio, refusing Gary Cooper.

His friendship with Ford did not spare him on set. Ford picked on him unmercifully to provoke a good performance out of him. "He dares you to do—to do it right—to do it good," Wayne told Peter Bogdanovich later. "And it's sort of a competitive thing. Nobody gets on better with the stunt people than Ford, but he's always playing you against them . . . I think this works, this sort of little seed that he plants in you. You're really sort of on trial all the time. And you really don't know what he's going to think of it. Actually, you don't know what's going to happen in the scene . . . It's a nervousness and it's intentional on his part . . . There's tension every place. Everybody's on edge."[5]

Ford kept Wayne on edge by his usual trick of making Wayne a victim until all the more experienced actors supported him and gave him the confidence that he was as good as they. Then Ford stopped picking on Wayne and tried to encourage his new assurance. At one romantic moment, when Wayne was having trouble showing his shy and honest love for Dallas, Ford just told him to raise his eyebrows and wrinkle his forehead. It worked, and Wayne used the same expression for the next forty years.

Ford wanted what he wanted on screen whatever the personal price, although he was always tight on the budget. Actually *Stagecoach* doubled its budget and cost more than half a million dollars—a rarity in a Ford production. Yet he knew he was making a fine picture and for once damn the cost. When the producer, Walter Wanger, made a rare trip to the location, Ford gave him what he demanded—a stuntman to double for Wayne in his more dangerous sequences on the stagecoach, in case Wayne hurt himself and stopped the shooting. By that time Ford had provoked Wayne enough into proving himself, and he could allow Yakima Canutt to double for his star.

Canutt was one of Ford's beloved stuntmen. He deserves a special credit for the action sequences of *Stagecoach*. The famous shots of the Apache falling between the galloping coach-horses and beneath the wheels of the stage show Canutt at his bravest and most graceful. Ford got the shot in one take by placing his camera correctly; he tried never to make a stuntman risk himself twice. It was the old army principle that a soldier will do anything for his officer, if he trusts him. Twenty-five years later, when stunt acts were recognized for their true value, one critic would compare Canutt's work on *Stagecoach* to "the beauty and precision of a ballet filled with danger."[6] It was because

Ford knew the cinema was, in essence, a *moving* picture that he encouraged his stuntmen to excel themselves.

To capture that mobility, Ford, the eternal innovator, used new techniques of shooting. There were no camera cars in those days, so Ford mounted his cameras on automobiles on the bed of the dry salt lake and shot at speeds of over forty miles an hour. The whole Apache assault on the stagecoach was recorded in two days. Ford later said that every critic asked why the Indians didn't shoot the horses to stop the coach, and that he always replied, "If they had, it would have been the end of the picture, wouldn't it?"

This explanation was, however, just for the critics—part of Ford's disguise as a hard-boiled professional, which hid his careful research and control over his scripts. In point of fact the Apaches were more interested in the horses than the passengers on the stagecoach. They needed remounts. "They fought on foot most of the time," Ford said, "and they needed horses. Besides, they were notoriously bad shots on horseback."[7] Rather like the Aztecs, who had tried to capture the conquistadors for ritual sacrifice instead of easily killing them off, the Apaches would always trade a useless coach for a live horse.

The shooting and editing of *Stagecoach* showed Ford's relentless economy with shots and words in his films. He said later of the film, "We dropped out only one two-minute scene in the cutting room."[8] He also cut in the camera by carefully selecting his angles and takes, and he kept Dudley Nichols, unpaid, on set to work on new lines with him. From the portentous original scripts he would remove everything which was unnecessary or unrealistic. Such care and selection made it the text for Orson Welles, who ran its sequences over and over again before directing *Citizen Kane*.

Wayne was overawed by Ford's analytical mind, such knowledge of the difference "between the trivia and the meat of a scene . . . He would have Dudley Nichols rewrite scene after scene after scene—this was before the picture started, and then just reach down and take a line out of this one, a line out of this one, and then three lines out of all this wonderful writing, but flowery language of Dudley Nichols—he'd just go right to the valuable thoughts."[9]

When *Stagecoach* was shown, it had the immediate recognition of *The Informer* and was a commercial success. It set the pattern of the classic Western for all time, making archetypes of its characters, primal conflicts of its situations, dream landscapes of its backgrounds. It had grown out of Ford's long experience: his boyhood as an observer of small men moving against the vast forces of nature; his transcontinental journeys over the land mass so tenuously linked by trail and rail; his awareness of the eternal bickering unto death between the regions and moralities and immigrant groups in America; his sense of pilgrim's progress through trials and adversity towards a nemesis; his instinct for land and for men and women who are part of it or set against it.

Finally *Stagecoach* paid tribute to Ford's terrible powers of command and resolute subtlety in taking advantage of every human mood, contour of ground, and change in the weather to fit his total plan for the film. "What a dirty, miserable, mean, Irish trick," Wayne exploded about one of Ford's ruses during the shooting. "That's the way he keeps you in your place."[10] If Ford had had to bury his legendary cowboy friend Tom Mix, he could resurrect the Old West with its courage and conflict and human decency by ruthlessly keeping everybody smack in the place he set for them.

9: The Semaphore of Democracy

Ford was always a cop hater, by religion, by belief. He had a big streak
of contempt for any kind of authority, any kind of paternal influence on
him—all the producers, all the money—they were the enemy.

—Robert Parrish

Ford always refused to admit that he had a historical point of view or
made films of social protest. This was a difficult position to maintain, once
he had completed *Young Mr. Lincoln, Drums Along the Mohawk,* and *The
Grapes of Wrath* in the years that Fascism began its attack on the surviving
democracies of Europe. "When I make a picture," Ford insisted, "I try
to find people I like in situations that I think are dramatic."[1] He would
say no more, stressing the fact that he was apolitical to the point of
incredulity.

Actually, Ford was something of a politician, who felt the pulse of his
country and his times. If his three Fox films of 1939 and 1940 were
suggested to him by Darryl Zanuck, he made them in his own image of
history and society. *Young Mr. Lincoln* was his most personal statement of
the archetypal American political hero. In it, he signaled for all time his
belief in liberty under the law, individualism in every circumstance, and
the opportunity of each man to prove his own worth. If his film did not
have the conscious semiology claimed for it by some modern critics, it did
have the instinctual semaphore of the artist and the professional and the
thinker who was achieving the boyhood dream offered to him by his
country.[2] "I do believe in the American Dream," he once said. "Definitely. Definitely. I think if you work hard enough, you will succeed."[3]

Sergei Eisenstein was the only director of the period who had begun
to present as personal and important a version of his country's history
from *The Battleship Potemkin* to *Alexander Nevsky* and *Ivan the Terrible.* For
him, a Communist and a revolutionary, *Young Mr. Lincoln* was the picture

he would have liked to have made. He found, in the signs hoisted by Ford from the tower of his film, an international human message which was entirely the work of the director. With some difficulty from the redoubt of the Stalinist cinema, which had imposed upon all film directors except himself a stereotyped image of Russian history, Eisenstein wrote:

> Give any master of "personifying" historical monuments the task of inventing an appropriate figure, devoid of false pathos, for a bearer of the ideals of American democracy, and he would never think of creating such an extravagant figure—an exterior reminding one simultaneously of an old-fashioned semaphore telegraph, a well-worn windmill, and a scarecrow, clothed in a long, full-skirted frock-coat, and crowned with a shaggy top-hat in the shape of a stovepipe.
>
> In all probability it is precisely through these external features that this historical figure can be shown as heroic and full of pathos, for he is so obviously free from all pose, free even from the slightest concern with himself. The business of this life was the most disinterested service in the interests of his people.[4]

Of course, after the director came the actor. Henry Fonda played the young Abraham Lincoln in his first role for Ford. He was the third male lead actor under contract at the Fox studio, and he thought himself unsuitable for the part after a screen test. Makeup and mime made him look like the young Lincoln, but his voice sounded wrong to him.

He was summoned to see Ford, who blasted him with the full battery of his authority, chewing on his pipe and on the corner of his old handkerchief, glowering through his tinted glasses in a fury. He cursed Fonda out, making him feel like a raw midshipman in front of an admiral disguised in a slouch hat. "He shamed me into it," Fonda said later. "Did I think I was playing the great emancipator, or something like that? He said, 'This is a young jack-leg lawyer from Springfield, for God's sake!' "[5]

So Fonda played it that way and made Lincoln come alive in the cinemas of the world for tens of millions of people, longing for the hope of democracy at a time when Fascism and Stalinism ruled and encroached upon the little liberties of mankind. "You are surprised to observe," Eisenstein wrote of his favorite film, "what accurate intuition and skill were shown by the pleasant-looking young Henry Fonda in transforming himself into this Don Quixote, whose armor was the U.S. Constitution, whose helmet was the traditional top-hat of a small-town lawyer, and whose Rosinante was a placid little mule that he straddled, his long legs almost touching the ground. This is a portrait finished with strength, pathos and life. The man has been reconstructed and passes alive before us on the screen."[6]

It was Ford's reconstruction and Fonda's playing of a script by Lamar Trotti that would have seemed trite seen through another director's vision. Eisenstein found in the film a classic harmony, the daguerreotypes of American history miraculously brought to life. He could not fault the craftsmanship or the rhythm of the montage corresponding to the quality of the photography, the flow of the muddy river, and even to the steady plod of Abe's little mule. He thought it a perfect blend of popular and national spirit, as though Ford had brought together in that quaint figure the total expression of American democratic belief.

The essence of *Young Mr. Lincoln* is that, like *Mary of Scotland* and *The Informer,* the known destiny and fate of the youthful Abe marks and informs every step of his homespun beginnings. The necessary premise of the film is that every spectator knows that Abe will become the President of the United States, win the Civil War for the North, and be assassinated in his theater box by the actor John Wilkes Booth—a scene shown in *The Prisoner of Shark Island.* The pathos of the film depends on this precognition. All of the jack-leg lawyer's clownishness and opportunism is leading him towards his maturity and tragic destiny.

Ford always regretted that the studio removed a scene of Celtic doom-saying from the release print of what he often called his favorite film. In that scene the young Lincoln stopped by a poster advertising the Booth Family playing *Hamlet,* and the young actor who was later to assassinate him walked out of the small-town theater and stared in wonder "at this funny, incongruous man in a tall hat riding a mule. And you knew there was some connection there," Ford said. "They cut it out—too bad."[7]

What was left in was a miracle of precise statement and rich recreation of rural America in the age of Andrew Jackson. The film opens with the usual Ford statement about its purpose. In this case it is a quotation from a poem about Nancy Hanks, Lincoln's dead mother, who is asking where her son is and what he has done. Throughout the film the young Lincoln will be looking for that lost mother-love. Failing to find it, he will strengthen himself to prepare to become the father of his country.

The next statement of the film is that we are in New Salem, Illinois, in 1832, a time when Washington is undergoing one of its recurrent periods of corruption. The young Lincoln puts himself up for office in front of the voters with a nonchalant phrase, his hands in his pockets, filling the screen with his negligent presence: "I presume you all know who I am. I'm plain Abraham Lincoln."

He stands for a traditional National Republican program, a protectionist tariff, the National Bank, and an opportunity for every American to get a slice of the pie. He believes in a poor man pulling himself up by his bootstraps. The law will protect him in his rising, the moral law of God, the natural law of the family, and the civil law, which is contained in the books given him by the mother of two sons whom he will later defend in the courts from a false charge of murder. For Lincoln the law is divine and human and practical—and even tricky. When he first is asked what he knows about the law, he replies: "Not enough to hurt me."

His affair with Ann Rutledge is one of the more economical and poignant sequences in the cinema. The whole affair is basically compressed into two tracking shots, the first ending on a river in springtime with the two young lovers walking and talking together, the second moving with the saddened young man alone by the icy current, stumping through the snow to kneel by his love's grave and talk to her ghostly presence. The passage of time between the tracking shots is shown in a visual shorthand in three takes, one of Lincoln skimming a stone across the river, the second of the spreading ripples as the stone sinks, the third of the dark winter torrent choked with ice.

Another brilliant device signals in the first tracking shot that Lincoln's love for Ann Rutledge is doomed. Ford leaves the pair talking behind the cross of a barred gate, eliminating them from the bright future stretching away on the shining river in the background. Yet when the grieving Lincoln moves along the riverbank to kneel by Ann's grave and talk to her headstone, the rails of the fence are now as regular behind him as the lines of his lonely way ahead. He even accepts his destiny by cheating on chance. He pretends to let a falling stick make the choice whether he will become a lawyer or not. In fact he tips the stick to fall on Ann's grave and make a sign to him of the fate that he has secretly chosen.

So the young Ford himself had talked to the pioneer gravestones on the Western Promenade in Portland during his games as a boy. "He loved certain scenes," Henry Fonda commented later. "He loved graveyard scenes. He loved a man coming to the graveyard, all alone, talking to the person. I've done that in two or three pictures for Ford."[8] It was his personal seal stamped on what he shot, his acknowledgment that he too was part of the great chain of the living and the dead, his work interpreting the past and showing it and talking of it to the present and the future.

Ford was conscious of the links between his various films, of the unity of his presentation of American history. So the young Lincoln, riding like Christ on his mule, is made to play a new catchy tune on his Jew's harp. It is "Dixie," actually not even composed at the time, but the tune of reconciliation the old Lincoln makes the band play at the end of the Civil War in *The Prisoner of Shark Island.* If Ford does not stress the messianic overtones of Lincoln's ride through the muddy streets of Springfield, he is certainly aware of what he is doing. "He deals a great deal in symbolism," William Holden said of him. "Not necessarily consciously."[9]

Yet symbolism was the signal for Ford to change pace and style, lest his film be thought symbolic. He admired Shakespeare, who so often mixed tragedy with farce. After Lincoln's entry into an Illinois Jerusalem, Ford immediately made a fond mockery of his own most cherished values. He set his hero at a Fourth of July procession as the old veterans of the two wars against the British Empire go by on parade. The veterans of 1812 hobble past, while the veterans of 1776 are three ancient men pulled along in an open carriage. Lincoln's future adversary and wife are introduced together, Stephen A. Douglas and Mary Todd—both are from the *haute bourgeoisie,* both alienated from the gawky young lawyer, yet linked inseparably to his future.

Lincoln then gives a display of his most human powers, Yankee cunning and frontier strength. He wins a rail-splitting contest at a country fair, eats the better part of two fruit pies while making a Solomon's judgment between their merits, and triumphs at the tail of a tug of war team by looping the rope onto a moving wagon at the critical moment. Trickery as good clean fun is fine for Lincoln, as is subtlety in interpreting the law; but finally, after the pleasant ruses and clever words, honesty must be all.

That is proven in his long set-piece courtroom sequence. He first prevents a mob from lynching the two accused brothers. He uses his fists and his humor and his reason. Both the law and the Bible support his arguments to the mob, which eventually disperses, leaving their battering ram on the ground in front of him—the symbolic rough rude tree of his later martyrdom. Then he attends a smart ball, where he stresses that he is poor unlike the rest of the guests, before he is asked to dance by his rich future wife. Ford always liked to make Fonda dance. "He just loved that in me," Fonda recalled. "I did it just joking the first time and he lapped it up. And he embroidered it."[10] The talk to the tombstone and the skip-hop to the fiddle were both habitual letters in Ford's signature on film.

In the selection of the jury the young Lincoln makes clear that only the quality of the people can bring justice. He chooses a trapper with the historic name of Boone because the old man says he drinks, has no job, does not go to church, approves of lynching, and is against the law. This is the sort of honest man Lincoln wants on the jury. Although the subsequent trial is played a little for farce and melodrama—the false accuser and real murderer is overacted by Ward Bond under the name of Jack Cass and his testimony is overturned by a farmer's almanac—Ford once again transforms Lincoln's wise foolery into an apotheosis, sending him after the acquittal transfigured and triumphant to meet the cheers of the crowd. Clever framing and lighting, indeed, cast an oblong of light behind the newly dominant figure of Lincoln, so that a horizontal line crucifies the tall vertical of his body at shoulder height.

The hero's final walk up a hillside in a thunderstorm, backed by the strains of "The Battle Hymn of the Republic," is overdramatic, yet effective—the necessary translation of a quixotic figure of fun into the stern father-figure of the nation on the final dissolve to the statue in the Lincoln Memorial in Washington. This transition has been foreseen by the audience since the opening shots of the film. Now Ford makes it clear in his final shot, sending his viewers back in their memory to the clues about the future destiny of Lincoln sprinkled through his images and text. As the editors of a *Cahiers du Cinéma* critique of the film discerned, although all is given and all is there, the language and images of the picture cannot be deciphered until it is seen for a second time with an eye that *knows.* Although their Marxist interpretation of the film is just, that it is a vigorous defense of Republicanism and money values and legal procedures, they do recognize that the basic text of the film is the image of Lincoln as the healer and unifier of the divisions of society, a man of Blackstone's *Commentaries,* not revolutionary manifestos.[11]

Ford made two more films with Zanuck and Fonda, deep in the American grain. The first was his only film about the War of Independence, *Drums Along the Mohawk.* It was Ford's first film in color, and it caused him no more trouble than the coming of sound had. He reckoned the new medium would be a cinch if he had any painter's gift for color or composition. This he had always had, since his early days by the ocean when his poor sight had blocked out the shifting masses of light and shade, cloud and sea and shore. Even so, he was always to prefer black and white photography as a more difficult medium and a better one for a good dramatic story.

Ford's success in *Drums Along the Mohawk* was to turn an ordinary costume drama with a miscast Claudette Colbert into an endearing and illuminating recreation of pioneer life in the backwoods. Part of his method was his use of the techniques he had developed on location in *The Iron Horse.* He pitched his camp for his hundred and fifty actors and technicians over nine thousand feet high in the mountains of Utah. He made the living quarters as much a part of the filming as the set. "Such morale," Fonda remembered. "It was like being a child again at camp."

Yet that was only at night. "During the day you were making a picture," Fonda said. "You weren't horsing around."[12] Ford would then exercise his full ritual of authority, arriving late accompanied by Borzage playing "Bringing in the Sheaves," waiting for his cups of hot coffee, considering his first shot without any consultation, being merciless to his actors while they read through their lines, practicing his regular gibes at his chosen victims to set his players on edge, insisting that everything emanate from his mood, that everyone jump to his occasional word.

Drums Along the Mohawk was not all of a piece, although it included scenes that seemed to have been drawn from the first woodsman's view of the primal American forest or the endless bright nightmare of the American child being chased by Indians through the trees. The thousand miles of forest which stretched west over the Appalachian mountains had been the first barrier and opportunity of the American pioneers on the frontier of civilization. They had lopped the trees and had dressed the trunks for their cabins and forts, they had grubbed up the roots with their horses and had cleared the ground for their crops of grain. All this necessary hard labor was shown by Ford in a paean to the toil that had created the American farms of the forest.

He then dealt with the Indian and Tory menace as if he were illustrating a child's history book, lurid with melodrama and broad with schoolboy jokes. His Indians are not the fierce centaurs of the Plains, but grotesque flat-footed buffoons, led by evil incarnate in the person of John Carradine, playing the Tory Caldwell with Ford's own black patch over one eye. Such a savage and crudely-colored crew is the stuff of boyhood terror and strip cartoon, a comic chorus backing the clownishness of Edna May Oliver in her role as a lusty rich widow. In one climactic scene the Indians break in to burn her out of her house, but she makes them carry her out to safety in her marriage bed, her farcical porters rather than her fearsome scalpers.

The American dream pervades the opening of the film with the credit titles presented as needlework samplers and the actual marriage of Fonda to Claudette Colbert setting forth the moral of the story in the clergyman's exhortation, "Bless them as they go forth into the wilderness to make them a new home. . . . Every generation must make its own way—in one place or another."

As Fonda drives his new bride on his wagon from her snug two-story family house through sunny meadows they run into a torrential storm before they reach the freezing log cabin that he is proud of having built with his own two hands. There he has to slap her out of a fit of hysteria, brought on by the sudden entrance of a huge Christian Indian chief, Blue Back, played by Chief Big Tree. The reality of the harshness of frontier life turns the bride's illusions into a nightmare and begins the contrasts that counterpoint the rest of the film.

Thereafter, the picture rides a roller-coaster ranging from unlikely romancing in the hay to flight from the attack of the fire-bearing Indians and Tories. Claudette Colbert suffers a miscarriage and poverty as a hired hand along with her husband in the snow, but they fight back with the rest of the settlers against the menace from the forest.

Ford particularly makes *Drums Along the Mohawk* his own in the military sequences, the new American regular army regiment marching down the road to patriotic music with the local militia tagging along behind, the women parting from the men going to war like the sailors' wives at the Portland docks, then waiting on their widow's walks for the husbands who will never return. "All the men going out to kill—to be killed!" Edna May Oliver explodes, thinking of her dead soldier husband, Barney. "Blast his eyes! Loving it!"

As usual, Ford does not show the actual battle, only the militia shambling back in heavy rain, apparently defeated, in fact victorious. Again he plays a scene he would replay in future films, the amputation in the ordinary home, in which General Herkimer has to lose his leg and shows his stoicism by asking for his pipe. To his distraught wife Fonda declares his horror of the battle they have just won. He has had to kill, but he is shattered to have seen a neighbor enjoying the killing: "He was having a good time." Of the six hundred men who have marched out against the enemy, four hundred will never return to the valley they have defended with their lives.

Light and shade now chase across the screen in a quickening tempo. Fonda's little jig with his first-born in his arms is a fond memory for us all. "Doggone," is all he can manage to say. "Well, I'll be doggone." But soon he is in the common nightmare of the sleepless, running through the darkness from his three Indian pursuers to bring help to the survivors in the valley, beleaguered in their little wooden fortress. Fonda runs and runs through the coming of dawn into the day, crossing forest and river and clearing. Behind him, vengeful as the hounds of hell, the Indians keep coming until he seems to gather speed with the sun and outdistance them, like a sleeper racked with bad dreams who springs awake to the joy of the morning.

The final sequences of *Drums Along the Mohawk* show Ford at his most populist and assured. The new American flag of independence is hoisted on a pole at the news of Cornwallis's surrender at Yorktown. The comment is underplayed—"It's a pretty flag, isn't it?" Then a succession of quick cuts shows a black woman and Chief Big Tree reverencing the thirteen stars on freedom's first banner. The moral is given in the words, "Well, I reckon we'd better be gettin' back to work—there'll be a heap to do from now on."

Then Ford plays his last private joke, setting up Chief Big Tree in a pulpit wearing the sinister black patch of the Tory officer. "Where's Caldwell gone?" is the question. The answer is—Behind the camera, because the patch is Ford's own patch, which has made him see from one good eye and one bad one the extremes of light and shade that make *Drums Along the Mohawk* such a bright-dark child's history of the War of Independence.

The Grapes of Wrath was another matter. Ford's masterpiece of contemporary history was assigned to him by Zanuck, after Nunnally Johnson had written a superb script from John Steinbeck's novel about the dispossessed dirt farmers of Oklahoma who emigrated to the false promise of orange groves in California. Zanuck was both proud and frightened of the project because of its social content. It was filmed under the title of *Highway 66,* the road the Okies used when they came to California. It was also given an optimistic populist ending by Zanuck himself in place of Steinbeck's bleak final scene, in which Rosasharn gives her milky breast to a starving boy because her baby is dead.

Zanuck even convinced Steinbeck of the necessity of the final change from despair to hope, although the story conference was interrupted by the terrible news of an accident on the Fox back lot. When Zanuck had to leave on the instant to solve the problem, Steinbeck consoled the studio boss. *"The Grapes of Wrath,"* he said, "is unimportant compared to Shirley Temple's tooth."[13]

Ford was assigned to work with Nunnally Johnson on Steinbeck's novel. He liked the project because it reminded him of the Irish famine —a story of simple people thrown off the land and starving as they wandered the roads. "That may have had something to do with it—part of my Irish tradition," he said later,"—but I liked the idea of this family going out and trying to find their way in the world. It was a timely story."[14] He also liked the subject because of his own infancy on a small farm in Maine. "I had complete sympathy with these people."[15]

The story was timely and the American people were sympathetic. Not since the hobo armies of the depression years of the 1890's had there been so many millions on the bum. There were even more millions of people living in the shack towns ironically called Hoovervilles. Most of these people were looking for work, as there was precious little welfare. The New Deal of Franklin D. Roosevelt was trying to create public works programs through the W.P.A., but it could never employ more than one in four of the jobless. The federal government was attempting to help, but America was still a country which believed in men helping themselves —though not out of poor men's pockets.

If the novel *The Grapes of Wrath* had echoes of radical discontent, the message of the film pointed toward a populist panacea by which the government would aid a dispossessed family get back on its own feet and land. After all their tribulations the Joads, in the script, finally come to a rest in an "apocalyptically sanitary" government camp for transients.[16] When they leave it, they leave it ready to do well for themselves again. They will certainly survive. "Rich fellas come up an' they die," Ma Joad says with matriarchal finality, "an' their kids ain't no good, an' they die out. But we keep a-comin'. We're the people that live. Can't nobody wipe us out. Can't nobody lick us. We'll go on for ever."

This closing speech was Zanuck's own addition and an afterthought to Nunnally Johnson's script. He even shot the sequence himself during Ford's absence on *The Araner*, for Ford had sailed off as usual after completing the shooting of the original screenplay. Ford agreed to the new hopeful ending as he had agreed to Zanuck's other cautious dele- tions from the novel. John Steinbeck's specific attacks on used-car sales- men, greedy camp owners, weighted scales, fixed slot machines, and even rogue policemen were eliminated. The hero, Tom Joad, no longer talked of keeping his decency "by takin' a sock at a cop." Instead, the Christ- figure of the failed preacher Casey carefully exonerated the regular depu- ties from strike-breaking and only accused scab security men, "them tin badge fellas they call guards."

An assault against social injustice is made to seem useless by Ford and his collaborators, because wrongdoing is no longer personal, as it used to be in a Western. "Then who do we shoot?" one of the evicted Okie farmers asks, only to hear the answer, "Brother, I don't know. If I did, I'd tell you. I just don't know who's to blame."

The times are at fault, not men. The banks are faceless, not villains on the run with their bag of money as in *Stagecoach*. In fact nature is the real villain with its drought and dustbowl and erosion. Radicalism is presented as an enemy as vague as capitalism. The squatters are evicted from their camp in the name of the Red menace, but when Tom Joad asks who the Reds actually are, a farmer answers him, "I ain't talkin' about that one way or another." The Reds are the Apaches over the horizon who never ride in for a final solution.

Ford's message in the film is religious populism, not socialism. He shows that angry Christ who scourged the moneychangers from the Temple, not the Bolshevik overthrowing an oppressive capitalism. The very first shot shows the small figure of Tom Joad walking toward a slick-wet crossroads, a tiny figure on the huge symbol of Christ's suffering laid on the barren ground. The first long significant two-shot in the Fordian tradition shows Tom talking to the failed preacher Casey in front of a willow tree as Casey tells him that caring for God has given way to caring for other men. "Maybe there ain't no sin and there ain't no virtue. It's just what people do."

If what some people do to Casey later is to kill him, the film shows what the people will do and must do, which is to endure. When Tom finally takes up the dead Casey's preaching role as a union organizer, he still gropes for messianic words rather than revolutionary ones. "Wherever there's a fight so hungry people can eat," he tells his mother, "I'll be there. Wherever there's a cop beating up a guy, I'll be there." It is only Ford's hatred of authority speaking, balanced by his respect for Roosevelt's New Deal, which had saved American capitalism instead of ruining it. Thus even Tom's last speech ends in the hope that everything will improve soon in the good old way. "And when our people eat the stuff they raise, and live in the houses they build, why, I'll be there too." He goes off to become a union organizer outside the law; yet he goes alone along a dark ridge, while the last shot of the film shows his enduring family driving in a procession of old trucks to search for a small farm again over the bright-dark horizon.

So Ford and his colleagues took most of the radical politics out of *The Grapes of Wrath* and made a universal film about how a poor family may yet survive through its qualities of courage and decency and love. Ford's new cameraman, Gregg Toland, used the documentary techniques of a Pare Lorentz or a Flaherty to capture the shabby eroded look of the land

and its threadbare people, blown off the soil by dusters and drained by mortgages. Ford shot his location sequences chiefly in the morning or the late afternoon, so that the scarecrow figures of the Okies stand in silhouette against luminous skies, their elongated shadows making bars against their possession of the land.

In one extraordinary tilting shot we move from the biblical image of three black shadows on the ground to a caterpillar tractor driving straight through the dirt farmer's home. (In a striking contrast to the Russian propaganda film, in which lines of advancing tractors always hymn revolutionary progress, Ford's sequence of the coming of the "cats" is fraught with doom and destruction, as though they were the advance guard of a Nazi *Blitzkrieg*.) And through the film Tom Joad is often seen trapped by the cabin of his old truck or the huts of the squatters' camp, caught in the frame within a frame which a great director uses to confine inner space.

Yet if Ford took the radicalism out of the text of *The Grapes of Wrath* and substituted his own agrarian yearning for the simplicities of time past, the images of his film were subversive and disturbing. The western dream is shown in its ghastly conclusion with the crashing gears of the old Joad truck crawling past the great sandstone bluffs where the cavalry and the Apaches once galloped. A slow tracking shot into the transient camp, with the starving occupants sleepwalking out of the path of the grinding truck, is a nightmare of deprivation, the counter-image of the lusty pioneer camps with their polkas and fiddles. The special constables and strikebreakers are presented like the stormtroopers of Europe, and Henry Fonda, playing Tom Joad, always seems ready to burst into an act of violence, as if he would pick up a club and break the skull of the whole rich man's misgovernment. He can say with quiet relish that he has served a term in jail for "Hom-i-cide" and that he knocked a man's head "plumb to squash" with a shovel. And when he does kill Casey's killer with a pick handle, his act is as quick and sure as the blow of a wildcat.

The enduring images of the noble dignity of the poor Okies oppressed and exploited by a greedy society do make Ford appear to suggest a revolutionary redistribution of wealth. Radical in style but conservative in text, *The Grapes of Wrath* showed Ford in the full power of his ambivalence and his mastery of that film dialectic which counterpoints word and shot and angle and movement and sound in a ceaseless argument for the understanding of mankind.

When the film was released in 1940, President Roosevelt was running for an unprecedented third term. The Axis powers were winning victories against the last embattled democracies of Europe, and the infamous pact between Hitler and Stalin to partition Poland, occupy the Baltic States and invade Finland made Fascism and Communism seem like bullies in harness. Ford's assertion of the values of democracy and human dignity, even in an age of depression, appeared as a text for the times.

The Grapes of Wrath was to be the apogee of those films of social concern which Hollywood liked to make occasionally in the late Thirties as proof that the studios also cared. Zanuck himself was scared by the radicalism of his own final cut of the film, directed by Ford in his unique way that only allowed one version to be edited from his footage. But Ford fought Zanuck tooth and nail to keep in all he had shot, and he won his battle. As Fred Zinnemann acknowledged later about this episode, "We owe the director's first cut to John Ford." Ford had ensured that by cutting in the camera, limiting his footage and angles, and struggling for the director's right to have all his chosen material included in the release print of an important film.

Although the studio bosses wanted some films of social protest, they wanted them in their own misleading image. As Scott Fitzgerald observed in his novel *The Last Tycoon,* at that time the studios feared mob rule. So they tended to put out films stressing the American values of the rule of law and the rights of property and the abiding worth of fundamental human decency. In his three roles for Ford in 1939 and 1940 Henry Fonda always represents these values. As a future President of the United States or as a poor Okie convict, he speaks the same language of idealism. Like any Founding Father, he preaches liberty, equality, and property rather than the dangerous pursuit of happiness.

Ford's daughter Barbara always quotes a saying attributed to Stalin. "If I could control Hollywood, I would never have to fire a gun." The men who controlled Hollywood and commanded the experience of directors like John Ford were probably the most potent propagandists for democracy and capitalism that the Fascist powers had to face. In that age before the coming of television the common international language was the American film. Most people in most developed countries went to the cinema at least once a week, and the Hollywood movie was the international medium of the eye.

John Ford had made more films about American history and the American way of life than any of his contemporaries. His message about liberty, equality, and property safeguarded by the law had been consistent. Working as a professional for his salary, he had also been working unconsciously as a messenger of democratic values. He was not only a preacher to his own people, but to many peoples. As Margaret Thorp wrote in 1939 in her illuminating book *America at the Movies,* Ford and his lesser contemporaries were furnishing humanity with a common body of knowledge:

> What the classics once were in that respect, what the Bible once was, the cinema has become for the average man. Here are stories, names, phrases, points of view which are common national property. . . . The movies span geographic frontiers; they give the old something to talk about with the young; they crumble the barriers between people of different educations and different economic backgrounds.[17]

To America and much of the world, *Young Mr. Lincoln* spoke while *The Grapes of Wrath* were about to be trod.

10:   Preparations for a Private War

*Making a movie is a damned sweaty process . . . I like to know what
I'm doing before shooting starts—get a close schedule and budget and stick
to it. I rehearse the cast carefully on all scenes and use a minimum of
dialogue. I believe movies are primarily pictures so I play them that way.
Let the pictures do the talking for you.*

—John Ford on the making of *The Long Voyage Home*

When most of the world except for the United States prepared to go to
war, John Ford began to bring together his secret life with his public one.
He aimed at organizing a private army of Hollywood technicians more
than two hundred strong, ready to serve their country by recording real
combat as expertly as they shot war films and Westerns. His problem was
finding an employer in Washington—just as difficult as finding a producer for any project of his own in Hollywood.

He had the luck of the Irish, for President Roosevelt was secretly
setting up a foreign intelligence agency through an Irish-American, Colonel "Wild Bill" Donovan. The group was originally called the Co-Ordina-
tor of Information, C.O.I., and later the Office of Strategic Services,
O.S.S. Through the Secretary of the Navy, Dudley Wright Knox, Donovan received word of what Ford had already done and was doing for naval
intelligence. He could not recruit Ford immediately because the United
States was not yet at war, and Congress had made no appropriation for
such covert operations. What little money there was had to come from
the President's secret fund. The nation might be expecting to fight, but
few were actually preparing for the outbreak.

As Ford could not yet find himself a military post in Washington,
he kept on working as a film director in California and preparing to
fight a future war from there. He still had to earn his keep while he

waited for his call to service. So he chose as his next project with Walter Wanger, the producer of *Stagecoach*, "a tartar" of a picture, which was close to his heart and relevant to the war effort. With Dudley Nichols he adapted four one-act plays about sailors by Eugene O'-Neill. These were set on a munitions ship, trying to beat the U-boat blockade and reach the blitzed London docks. Ford seemed to have forgiven the British Empire in its last-ditch struggle to keep democracy alive in Europe. He was using Irish-American plays and players to praise English patriotism.

By the terms of his contract with Fox, Ford was allowed to make one feature a year outside the studios. To finance the O'Neill plays, he set up with Walter Wanger his own independent film company, Argosy—a name that harked back to rich commerce on the high seas. To publicize his picture, released under the original O'Neill title of *The Long Voyage Home*, he gave one of his rare interviews. It was a good summary of his method of making pictures.

O'Neill had won the Nobel Prize for Literature in 1936, and Ford went up to Oregon to meet him for the first time. "He turned out to be a grand guy," Ford commented. "Right away he said, go ahead and make the picture, and then we spent four days talking about his old man and my old man, two swell gents. Gene said he'd trust Dudley Nichols and me and he never came to Hollywood or saw the script. Dudley wrote the script after we talked together like this for six weeks, mulling over photos of real wharves, bars, and so forth.

"After these conferences, Dudley locked himself up sixteen hours a day for twenty days and turned out the first draft. Then we took a week and knocked it apart, and then another month to put it back together again. The final shooting script was changed very little during shooting. Then we hired the actors, ordered the scenery, and gave every actor instructions to read the entire script very carefully, before we began.

"We had one particularly bad break during the shooting. In the storm scene John Wayne, playing the part of Olsen, was knocked out. His injuries kept him laid up for a week. But everybody in the cast did his best under the circumstances. I rarely have trouble with actors, anyway. Those working with me chip in with their ideas as to how to get the best effects."[1] What Ford did not say in his interview was that he rarely listened to the ideas that any actor dared to chip in. He met the refugee French director Jean Renoir shortly afterward with the dictum, "Don't ever forget what I am going to tell you—Actors are crap." He meant it, even if Renoir only thought he meant bad actors.[2]

Like *The Informer*, the film opens with the titles spelling out its theme:

> With their hates and desires, men are changing the face of the earth. But they cannot change the sea. Men who live on the sea never change. They live apart in a lonely world, moving from one rusty tramp steamer to another.

So Ford and Nichols set the drama of a group of men opposed to an indifferent nature. For Ford, the ocean was like the wilderness, immutable and uncaring, not like the land, which could be put in harness by the toil of the pioneers of the Mohawk Valley or the Far West. His sailors want to believe that they may escape from the sea to the soil, but none of them do except for the golden Swede, played by John Wayne, who actually has a home waiting for his return. Despite their illusions of a final landing the others must sign on for another dangerous voyage along with the Donkeyman, the only one of them wise enough to know that they will always go back to the sea.

At the opening of the film the sailors leave the South American delights of brawling and sprawling with bumboat women for a trial by storm in a submarine-haunted ocean. Ford and his cameraman Gregg Toland show the sailors as prisoners on their rusty freighter, the S.S. *Glencairn,* trapped between the rails and hawsers of the deck or the iron piping of their bunks below. They suspect that a British ex-naval officer is a spy, but he is exonerated and dies heroically in an air raid on board, to be finally buried like Tom Mix, wrapped in his country's flag—only this time Ford shows a change of heart by using the Union Jack and playing "Rule Britannia" on the soundtrack. It is a long voyage from the strong rebel feeling of his Celtic trilogy, but this time Britain was fighting Fascist oppression.

Once the ship has reached London, Ford shows that the docks are a worse trap than the freighter itself. Pabst's techniques of fog and chiaroscuro are used again to hide the blatant flats of the studio sets, so that the sailors are snared like Gypo Nolan in a dark jail in an artificial city. They intend to settle down and never sign on again, but they give way to the blandishments of the crimp and go to his dive and his drugged drinks and his women. They manage to get the odd Swede out, however, onto his ship for home, while they must sign on again to their inevitable doom afloat. Already the Donkeyman has seen that the savior of the

Swede has been torpedoed on another boat, and he tosses into the oily screw-churning sea the newspaper prophesying that they will go down with all hands. The sailors have chosen the fate they have to choose. Men who live on the unchanging sea can never change. As the final title states: *For some, the long voyage never ends.*

Ford's film of the O'Neill plays is more brooding and powerful than *The Informer,* but it lacks the hypnotic unity of its predecessor. The caper with the bumboat women, the plummy heroism of the ex-naval officer, and Wayne's uncertain Swedish accent are all exaggerated, so that the film is often unrealistic without being hallucinatory. It is certainly eloquent and poetic and tragic, but it does not convince as a whole. A noble failure, it did not succeed at the box office, as if the mass audience objected to its splendid simulation at the time of a real world war.

Zanuck then asked Ford to try and repeat his success with *The Grapes of Wrath* by making a film from another best-selling novel about poor people, Erskine Caldwell's *Tobacco Road.* Yet there was an essential difference between the two projects. While Steinbeck's book had dealt with dispossessed small farmers trying to get on their feet once more, Caldwell's book and its successful Broadway adaptation was a comedy about shiftless poor whites in Georgia, who would rather lie down than lift a finger. Even Nunnally Johnson could not give a social purpose to the script, which showed Jeeter Lester's family as feckless and mindless, the true rural lumpenproletariat that even the Reds despaired of raising to political consciousness. As in Gorki's *The Lower Depths,* the people of Tobacco Road seemed better off dying than trying.

Except for the sexuality of the young Gene Tierney and the antics of Charlie Grapewin, who seemed determined to bury his fine performance as Grampa Joad under the barnyard buffoonery of Jeeter Lester, there is little that is memorable about the film, and much that is embarrassing. The material encourages the audience to laugh at the indolence and supineness of the very poor. It was, as one critic wrote, "an economic circus in which poverty was clown."[3] Even if a war boom was beginning as America supplied the Allies and started to rearm itself, the memory of hard times was too recent to make *Tobacco Road* seem tolerable. Yet Nunnally Johnson was able to garner one good line at the expense of an indignant Southern lady, who rightly complained about the white-trash setting and asked if Johnson himself came from such a background. "Ma'am," he replied, "where Ah come from, we call that crowd the country club set."

Before he was engulfed in the war, Ford's last assignment for Zanuck was also about poor people, completing his quartet about Okie farmers and tramp sailors and southern crackers. *How Green Was My Valley* was another best-selling novel, this time about mining families in Wales. To simulate the background, a whole village was built up the hill on the old Fox ranch, a careful curve of cottages leading past a chapel to the gaunt scaffold of the cage-lifting mechanism at the top. Unfortunately the cottages were backed by obvious Californian dry hills and trees, while the way up to the mine looked no more real than a black-brick road to a Celtic land of Oz.

Ford, indeed, played his sentimental material like a musical, with lines of Welsh miners singing on their way to the shaft and pay day, and sweet hymns sounding as regularly as cuckoo clocks from his chorus of shawled women. His cast of mixed Irish and English and Americans spoke oddly against the scattering of Welsh players, so that a strange conflict of accents added to the unreality of it all.

The script by Philip Dunne was wordy and overwrought with Ford too light on the shears throughout the romantic rhetoric. Only the fact that the whole film is presented as the nostalgia of a mysterious voice off-screen, remembering how green his valley was and no longer is, makes such a treacle of time past tolerable in time present. The Great Depression was over at last—the movie seemed to say—and long live its sweet memory.

Yet the genius in Ford partially glowed through the sticky morass of his subject. He told Anna Lee, who played Bronwen for him, that it was the happiest picture he ever made because the whole thing was exactly like a family.[4] He managed to melt his polyglot players into a pool that reflected the true emotions of the hearth and home. The success of the film lay in this direct appeal to common sentiment in the village births and marriages and deaths, the raising of a family and its going away and its dying.

Donald Crisp's playing of Mr. Morgan, the strong miner father of one daughter and many sons, is an affecting portrait of strength and goodness and idiosyncrasy. When he walks a chalk line with the exquisite caution of the drunk, he is unforgettable. When he is caught with his bare feet in a mustard bath by the mine-owner, come to ask for his daughter's hand for his son, he treads an exact path between embarrassment and dominance. From him, Maureen O'Hara, Anna Lee, and the child Roddy McDowall, Ford drew the performances of tender resonance that always keep his films from becoming saccharine and sentimental.

Ford's success with human emotion was matched by his failure with realism. The words might say, "As the slag spread over the valley, so a blackness spread over the minds of my people." But Ford never showed that slag nor the true blackness of the coal pit. His few scenes down the mineshaft do not bear comparison with the claustrophobia of the trapped miners in Pabst's *Kameradschaft* or in Carol Reed's *The Stars Look Down.* His criticism of the owners' exploitation of the miners is muted by Crisp's royalism and pride in the British Crown. If the sons leave the house to form a union and go overseas, the father leads the village choir in singing "God Save the Queen."[5]

As if he acknowledged the artificial quality of his mining drama, Ford could not restrain his symbolism. He carefully posed Walter Pidgeon and Roddy McDowall in the shape of a human cross framed by wooden crosses as they bring up the body of Donald Crisp from the depths of the flooded mine. "He had to do it on purpose," Anna Lee says. "He always swears he didn't, but I know it was a deliberate composition." Of course it was, as were the fields of unlikely daffodils springing in the Klieg-light sun when Walter Pidgeon forces the young boy to walk again so that he can come to chapel and pray. "Prayer is only another name for good, clean, direct thinking," Pidgeon says, turning himself into one of the most righteous and improbable of Ford's heroes.

How Green Was My Valley put Ford at the peak of his acclaim in America. The film won six Oscars all told and Ford's fourth award from the New York Film Critics. In the Academy Awards it defeated *Citizen Kane* as the best picture, and Ford defeated Welles and Wyler, Chaplin and Hitchcock, Cukor and Capra as the best director. It was as though the Academy voters and the mass audience wanted to say a fond farewell to the Depression years, to exorcise them with a nice cry over a crippled boy who gets onto his feet again. The past needed to lose its hard edge, to be wrapped up and stowed away. War was the next business of America.

With Zanuck as his producer Ford had already shot a thirty-minute documentary for the U.S. Army on *Sex Hygiene.* Clinically and unpleasantly it shows army recruits how to avoid venereal disease—and what it looks like if they catch it. If the subject was not a labor of love for Ford, it was a job of duty.

The private combat group of technicians which he was organizing and training made his vision grow with his authority. Instead of just recruiting photographers, he wanted to put together a whole motion picture group for war service—writers, directors, cameramen, makeup specialists, editors, full movie crews. Aerial reconnaissance would only be one of their functions. Ford's objective was "to record the history of the navy in World War Two and the role it played."[6]

He made several trips to Washington in 1940 and 1941 to find a backer for his group. Eventually he secured permission to set up a historical unit in the Naval Reserve. To assist him, he hired one of his regular character actors, Jack Pennick, an ex-Marine who was responsible for recruiting and drilling his volunteers. The unit ended with 35 officers and 175 enlisted men. Working with borrowed equipment, it met once a week on a vacant stage on the Fox back lot in order to train and get to know one another.

"Men in that unit were over age and rich, people who could never have been drafted," Mary Ford remembered. "But when Jack said, 'Let's go,' they obeyed him."[7] He had always run his film unit like a guerrilla training camp, and now he was obeyed while he was rehearsing his men for actual combat. "Everyone had to be able to do everybody else's job," recalls Mark Armistead, one of Ford's aides, who was then a young man in the camera rental business, expert only in loading magazines with film stock. Ford wanted everybody to be able to take over from a wounded comrade and to record a battle on his own. So he trained his unit to readiness for its pictorial history of the navy—then found that the navy did not want his gift at all.

Colonel Donovan, however, was expanding his foreign intelligence agency into the hydra-headed Office of Strategic Services. He began making arrangements to recruit Ford with his ready-made surveillance group under the title of the Field Photographic Branch. This group never had a precise directive, although it was chiefly responsible for all operations overseas that needed photographic records. Before the United States entered the war, Ford's camera teams were already documenting naval strategy in Iceland against German U-boats, and making a photographic report on the defenses of the Panama Canal.

After moving his unit from the Fox lot to Washington, Ford recruited a rough ex-bosun's mate named Benjamin Grotsky to lick his odd Hollywood crew "into some sort of military semblance." Grotsky was "strictly a dese and dose guy," but there was no boot camp for the unfit recruits, only some hard drill.[8] The Field Photographic Branch was rapidly prepared to go into action. It had fifteen complete film crews and its own processing laboratory in the South Agriculture Building on December 7, 1941.

On that Sunday Mary Ford was lunching with her husband at Admiral Pickens's old house in Alexandria, Virginia. In that house seven wars had been announced, beginning with the American War of Independence. The telephone rang and the admiral rose from the table to answer it.

When he returned, he said, "Gentlemen, there has been a bombing of Pearl Harbor by the Japanese. We are now at war." All the men left the table immediately. Mary Ford knew that "their lives had changed that very minute." So many of Ford's film technicians turned up in their Washington hotel suite that evening wondering where to report for duty that Mary Ford had to give an impromptu cocktail party to welcome the outbreak of the war.

Ford himself knew Pearl Harbor well. He had done photographic reconnaissance there, and he had watched the American navy planes make mock bombing runs on the base early on Sunday mornings. Japanese spies had also noticed these runs, so they could bring in their own assault planes one Sunday to confuse the American defenses. Their sneak attack sunk or damaged seven battleships, two destroyers, and three cruisers. Much of Ford's prized Pacific battle fleet lay on the sea bottom. There were no American air patrols flying, and the antiaircraft guns had no gunners to man them and no ammunition. All of Ford's personal intelligence reports and Hollywood film propaganda about the lack of naval preparedness had fallen on deaf ears and blind eyes.

So an act of war made Ford's clandestine commitment to the navy become his public service. The most experienced and praised director in Hollywood became the head of the best photographic reconnaissance unit yet seen. He moved from simulated to practical warfare as if the illusion had always been the real thing. As close-mouthed as ever, he never even told his wife that he was the chief of the new "official eye of the American high command."[9] He just said to her casually, "I am going to Washington for a couple of days," and then she found herself only meeting him for twenty-four hours in the next three-and-a-half years.[10] He carried official secrecy to the point of conspiracy against his own family.

If Ford had failed to prepare his country for the inevitable combat he had prophesied since 1939, he had prepared himself and his men. The minstrel boy to the war was gone with his camera slung behind him.

11: Theater of War

BRICKLEY:

The Japs have us swamped—ships, planes, machines, men. Our job is to tie them up as long as we can. That means we'll fight it out in the Philippines—to the last boat and the last man. We're expendable, fella.

RYAN:

I see. We'd better keep it to ourselves. There's no sense breaking the men down with bad news.

BRICKLEY:

Check.

—Frank Wead's and John Ford's script of They Were Expendable

Ford's four war years used his powers at full stretch. His professional skills made him adept at developing new reconnaissance equipment and getting back excellent documentary footage. His inherited talent for politics was essential in dealing with a difficult President of the United States, a jealous navy, and a host of competitive intelligence agencies. His gifts for command had to be spread thin across the globe, forcing him to pick good aides and devolve control to them. "He could delegate authority," Leon Selditz recalls. "He was never one to be the overall king."

He had always been brilliant at picking a film crew and cast, and he showed the same uncanny instinct at choosing the right field officers. The young Mark Armistead, for instance, found himself abandoned by Ford to run the Field Photographic Branch in England for two years on his own. His only instructions were ambiguous, "Do a good job for the O.S.S. and the navy." Ford believed in giving local commanders total authority as long as they were successful. He was not interested in their failure any more than his own.

Armistead had become friendly with Ford as his unwilling landlord and lackey. Finding nowhere decent to live in an overcrowded Washington, he had managed to buy a useless luxury yacht called the *Saramia* and anchor it in the Potomac River. He rented out its cabins to his brother officers and kept the master bedroom for himself. Ford heard of the yacht, inspected it and as his superior officer, commandeered Armistead's room, relegating the yacht owner to a broom closet.

Ford now had a servant at hand and used him to satisfy his midnight cravings. "He didn't sleep at night," Armistead recalls. "Only naps during the day." Early on his first morning aboard Ford sent young Armistead out for chocolate bars, on the second for pipe tobacco, on the third for ice-water. Surrounded by a mess of shredded special Virginia mixture and Hershey wrappers, Ford would hold forth through the small hours to the sleepy Armistead from his littered bed in his stained pyjamas. "He was never a tidy man," Armistead says, "and he never changed his sheets."[1]

Those who worked for Ford loved him for breaking every rule, just as most of the regular military brass hated him for the same reason. "He never wore a uniform if he could help it," one of his friends recalls. "He fell in love with the baseball cap the U.S. Navy wears. Yet he could be just as grand as anyone in full uniform."[2] Ford used his unpredictability of dress as another of his weapons of authority. He kept everybody off balance by his usual disreputable look before making a sudden switch to the braid and brass of a full navy captain. He was only upstaged once in the war, by the British Orde Wingate, who received him stark naked in Burma.

Ford was something of what his daughter calls "a ribbon freak." He publicly despised and secretly revered his decorations, even one from the King of the Belgians who had surrendered his kingdom to the Germans. The King had made Ford a Chevalier de l'Ordre de la Couronne in 1940, and consequently Ford always defended the royal surrender as an act of compassion for his countrymen rather than personal cowardice. Whatever they had done, Ford was always loyal to those who had honored him or served him.

The Field Photographic Branch's fifteen film crews were rapidly deployed across the world to do aerial reconnaissance, report combat operations, or make training films such as *How to Operate Behind Enemy Lines* or *Living Off the Land.* Ford even had one of his crews in Hawaii six days after the Japanese attack on Pearl Harbor in order to find out the reason for American unpreparedness. He and the newly commissioned General Donovan, however, particularly wanted to test the limits of their authority at home. So he sent out his ex-editor Robert Parrish with a petty officer

to make a photographic report on the old State Department building next
to the White House. Officially the O.S.S. was forbidden to engage in
intelligence within the United States, but Ford wanted to challenge this
presidential directive and also annoy the desk-bound admirals who had
refused to include his outfit in their navy.

So Parrish and his assistant shot some film from a Cunningham camera
with a long-focus lens that looked rather like a machine-gun mounted on
its tripod. The footage showed the U.S. Marine guards on duty playing
cards, then running about in panic and confusion once they had spotted
the camera shooting at them. Parrish and his assistant ended up in deten-
tion cells and were brought for court martial in front of Ford and a Marine
Corps captain. Ford said that the footage was excellent and showed
exactly how well the Marines were guarding important government buildings. The uneasy Marine captain recommended that the court martial
charges be dropped. Ford used the film footage as proof that the O.S.S.
should be allowed to operate within the United States to preserve security, but President Roosevelt stayed firm. Ford's men should only work
overseas, where they might be less embarrassing.

Ford, however, soon won over the President and many of the admirals
in Washington. He would arrange showings of his best and more patriotic
movies for the White House and for the top navy brass. He would attend
the showings, pretending that he had never seen the final film because
he had always been too busy working on another one. He would then
wipe away a tear at the end of the screening of Young Mr. Lincoln or The
Long Voyage Home and say to the assembled dignitaries, "I'm glad I waited
until I could see it with you."3

This was a politic performance, but he won the respect of the President
by an act of personal heroism. Naval intelligence expected the Japanese
to assault the American-held Midway Islands in May 1942. Ford flew
there with a cameraman to film the defense. The Japanese codes had been
broken and the Americans knew where the enemy was going to attack. So
Ford was waiting for the assault on the naval air station.

As a boy, he had watched from the Portland observatory the first
military flights over the army and navy camps and the forts flying the
American flag in Casco Bay. Now from the exposed top of the power
plant in Midway he recorded a boyhood dream of heroism, the raising of
the flag by bluejackets in the middle of a storm of shot and shell. He was
wounded himself in the left arm.

Ford's shot of the raising of the flag on Midway was the synthesis of
his life. He had been blown up as a young stuntman in his brother's serial

wars, he had rehearsed battle scenes in his own films and recorded them on set. His sense of the dramatic and his patriotism had also taken him into surveillance work for the navy. Now he had actually been hit in combat and filmed a scene of the navy's courage under fire that would have seemed excessive in one of his own movies.

The flag in the documentary of *The Battle of Midway* is hoisted as if the military personnel were extras under Tory fire in their wooden fort in *Drums Along the Mohawk* or cavalrymen holding their banner high in the charge in *Stagecoach.* The heroism of Ford's American movies had already taught his country's soldiers and sailors the form of brave acts. If they now did these and Ford recorded them in actual war, they had been inspired and he had learned his skills from Hollywood artifice. At the battle of Midway illusion and fact were one.

Ford's second citation from Rear Admiral Bagley of the Fourteenth Naval District at Pearl Harbor listed his military and his directorial achievements. He was commended "for distinguished service in the line of your profession when on June 4, 1942, the Naval Air Station, Midway Island, was bombed and strafed by Japanese aircraft. Despite your exposed position you remained at your station and reported an accurate account of the attack, thereby aiding the Commanding Officer in determining his employment of the defending forces. Your courage and devotion to duty were in keeping with the highest traditions of the naval service."[4] Ford was decorated with the Purple Heart and the Air Medal for his action, as well as receiving a special Oscar for the film he made from the Midway footage. He could not have been honored more.

On his return from Midway Ford was able to see his wife for the first time in six months. He had a code signal for her to meet him at the Mark Hopkins Hotel in San Francisco. She saw him with his bandaged arm, which he explained away as a scratch from a piece of shrapnel. The Fords spent twenty-four hours together. After that brief time she did not see him again until the end of the war. She returned home to see her son Patrick into the navy and to become vice president of the Hollywood Canteen, a remarkably successful organization of film people which entertained all the armed services passing through Los Angeles and Long Beach. By ceaseless activity she survived well the loneliness of the war while many of the Hollywood wives drifted away into drink and adultery. "You're doing a lot for the Canteen," she was told. But she always replied, "Are you kidding? Look what the Canteen's done for me."[5]

After leaving his wife Ford treated his footage from Midway like a personal statement. He hid it from the navy and arranged for Robert

Parrish to edit it secretly in a Hollywood cutting room under armed guard. Parrish asked Ford if he wanted a documentary or a propaganda film, but Ford ducked the question and answered that he wanted to show the mothers of America that their country was beginning to hit back against the enemy.

Ford then called in the radical writer Dudley Nichols and the reactionary James McGuinness to do two alternative scripts. He recorded parts of each script with his favorite available stars—Henry Fonda was one of them. The background music was to be his darling folk and patriotic songs from "Red River Valley" through "America" and "Anchors Aweigh" to "The Marine Hymn." Each one of the four armed services had to have the same amount of footage cut into the film to prevent any jealousy among them about their role in the victory at Midway. Secrecy was paramount, in case the footage was seized by one of the rival services and never released.

Parrish did his editing job and Ford made a final clever addition. He produced a close-up of the President's son, Major James Roosevelt of the Marine Corps, at the salute on Midway Island. Although the major had not been there officially during the battle, Ford cut him in at the moment when the flag-draped coffins of the American dead were slipping into the ocean off the sterns of the PT boats. When the President saw the film, along with the Joint Chiefs of Staff, he showed little interest until he saw his son saluting the sea burial of the brave. Then he said, "I want every mother in America to see this picture." Five hundred prints were made, and many American mothers did see Ford's picture and the President's son.[6]

So Ford won over Roosevelt through his courage and his diplomacy. He even had private dinners with the President in the White House and was impressed by Roosevelt's bravery in coping with his paralysis and his wheelchair. "I don't know if they were intimate," Mary Ford said, "but they were great admirers—they were friends." This presidential admiration was increased by Ford's flying in the Doolittle squadron on the Tokyo raid in order to make a film on the aerial counterattack on the heart of Japan. Ford did not like being shot without reprisal. He also took part in the raids on Marcus Island and Wotje Atoll, so expensive in American lives. He saw how bloody it would be to take back the Pacific Islands, so easily lost because the American high command had not been prepared before the war.

This preoccupation made him lose Roosevelt's support. He remained particularly angry at the navy's failure to guard against the initial disaster at Pearl Harbor despite his warnings. So he had cut together from material collected by Gregg Toland a two-hour documentary called *December 7th,* showing in detail the slipshod precautions and glaring mistakes that had allowed the Japanese surprise attack to be so successful.

One of Ford's action cameramen, Brick Marquard, saw the full documentary before it was suppressed. "It was political dynamite," he says. "It showed the cause and effect of Pearl Harbor, the total carelessness."[7] When it was viewed by the Joint Chiefs of Staff and reported to the President, it led to a directive from the White House that all Field Photographic Branch material was to be controlled and censored in case it had a bad effect on national morale. *December 7th* finally appeared as a twenty-minute short and won another Academy Award for Ford, although its final shape was almost as innocuous and routine as the other Branch documentaries like *We Sail at Midnight,* an account of the merchant marine in war zones.

Ford had never been popular with the high command of the Atlantic Fleet. He was disliked for his willfulness and disrespect for authority. He would often fail to appear at important meetings of the heads of the O.S.S. branches with the Washington admirals and generals in charge of European operations. The furor over *December 7th* gave them their chance to move against him.

He was sent out to cover the invasion of North Africa with ten of his combat film crews. In Algiers he met up again with Darryl Zanuck, now a colonel in the Signal Corps. "Can't I ever get away from you?" Ford complained. "I'll bet a dollar to a doughnut that if I ever go to Heaven, you'll be waiting at the door for me under a sign reading Produced by Darryl F. Zanuck."

Ford and Zanuck formed an advance outfit for the attack. Once they were far in front of the lines in Zanuck's personal blue Chevrolet, which he had commandeered in Algeria. They found a beautiful old church, which they thought would make a significant background shot if the German artillery did not destroy it first. Ford had run out of cigars and demanded that Zanuck share his last one with him. "I'm not a Catholic," Zanuck said, "but you are. And what greater place for a Catholic to get killed than in a Catholic church?" So Ford walked toward the church with a camera, just as a bomb landed near them. The camera was destroyed, but he and Zanuck picked themselves up, more or less in one piece at the bottom of a cliff. "Did it hurt the cigar?" Ford asked.[8]

His North African adventure only lasted for two months, and Ford found himself still out of favor in Washington. He was recalled to New

York, then put on a slow boat to Calcutta. It seemed to be a calculated slight—a forced long voyage away to avoid official censure. For the head of an important section of the O.S.S. to spend nearly two months on an unescorted munitions ship ambling toward the Far East would have been an improbable mission, if Ford had not been directed by Donovan himself to lie low until the heat was off him. The freighter left New York on September 19, 1943, and took fifty-five days to reach Calcutta after calling on the way at Cuba and Australia and Ceylon. One of the combat cameramen with him on the voyage, Jack Swain, said that none of Ford's men could understand why they had to cross the Pacific that way. Flying would have taken them less than a week. "We didn't know if we were top dog," Swain said, "or lost."

Ford may have been in the doghouse in Washington, but he was popular with Admiral Nimitz and the Pacific Fleet. He had done valuable intelligence work in the Thirties on his private trips around the East, and most of the Pacific admirals admired initiative and disliked protocol almost as much as he did. Many of them were old friends of his and Mary Ford's from prewar years, when they used to come aboard *The Araner* to be entertained each time the fleet sailed in to Honolulu. Ford was not responsible, in fact, to anyone except Donovan, and he was a long way away from his enemies in the nation's capital. "We wanted nothing to do with MacArthur," Swain said. "We were always on detached duty."

Ford went with his camera crews up to Nazira in Assam, and then proceeded to the Burma front. He turned his men over to Carl Eifler, now colonel in command of the O.S.S. in the Far East. Eifler's biography confirms the rumor that Washington was glad to ship Ford off to the battle lines, where he might rub against the enemy and do some damage to them instead of rubbing the top brass the wrong way at home.[9]

There were also political reasons behind Ford's mission to the Far East. Donovan himself flew out to confer with Eifler and go behind the Japanese lines in Burma with his guerrilla fighters. Large appropriations had been voted to the O.S.S., and Congress wanted to see some vivid proof of action to justify its outlay from the public purse. Eifler was a daredevil and his men were engaged in a desperate jungle campaign. Ford's cameramen could record that and send the film back. Eifler himself was soon to be recalled to Washington to present the documentaries that showed the O.S.S. ambushes of the Japanese and the brutish survival war behind the lines. With such evidence before its eyes Congress could approve in safety the courage and casualties brought by its vote.

After Burma, Ford himself proceeded to Chungking to check on the

Field Photographic Branch on the Chinese front. The first camera crew dropped by supply planes had all been killed. Ford had to replace the dead men with more crews, flown in to make propaganda films about the efforts of General Stilwell's forgotten army fighting for Chiang Kai-shek. These documentaries were also used to try and influence the military and Congress at home to send more reinforcements and supplies to China.

Ford then moved back to organize his men and record with them the American counterattack across the Pacific. Wherever the armed services were pressing the Japanese early in 1944, Ford or his cameramen were there. The footage was so excellent that Ford found himself popular again in Washington, which had found other scapegoats in his absence at the front. He was pulled back by Donovan to return to Europe and become "the official eye of the American high command" on D-Day, the largest amphibious invasion ever prepared in human history.

In London Mark Armistead had set up an operation on his own. A secret laboratory was installed at Denham Studios for developing classified film stock, which could also be edited and projected there. Armistead and his men had made various documentaries before 1944, including one on the North African invasion called *Dunkirk in Reverse* which was suppressed for security reasons. His first important job was to fill a surprising gap in British intelligence work. Incredibly, the War Office had no detailed maps of the Normandy beaches where the Allied armada intended to land—only a few picture postcards and reports from holidaymakers.

Armistead began to develop with Gerald Juran an aerial reconnaissance technique which was called "low-level-oblique." All the French coastline on the Channel was covered by a series of photographs, shot from fixed cameras flying at a height of two hundred feet above the ground. As the height and the shooting angle were fixed, the size of buildings or blockhouses and the width of piers or bridges could easily be calculated from the developed photographs. So precise were the images that the depth of rocks under the sea could also be estimated.

Low-level-oblique reconnaissance provided the data for the invasion maps of the Normandy beaches. Armistead also arranged for five hundred clockwork Eymo cameras to be mounted on the front of landing craft so that the mechanism would be triggered by the ramp going down on the beach. With this device five hundred takes of the troops charging into France would actually be shot, each providing four minutes of film. No cameraman needed to be present; the clockwork would do the job.

At this point Ford turned up in London and took over after two years of absence. "I'm in command," he told Armistead. "You're second. I'll take the toughest spot, you take the second toughest spot."[10] Actually, the toughest spots were assigned to two cameramen, Brick Marquard and Junius Stout, who were specially chosen by Ford to go in with the Rangers on the day before the main invasion so they could pick good camera positions to film the major assault. In fact, Ford had set up his cameramen *before* D-Day even began, making them choose their angles and "whatever cover we could get."[11] Ford could not allow the largest landing in military history to occur without putting his cameras in place.

He already knew where he would put himself after D-Day. He had arranged to meet the most decorated man in the whole U.S. Navy, Commander John D. Bulkeley, the hero of the fighting retreat of a squadron of six PT boats during the Japanese conquest of the Philippines. Ever since an account of Bulkeley's exploits had appeared under the title *They Were Expendable,* Metro-Goldwyn-Mayer had been pestering Ford to make a film about him, starring Robert Montgomery and John Wayne. Wayne had already worked on a picture about another "splinter fleet" with Ford, *Submarine Patrol,* and he wanted to do something for the war effort more than the one special intelligence mission on which Ford had sent him.

So Ford had both his careers in mind when he arranged for Bulkeley to take him across the Channel to Occupied France in a PT boat before D-Day. He needed to complement Armistead's maps with an intelligence report from the Bayeux area, and Bulkeley was delighted to take him there personally. "We used to go back and forth," Ford said later. "We'd go in there on one engine, drop an agent off or pick up information, and disappear."[12] Once he asked another Hollywood director at war, George Stevens, what he wanted from Occupied France. "Two bottles of booze," Stevens said; he received them the next day.[13]

After a brief spell on the cruiser *Augusta* to take advantage of its superior communications system Ford transferred to Bulkeley's PT boat for the rest of the Normandy landing. They became close friends. Once again Ford met the real McCoy, the man who had fought what Ford would film. In the theater of war off the Normandy beaches Ford met the hero of his next drama for the theaters of America.

On Omaha Beach, Marquard and Stout were filming extraordinary footage of the first days of the invasion, some on color stock. One day Marquard heard his name shouted over the beachmaster's bullhorn. "There's a crazy guy out there on a PT boat," the Beachmaster told Marquard, "who wants to know how you are—and get your ass back to

England with the stuff." So Marquard put together the footage and brought it back to Portsmouth, receiving a Silver Star for his trouble. He saw some of his film on the British newsreels the following week, but most of his material was impounded and disappeared because of Roosevelt's restraining order on material shot by the Field Photographic Branch.[14] To risk one's life was not enough; the military censor had the last word.

Ford was only to be in one more theater of war before Hollywood dramas claimed him back. His new intimacy with Bulkeley led him on a PT boat operation to support the Yugoslav partisans, who were increasingly falling under the control of Tito. Ford was anti-Communist and supported Tito's rival, Mikhailovich, but the émigré leaders were hopeless and British intelligence was antagonistic. The whole operation was "too full of lousy Oxford dons and aristocracy," Ford said later. "Princes and dukes and God knows what kind of White Russians." Ford was offended that such people could claim to liberate or lead "the proud, brave people of Yugoslavia."[15]

It may well have been his new quarrel with the Allied high command in Europe over the liberation of Yugoslavia that made James T. Forrestal himself, the Irish-American Secretary of the Navy, detail Ford to make a film about Bulkeley and the PT boats. Victory in Europe was already probable, with the Allies advancing quickly through France and the Russians through Eastern Europe. In the Pacific, however, the cost of reconquering the islands won by the Japanese in 1942 was proving high, and the American public did not understand why so many lives and so much time were necessary to regain what had been lost in a matter of months.

Ford shared popular opinion. The shame of the American defeats after Pearl Harbor had prompted his version of the disaster, *December 7th,* and his disgrace in Washington. Much of his men's best material from the war had been impounded or censored or disappeared due to Roosevelt's directive and the bickering of the various armed services. Although the Hollywood system imposed its own censorship, it followed the box office, not the propaganda line. When Captain Ford, U.S.N.R., was ordered to leave active duty and make a Hollywood film to help recruiting and boost public morale over the fighting in the Pacific, he decided to use it as a vehicle for his own suppressed opinions about the failure of the prewar military leadership.

Ostensibly, *They Were Expendable* was the story of Ford's shipmate after D-Day, John Bulkeley's heroic last-ditch stand against the Japanese and his evacuation of General MacArthur from the Philippines in the nick of time. If Bulkeley was the primary hero of the film along with his second-in-command, played by John Wayne, General MacArthur played the role of superhero and semi-divine presence. Ford was to be so impressed by MacArthur on a later mission to Korea that he would demand an autograph for the first and last time in his life, imitating the young sailor in a PT boat who asks the MacArthur figure to sign his navy cap.[16]

In the script of *They Were Expendable,* which Ford wrote with his old friend Commander Frank Wead in 1944, the film was to end with MacArthur leading the reconquest of the Philippines and saying to the PT boat commander on Leyte, "It's wonderful having you here." But the film was not shown until a year later, when victory had already been won against Japan. This stood the release print of *They Were Expendable* on its head, turning epilogue into prologue. Instead of starting with a heroic retreat and ending with a march of triumph, it started with the victorious MacArthur trying to make Americans remember the forgotten warriors who had been unnecessarily wasted in the first disasters in the Pacific. The progress of the war itself had made the purpose of the picture expendable. "Now with the war concluded and the burning thirst for vengeance somewhat cooled," Bosley Crowther wrote at the première late in 1945, "it comes as a cinematic postscript to the martial heat and passion of the last four years."[17]

So the passage of time and the final inversion in the release print made *They Were Expendable* seem out of date and even subversive. The film now began with a recent quotation from the conquering MacArthur, which could not have been in the original script.

> "Today the guns are silent. A great tragedy has ended. A great victory has been won. I speak for the thousands of silent lips, forever stilled among the jungles and in the deep waters of the Pacific which marked the way."

So MacArthur's words in victory already relegated into time past the meaning of the film Ford shot off Miami late in 1944, while the slow Pacific war was still continuing. The following title, superimposed on a shot of torpedo boats racing across sunny seas, also had a sense of Christian destiny and recall:

> Manila Bay in the Year of Our Lord 1941.

God's will in MacArthur's triumph had been superimposed onto a personal statement by Ford that could well seem defeatist in its resignation to the hidden motives and apparent idiocy of orders from the high command that had to be obeyed. "We little guys," one of Ford's characters is made to say, "the ones who are expended—never get to see the broad picture of the war, never find out the reasons back of the moves or failures to move. We only see our part—look up through the palm trees at the seamy side of it."

Ford himself had seen something of the broad picture of the war, but he had not usually liked what he had seen. He had obeyed orders because he had always been a professional, both in the studio and in uniform. In the most significant speech in *They Were Expendable,* the admiral says to the PT boat commander, "Listen, son. You and I are professionals. If the manager says sacrifice . . . our job is to lay down that sacrifice. That's what we were trained for, and that's what we'll do."

Yet Ford remained a populist at heart and a fierce defender of his men. He wanted to show in *They Were Expendable* the tragedy of wasting the lives of brave people through unpreparedness and bad judgment. The sudden victory over Japan may have altered the significance of the script as official propaganda. In a sense the dropping of two atomic bombs made all acts of individual heroism pointless. But Ford had still made his rebellious statement about the tragedy of individuals sacrificed at the hands of an inscrutable high command whose judgment was suspect, outside of the person of the godlike MacArthur.

The actual PT boats begin the film, despised by traditional navy people as a plywood dream of speedy crackerboxes. The news of the disaster at Pearl Harbor comes to their Commander Brickley—played by Robert Montgomery, a much-decorated PT boat captain who was taken off duty like Ford was and ordered to play the role of the actual John Bulkeley. In the film Brickley has to listen to a chorus of disbelief that the Pacific command could have been caught so unprepared. The script calls for "Voices" to ask all the unpleasant questions Ford had tried to ask in the original version of *December 7th:*

> "How did they get in undetected?
> *"Where* were our search planes?
> "What about our carriers?
> "They're set to invade the West Coast now.
> "And they got away scot-free."

Brickley tells his second-in-command, Ryan, that Pearl Harbor was "the worst naval disaster since the Spanish Armada," and Ryan answers that the destroyers of the Asiatic Fleet in the Philippines did not stand by but disappeared "like a rat race."

In the final version of the film an immediate Japanese air attack destroys the American naval base at Cavite—Ford took advantage of a coastal brush fire to shoot the background of burning Manila. The six PT boats put to sea and shoot down three Japanese bombers. Hourly they expect support from the American Asiatic Fleet and air force, but none comes. At first the local admiral misuses them as messenger boys, then looses them on death-or-glory sorties against the Japanese invaders. Interestingly enough, Ford does not treat the Japanese as cruel Orientals, but as the avengers of American carelessness, as invisible outside their machines of war as the lethal Arabs in *The Lost Patrol* or the menacing Apaches before their attack in *Stagecoach*.

The PT boats rapidly prove their worth, knocking out a small aircraft carrier, a cruiser, troop transports, and barges. When they run short of torpedoes, one of them is loaded with explosives and rammed like a fireship into a Japanese freighter. Finally the surviving three boats are detailed to carry the MacArthur figure and his staff back toward a safe island, so that he can command the regrouping and counterattack of the American forces. In an ironical final action another Japanese cruiser is destroyed and Brickley's last PT boat is taken to pieces and put on the back of a truck to serve on an inland lake. All acts of personal bravery end in accepting stupid orders because sailors are ultimately professionals.

Because of their success with their squadron Brickley and Ryan and two young ensigns are unexpectedly flown out with MacArthur in order to supervise the building of a fleet of PT boats. Their salvation at the last minute comes at the price of abandoning their heroic crews to death or imprisonment at the hands of the attacking Japanese. In the original script by Wead and Ford, Brickley and Ryan feel like "a fine pair of heels" when they are ordered to leave their men. "We should have been Hawaiian musicians," Brickley says. "All we've done in this War is say goodbye." But when Ryan tries to leave the airplane and rejoin his men, Brickley asks him, "Who are you working for? Yourself?" Ryan obeys orders and saves himself.

So Wead and Ford felt themselves. Although crippled, Wead had arranged to be returned to service aboard the pocket carriers he had helped to conceive, while Ford had been with his combat camera crews in most theaters of war. They felt expended in being ordered to make *They Were Expendable*. But in the final release print Brickley's bitter farewell to his men has been cut. He no longer takes off in a Flying Fortress, making a sad checklist of the men he has had to leave behind him, but roars away over the abandoned crews to the strains of "The Battle Hymn of the Republic" on the soundtrack, while MacArthur's famous words of defiance are echoed and superimposed, *"We Shall Return."*

Ford's private message about valiant self-sacrifice for inscrutable commands is inverted and then perverted by the film's beginning and end, added by the studio in the flush and forgetfulness of total victory. Yet the film remains to haunt us with its realism and its images. Ford had now served with the navy on its little boats. He knew the sailors' conversation, its understatement and its banter. He allied the small talk of men at war to his sense of ritual and his brooding eye.

The results led to some of the more moving scenes of comradeship on the seas, courage in field hospitals, and community in defeat that have ever been put on screen. One of the film's first champions, Lindsay Anderson, set down its qualities well:

> The film he made, which was shot for him by his old associate Joseph August with a nobility of style that forewent completely the earlier photographic mannerisms, had from beginning to end the vividness and force of profound personal experience. Although (presumably) a recruiting picture in intention, it transcended its origins completely: fundamentally, the values and human responses of the film were those of *The Grapes of Wrath*— love and comradeship, devotion to a faith, the spirit of endurance that can make victory out of defeat. In its sustained intensity of expression, it was perhaps even superior as a poetic achievement.[18]

The war was not yet over for John Ford. He returned to duty in Europe to see what the Field Photographic Branch had been doing on its own initiative in his absence. In a sense the war would never be over for John Ford. His men and his experience were simply not expendable.

12: They Were Not Expendable

He was the only one of the Hollywood directors that fought who did not forget his men.

—Mark Armistead of John Ford

While Ford was detached to make a personal and official statement about the war in Hollywood, the Field Photographic Branch in Europe was engaged in official and clandestine missions. Most of the cameramen traveled with the American forces, shooting footage for newsreels or archives and examining the effects of the thousand bomber raids on German factories and communications. Wherever they went, they made a record of the devastation of the world war. Two assignments were particularly important, one overt and one secret. Robert Parrish worked on the first, Mark Armistead on the second. Both have left accounts of this strange final year of Ford's technicians at war, when friend and enemy, loyalty and deceit were most confused.

Parrish and Budd Schulberg and other members of Ford's group were to try and find photographic evidence against the Nazi war criminals indicted at the Nuremberg Trials. They searched through the shambles of Germany in 1945, looking for the scarce footage of the Nazi leaders that had not been burned. They soon realized that the Russians had seized most of the film clips of the torture and execution of the conspirators against Hitler of the July Plot of 1944. They were making no progress with the Russian liaison officer until they began talking about their commanding officer. The Russian happened to be a devotee of Ford's films and immediately handed over thirty thousand feet of vital documentary material in homage to Ford's work. This evidence was used at the Nuremberg Trials, which were also photographed by Ford's cameramen—the real material which Stanley Kramer would remake artificially in his film *Judgment at Nuremberg*.[1]

The American conquest of most of Europe, which was called a liberation, gave Mark Armistead a chance to use his new aerial reconnaissance technique. After all, who knew when the American military machine might not be forced to intervene in Europe for the third time? Armistead went to Colonel David K. E. Bruce, then Chief of Operations for the O.S.S. in Europe, and secured from him an unofficial authorization to proceed. "Of course, you realize you're spying against friendly countries," Bruce said to Armistead. "If you're picked up, I don't know you."

Armistead began to borrow airplanes from anyone who had one to spare. He secured a Grumman Goose from Admiral Wilkes, and also borrowed a B-26 bomber and three other war planes—all officially "lost in John Ford's air force." Actually, Ford knew nothing about his new squadron because he was making *They Were Expendable.* On his own initiative Armistead set up an air base and laboratory at the small French village of Coutainville and an official headquarters for the Field Reconnaissance Branch at a luxury Gestapo headquarters in the Avenue de la Belle Gabrielle in Paris.

The Allies thought Armistead's reconnaissance planes were photographing Europe to help the repair work on devastated cities and communications. He was even to receive the Croix de Guerre for turning over copies of his low-level-oblique photography to the Gaullist government in order to aid them in rehabilitating France. In fact the private Ford air force was supplying to the American high command photographic details of all the ports and coastlines and communications and military bases of Western Europe.[2]

The value of this work to American military intelligence was inestimable. One American brigadier general wrote to another at the beginning of Armistead's surveillance. "I can assure you that this is beautiful work and would be of inestimable value, if we ever have to repeat our last few years' performance again."[3] The Supreme Commander in Europe, General Eisenhower, personally informed Ford's chief, General Donovan, that this photographic reconnaissance work alone justified the whole creation of the O.S.S. (which was later to evolve into the Central Intelligence Agency.)[4]

Early in 1945 Ford had finished making *They Were Expendable* and returned to Europe to find out what his men had been doing on their own initiative. He wanted to make a long documentary about the Nuremberg Trials from the reams of excellent footage, but the material seemed damaging to future relationships with West Germany. As for Armistead's work, Ford had to save his subordinate from a court martial when some of the Allied governments began to suspect what "John Ford's air force" was actually doing. Before he was stopped, Armistead had already begun on low-level-oblique surveillance of Russian-held Eastern Europe. It was a beginning of the overflights that would lead to Gary Powers's crash in the U-2 and the satellite eyes forever spying from outer space. If Ford did not approve of the surveillance of friendly countries, he did defend his man. That was his nature.

Ford's final duty was to oversee the demobilization of the Field Photographic Branch and the return of his Hollywood technicians to their peacetime occupations. The camera equipment and aerial photographic techniques developed by the Branch were taken over by the American air force and later by the Central Intelligence Agency. Ford rightly took the credit for the achievements of the Field Photographic Branch. He had chosen his technicians, worked with them on many of their projects, and given them local control during his necessary absences. He was responsible for their mistakes as well as their successes, and he never deserted his own men. For his four years of exemplary service he was awarded the Legion of Merit. The Secretary of the Navy, James T. Forrestal, sent him the award, stating that it was given:

> For exceptionally meritorious conduct in the performance of outstanding services to the Government of the United States as Chief of the Field Photographic Branch, Office of Strategic Services, from September 1941 to September 1945. Voluntarily recruiting and organizing approximately three hundred technicians as a Naval photographic group, Captain Ford greatly aided in establishing the photographic branch of the Office of Strategic Services and, exercising close and careful supervision of numerous branch projects, developed valuable new equipment which is now in use by the U.S. Army Signal Corps. Energetic and resourceful, he worked tirelessly toward the preparation and direction of secret motion-picture and still photographic reports and ably directed the initiation and execution of a program of secret intelligence photography. Participating in the Battle of Midway, the Tokyo Raid, North African Invasion and Invasion of the Norman Coast, Captain Ford controlled all seagoing photography of United Nations operations in these major battles, rendering this vital service under extremely difficult and dangerous combat conditions . . .
>
> By his brilliant service in a highly specialized field, Captain Ford contributed materially to the successful prosecution of the war.
>
> Captain Ford is authorized to wear the Combat "V."
>
> For the President
> James Forrestal[5]

Ford was still at war after his return home in October 1945. He had hurt a leg and exhausted himself; he also found it hard to adjust himself to civilian life. "Living in Hollywood, that is a bit difficult," he wrote to his cousin Lord Killanin, "but now I am rested, my health is better, I have discarded my crutches and am walking now with only the aid of my father's old blackthorn from Spiddal." He found it difficult to give up the habit of command and the comradeship of active service; working for private gain seemed to destroy the values of combat. His battle experience would inform all his future pictures and personal relationships. As *They Were Expendable* had already shown, a new austerity of style had come with his knowledge of the actual hardships of fighting. In the war Ford had found a deeper faith in loyalty and fellow-feeling and endurance, and, above all, a new compassion for the dependent and the maimed.

"He was the only one of the Hollywood directors that fought," Armistead recalls, "who did not forget his men." Because of his friendship with the crippled Spig Wead and because of his respect for the crippled President Roosevelt, who had died in the White House just before the victory, Ford wanted to help the permanently maimed as well as those who had served him. He knew of the dreadful lottery of war, which marked some for the rest of their lives and allowed others to go home in one piece.

Since he was still on military pay while making *They Were Expendable,* he made an extraordinary deal with Louis B. Mayer, whose studio was financing and presumably profiting from the picture. As the director, Ford asked Mayer to pay him a quarter of a million dollars and to throw in a further quarter of a million dollars of conscience money because Ford and his Hollywood men had been fighting Nazis while Mayer and his men had been making money and movies at home. Ford wanted the entire half million to go to the Field Photo Farm, first located at the old Eastman House, then at the Briskin place, eight acres at Reseda in the San Fernando Valley. The old farmhouse there was to be converted into a clubhouse for the O.S.S. veterans and as a recuperation center for the paraplegics forever condemned to the nearby Birmingham Hospital.

Mayer paid and *They Were Expendable* was shot. John Wayne starred in the film for little salary. He remained grateful to Ford for *Stagecoach* and angry that he had hardly been able to serve in the war, so he did his celluloid detail. The result was that the Field Photo Farm was initially well-endowed as "a lovely communal sort of a house" in Brick Marquard's words, "a little bit of everything—all we needed."[6]

Studio art designers and set-builders helped Ford and the veterans to construct a non-denominational chapel from an old gatehouse. The stained glass windows came from the chapel in *How Green Was My Valley*. A long tree-shaded drive led up to the entrance of the remodeled farmhouse with its five bedrooms and outdoor swimming pool and stables. The showpiece was a large pine-paneled room with a huge fireplace at one end. Meetings were held there under the medals and war photographs of the veterans on the walls. "It was a sort of shrine," Jack Swain's wife remembers. Over the hearth a huge portrait of John Ford hung, painted during the filming of *The Long Voyage Home*, hands on hips and pipe in mouth under his navy cap, a Mitchell camera seeming to blow a gale behind him so that his old clothes were sails on the canvas. "It was as if the whole man filled the room through that portrait."[7]

Of course Ford's private charity could not compete with the government's benefits to veterans. But it filled a need for those three hundred technicians, who Ford felt had served him personally and whom he could not forget. Women were excluded from the farm at first, except on visitors' days. In the immediate postwar period many of Ford's men moved into the farm's bedrooms for a while during the frequent divorces that took place because the war had unfitted them for a return to domestic routine. "It was the most extravagant doghouse in the world," Brick Marquard recollects, "if you'd had a fight with your wife."

In the beginning of the farm there were many all-male parties, where "booze cost peanuts" and the freedom of military life in the mess was briefly regained. Yet most of the veterans soon acquired or accepted their wives and families, and there was great pressure from the women and children to make their men leave the farm or "exclude them in," as Sam Goldwyn might have said. Robert Parrish even suggested to Ford that the farm be divided into fifty-foot lots to provide low-cost housing for the veterans' families, but such insubordination was too much for Ford. He rarely spoke to Parrish again.[8]

The farm was his last command: he was master of his generosity and his ground. As peacetime values took over and the veterans began to adjust to domestic life, their wives and children changed the purpose of the place from a nostalgic male club to a community outing. Although there were still military rituals on Memorial Day and regular entertainments for the paraplegics from the veterans' hospital, there were more and more family occasions.

Jack Swain's wife remembers that every Sunday the members would drive their families early to the farm. They would all sit having a picnic under the trees, "when all of a sudden, this little whisper would travel

around, 'The Fords are here, the Fords are here.' And then we'd all get
up, and we'd go and welcome John and Mary. It was just a touching thing,
we loved this man and Mary. He had an aura about him that created this
kind of a feeling among the men and their wives. Mary was so regal. It
was like the King and the Queen visiting the farm, and Barbara [Ford]
like the Princess."

The running of the Farm took a great deal of organization, and Mary
Ford was mostly responsible for that. "She was the actual heart and soul
of the farm existing as a living memorial," in Patricia Swain's words. "She
was truly the mother." She saw to the buying of the Early American
furniture and the hiding of the colored eggs for the Easter treasure hunt,
she looked after the catering and the decorations and all the details of the
ceremonies.[9]

Through her efforts life at the farm became a genuine community for
the young families of the Hollywood veterans, who had had to start all
over again at the end of the war unlike those who had stayed behind on
the set. Most of Ford's men would not consider missing a St. Patrick's Day
or Christmas Eve at the Farm, especially since Ford would arrange for a
stagecoach to roll down the avenue and pull up in front of the waiting
children. Out of its interior would step an actor like Andy Devine dressed
up in red robes and flowing white beard, and dispense gifts to all and
sundry. He would be followed by a rodeo cowboy like Monty Montana,
twirling his trick rope, then by stars like Wayne or Stewart or Widmark,
and always in the background there would be Danny Borzage, playing
carols on his accordion—and "Red River Valley."

The farm was both a matriarchy and a patriarchy. Ford's heart and soul
lay in Memorial Day, when the ritual element of his films became real in
memory of the dead men he had known. From far down the avenue the
bagpipes would play as they had once played in Portland when the Black
Watch had marched down to the docks and the Great War. Then the
kilted pipers would come to the open square where the Stars and Stripes
hung at half mast from the flagpole. There the veterans would be standing in their old uniforms and John Ford in his full naval blue and braid,
medals, and ribbons and all. The names of the fallen would be read and
taps would be sounded on forlorn brass in memory of those who had died
for those who had lived. Then a black choir would sing "Glory, glory,
hallelujah . . ."

The Fords made the farm into a ritual and a community occasion. He
subsidized its running to the tune of some ten thousand dollars a year
from his own pocket. It kept the feeling of the war alive in him. He would

not forget what he and his men had expended. His strong sense of past sacrifice inherited from his Irish rebel tradition had been tempered by his combat experience. It would mark him forever afterward. "You can see it in the subsequent films," a leading historian of American military intelligence has said. "All were acting out some of the themes subsumed in the Second World War."[10]

Before the war, Ford had made other personal statements about the American West. Harry Carey and Tom Mix had been his John Bulkeley, Wyatt Earp and Pardner Jones his Spig Wead. He had learned from them of how the West had actually seemed to be before he had recorded it on film. Their experiences had become his experience at second hand and on celluloid. The West was his peacetime nostalgia.

Not surprisingly, he reverted to this past in order to describe his feelings as a man coming back from war to the alien values of a settled community. As his first project after demobilization he had wanted to remake one of his early two-reel Westerns, *The Last Outlaw,* which he had shot in 1919, at the end of the First World War, under the working title *A Man of Peace.* Its plot dealt with an unwilling outlaw who hangs up his guns for love's sweet sake, then blasts away attacking night riders by throwing sticks of dynamite. The remake at the end of the Second World War was to bring the aged Harry Carey back to the screen in the role of an ex-convict riding home to discover that the values of his family and his small town had entirely changed.

The project aborted. Ford was not able to find the financing for the film, so he accepted from Fox an assignment to remake the story of his old friend Wyatt Earp at Tombstone. Allan Dwan had already shot Earp's story in 1939 under the title of *Frontier Marshal,* but Ford had the script extensively rewritten to suit his memories of Earp and his feelings of men coming back from the wilderness of war into the abiding values of domesticity and small-town life. The result, *My Darling Clementine,* is a Western about the adjustment of natural outsiders to the rule of law and church and family.

Although the real Earp and Pardner Jones had told Ford the truth about their Tombstone days and the gunfight at the O.K. Corral, Ford was always more interested in a good story than in true history. He liked to film myths, so wrapped in correct period detail that nobody could see the poetry for the dust on the old cowboy boots. Like the Ku Klux Klan rider he had played in *The Birth of a Nation,* he disguised his message under a white hood of denial that there ever was one. "We tried to do it the real way it had been in the West," Ford declared of the film, "none of this so-called quick-draw stuff, nobody wore flashy clothes and we didn't have dance-hall scenes with the girls in short dresses. As Pardner said, 'In Tombstone, we never saw anything like that.' "[11]

Yet Pardner Jones and Earp had never seen anything much like Ford's Tombstone either, a town suggesting a skeleton of things to come, sloughing off its old skin of weathered boards to reveal the stark horizontal and vertical ribs of doorways and the frames within the frame in which Ford had always placed his heroes to express visually their point of emotional reference. When Henry Fonda as Wyatt Earp does his skip-and-hop dance in front of the bare bones of the unfinished church like an overwound mechanical toy, he signals the free man's acceptance of the confines of social rituals. Until that moment Earp has come to town. After that he has come home to stay.

Although the release print of the film shows Earp in a traditional final shot riding away along the infinite road toward the future, this was not Ford's intention. "The finish of the picture was not done by me," he said later. "That isn't the way I wanted to finish it . . . I wanted Wyatt to stay there and become permanent marshal—which he did. And that was the true story. Instead of that, he had to ride away."[12]

Yet Ford did make a myth from the truth. He admitted, for instance, that he knew Doc Holliday had not died at the O.K. Corral, but eighteen months later from tuberculosis. "Ford would bend history," his editor Leon Selditz says. "He would take an incident and glorify it. Wyatt Earp wasn't the great hero Ford made him out to be, and Holliday was never at the O.K. Corral. There were only two Earps there and three Clantons. I once talked to the old Tombstone guys who said there was no pistol shooting, only shotguns. Ford was making a myth based on fact."[13]

Once again Ford chose Henry Fonda to play his lone hero. Fonda had also been changed by the war, ending as a senior navy lieutenant and an air combat intelligence officer in the Marianas. Although Captain Ford was his superior officer, Fonda had toughened and took direction less well. He had not lost respect for Ford, but he was more sure of his own value and ground. The character of Wyatt Earp in *My Darling Clementine* was Fonda's best performance and creation, a tense whippet of a marshal who seemed to muzzle his fierceness and unleash his spurts of action like a microcosm of the town itself, as if his own body represented the struggle in Tombstone between surface order and hidden anarchy.

"Ford never gave you readings or interpretation," Fonda recalls. "He somehow gave you a piece of business or something that made the scene —there was only one way to play it. That was one of the great things about Ford—the things that weren't in the script." Off the cuff Ford invented Fonda's two best bits of business as Wyatt Earp. The first was Ward Bond sniffing for desert flowers and Fonda replying, "That's me." The second was Fonda's "little choreographed dance of pushing away, changing the position of my feet" against the porch post, as he leans back in his chair and waits for the girl to come along the sidewalk. "That's typical Ford—" Fonda says, "dreaming up little moments that are the memorable ones when it's all over."[14]

With the full authority of a war commander Ford's signature is writ large on the rest of *My Darling Clementine*. He has his actors replay most of his favorite and obsessional scenes in cemeteries and at country dances and back-room medical operations. Once again Fonda talks to a gravestone, this time of his brother, pledging his spirit in the words of the dead Roosevelt rather than the dead Lincoln, "to make a country where kids like you can grow up safe." Roosevelt had promised a peace so that all men in all lands might live out their lives in freedom from fear and want, and Wyatt Earp would see to that in Tombstone, becoming the marshal and choosing his brothers as his deputies, putting an end to the chaos caused by drunken Indians and the evil Clanton family, who had killed his kid brother.

Two archetypal conflicts and one resolution make *My Darling Clementine* resonant in our memory. There is the battle of the virtuous Earps against the wicked Clantons, as just a struggle as the Allies against the Axis powers in the Second World War. It ends in a shoot-out at the O.K. Corral and the killing of the Clantons and of the neutral moralist Doc Holliday, the reluctant ally of the Earps.

In developing Holliday's character, Ford also shows the maturity of judgment given him by his war years. Before *My Darling Clementine* his drunken doctors had been gentlemen buffoons, wrapping the shreds of their self-respect around a whiskey glass and only being saved by a back-room operation which was always successful. This time the saturnine Victor Mature plays Doc Holliday as a poetic Lucifer, meeting Earp in his gambling saloon with the biblical question—Has Earp come "to deliver us from all evil?" This begins a second Manichean conflict between Heaven's favorite fallen angel and the godlike Earp, until Doc Holliday loses his patient, Chihuahua, after operating on her while he is drunk. His remorse makes him join the Earps in their showdown with the Clantons and sacrifice his own life in place of the one he has willfully given away. Holliday is even made to quote Hamlet's soliloquies to emphasize his role between life and death, eliciting self-mockery from Ford, who makes an unseen spectator observe, "Shakespeare—in *Tombstone!*"

The archetypal resolution in *My Darling Clementine* is the final victory of family and the duties of kinship. All of Ford's films exalt the role of the father as the source of authority, from God the ultimate Father through Pa Joad in *The Grapes of Wrath* to the invisible Pa Earp, who never appears but has to be told of the death of his young son and the stealing of the gold cross from the boy's neck by the murdering Clantons. Wyatt Earp even offers to spare the evil Old Man Clanton once his four boys have been shot down, but the Old Man tries to avenge his kin and is slaughtered, the good son killing the devil father for the sake of family peace.

Yet such interpretations are after the fact. Ford did not consciously plan archetypal and social conflicts of significance, civilization against anarchy, East against West, town against wilderness. These contrasts grew out of his search for a good story, which he instinctively framed and directed to show the message through the medium. He sensed his mythology, then defined it within the structure of his shots and the business of his actors and the laconic force of their speech. He pruned absolutes into the little sequences of the edited film. His black-and-white shots show both the inevitability of human conflict and the inscrutability of moral choice.

With the death of Tom Mix, Ford had buried the Old West. Now Harry Carey had died at last, after playing with John Wayne in *Red River* and suffering a heart attack caused by the bite of a black widow spider. So Ford decided to bury the West again in the ground bought for the veterans of his campaigns. He made a ceremony of it all, bringing together Tombstone and the navy in a bold mixture of his favorite rituals. Harry Carey's horse was tied to the hitching-post outside the chapel on the Farm at Reseda, while an honor guard of Ford veterans mounted an all-night vigil over the old cowboy's coffin. The guard was led by Harry Carey, Jr., whom Ford was to use in his future Westerns to replace his father.

In the morning the mourners came in their war outfits. Taps was not played in the background, only "Red River Valley" on Borzage's accordion. The pallbearers were Ford himself and Henry Fonda, Ward Bond and Spencer Tracy and John Wayne, who also recited Tennyson's

"Crossing the Bar" at the burial service. Afterward Ford took the salute before inspecting the survivors of the war and the old Hollywood. Then he resurrected another tradition by breaking out the beer for an Irish wake. To him life was made significant by a succession of rituals, binding men together in memory and community against the outer chaos of dying and war and wilderness.

13: Faith and the Family

It is clear that many gifted people, such as . . . John Ford, grew greatly
during the war. From now on we shall see what they can do with this new
maturity during the next interval of peace. My best wishes, God knows,
are with them; my bets are against them. Once in a while, quite certainly,
a good film is sure to get made: but my bet is that the next ten years or so
will be even harder for good people to work through than the last; that
soon there will no longer be a place on earth where honest talent will be
allowed to break loose from the asylum for more than a male nurse's
afternoon off.

—James Agee, "Movies in 1946"

For Ford the Catholic Church guarded the soul as the American navy
guarded the shores. To him the cardinal and the admiral were the two
paramount figures of authority, the priest and the sailor the two bond-
servants of duty. Once, in *The Hurricane,* Ford had managed to show a
church literally battered by stormy seas, the tidal waves crashing against
its buttresses and C. Aubrey Smith, as Father Paul, playing the organ as
the holy building sank with all souls aboard. If finally the only survivors
in the film were those who floated off on trees or boats above the flood,
the church was the last refuge of those who put their faith in the land and
did not put to sea.

His naval combat experience had led Ford into a total assurance about
his own powers and a firm belief that his Catholic faith would carry him
through every trial and danger. The Irish sense of martyrdom inherent
in *The Informer* and *Mary of Scotland* was printed on the images of *The
Fugitive,* the first film Ford made for Argosy Productions, his new independent film company set up with Merian C. Cooper, whose combat and
film experience matched his own. Cooper had been the producer and
co-director of *King Kong* and other features and had spent his wartime

more adventurously than Ford as a pilot and commander of American air
support for Chiang Kai-shek in the China theater. He was a resourceful
and aggressive man with large ideas, a partner on whom Ford could
wholly rely.

Ford's error was to launch Argosy with a film that mirrored his commitment to his religion. He hired Dudley Nichols to write a screenplay based
on Graham Greene's *The Power and the Glory,* the story of a hunted priest
during the anticlerical years of the Mexican Revolution. Ford chose to
ignore the fact that his previous two independent pictures with Nichols
had failed, *Mary of Scotland* and *The Plough and the Stars,* partially because
of their heavy involvement with Catholic martyrdom. "It came out the
way I wanted it to," Ford said later about the film. "That's why it's one
of my favorite pictures—to me, it was perfect. It wasn't popular."

From the start of the scripting there were problems. The Greene novel
gave the persecuted priest a mistress, whom Ford had to exclude. "You
couldn't do the original on film," Ford asserted, "because the priest was
living with a woman."[1] Ford could not offend his American Catholic
audience in 1947 with the spectacle of a sinful priest. Thus he and Nichols
had to take the sense of shame and corruption out of Greene's hero and
replace it with the sin of pride and the pictorial version of the Stations
of the Cross, "an allegory of the Passion Play, in modern terms, laid in
Mexico, using as much of Greene's story as we dared."[2]

Ford shot the film, now called *The Fugitive,* as a coproduction with the
Mexican director Emilio Fernandez and his cameraman Gabriel Figueroa.
Two Mexican stars, Pedro Armendariz and Dolores Del Rio, joined his
regular players, led by Henry Fonda and Ward Bond. This time, however,
Ford played his obsessive themes of the Crucifixion and the Good Thief
without any of his usual disguises and restraints. Over the first shots of
Fonda riding awkwardly toward a Mexican village on his mule, a commen-
tary makes clear that the ride is toward Calvary, not Springfield, Illinois:

> The following photoplay is timeless. The story is a true story. It is also a
> very old story that was first told in the Bible. It is timeless and topical and
> it is still being played in many parts of the world.

As Fonda walks into the looted village church he pushes open both
doors, making the sign of the cross with his gesture and body and shadow.
Dolores Del Rio, playing the Magdalene dressed as a Madonna with
Child, is waiting at the broken altar with her unbaptized baby. She asks,
"Who are you? Why are you here?" She knows the answer from the

images Ford has already shown. Fonda is playing the persecuted Christ in the person of his hunted priest.

Fonda tells her who he is and that he is afraid. Yet he rings the church bell to summon the village faithful, and he gives them the sacraments and baptizes the child of the Magdalene and Madonna. The village women come into the vaulted church as if into Christ's tomb to wash His body and bear it away. Each shot of Fonda in his ritual role is stylized into the positions of the Passion, culminating in the moment when Dolores Del Rio kisses his hand in farewell beside three carefully-placed wooden crosses, which make an arch above their two bodies to complete a curve of submission to martyrdom.

So Ford displays his Catholic iconography as if painting the Passion on the walls of a cathedral. Yet when he deals with the role of the Good Thief, played by Ward Bond, he reverts to the iconography of *The Informer,* particularly using repeated shots of the police posters of the two wanted men, bandit and priest, to show their linked destiny. In the script Fonda does actually reach safety over the border, only to return deliberately to his death in order to give the last sacraments to the dying Bond, who has sacrificed himself to cover the priest's escape. The words are explicit:

> PRIEST *(Fonda):*
> Listen to me. You believed once—try another stand. This is your last chance—at the last moment like the Thief on the Cross. I know that you have sinned a great deal, but that only belongs to this Life—
> GRINGO *(Bond):*
> Forget it—forget about me, Father. Skip it—skip it—take care—

The third graphic element of the story is the Mexican police led by the revolutionary lieutenant, played by Pedro Armendariz. Ford again returns to the iconography of his Westerns, bringing in the police horsemen in clouds of dust out of the wilderness to raid the Mexican village which is harboring the priest. They are shown in a whirl of savage motion as they attack the market under the grace of the church above. When the lieutenant finally imposes his order on the rebel villagers by lining them up in order to pick out a hostage as a scapegoat for their religious sins, Ford shoots the people in a horizontal bar crossing the church wall at their backs.

The lieutenant is actually the father of the Magdalene's child. Although blinded by his own fanaticism, he is shown with a strength of faith in the revolution even greater than the priest's assurance of his own role within the Church. Armendariz shouts to the silent villagers:

> "Can't you see I am one of you—I am doing this for your own good. This priest is a coward. If he was half the man you think he is, he would have given himself up to save you. Is it worth dying for a man like this? Why don't you trust me? Give him up—I don't want to see any of you die. You are my own people. Can't you understand? I want to give you everything."

Yet he cannot give his people what they want, the religion that only the priest can give them. When the priest tries to sacrifice himself in the place of the chosen hostage, saying that he is no good, he is rejected by the lieutenant: "If you are no good as a man, you are no good as a hostage." The conflict between what James Agee called Fonda's "creeping Jesus" and the *macho* Western representative of necessary order is Ford's own conflict between his faith in the humility of his religion and his admiration of the courage of a man of conviction, upholding the law, whatever it may be.

This basic opposition should have led to a remarkable confrontation at the end of *The Fugitive*. There ought to be no compromise between Caesar and God, but Ford allows the argument to be resolved by an easy religious answer. His harsh lieutenant becomes sympathetic at last when he finds out that the priest has baptized his daughter by Dolores Del Rio. He finds it difficult to deny that he believes in God, because he tries to kill Him always in the person of His servants. And finally, when he hears the shots of the firing squad that executes the priest, he is shown crossing himself. It is suggested that the priest's example has begun his conversion. Like Paul on the road to Damascus, the persecutor will become the zealot for the faith.

The Fugitive is important in Ford's career as the film in which he portrayed most powerfully the pictures that ruled his mind. Since his boyhood near Portland Cathedral he had lived under the Stations of the Cross and Catholic iconography. Here he set out the groupings and symbols of his faith. He had also been brought up in the glorification of religious martyrdom. At a time when the Catholic Church was being persecuted by the new Communist governments of Eastern Europe he felt the need to make a statement about the endurance of his faith. Yet finally his conviction of the need for law and order even in a revolutionary and godless state made him show the police lieutenant as strong in image and righteous in belief as any sheriff in Tombstone.

The Fugitive may have been too obvious in its symbolism, yet it impressed so penetrating a critic as James Agee as one of the ten best films released in America in 1947, along with other classics such as *Ivan the Terrible, Zéro de Conduite, Shoeshine,* and *Odd Man Out.* Agee had his reservations about the blatant allegory of the script and the photography, but his judgment has stood the test of time: "I have seldom seen in a moving picture such grandeur and sobriety of ambition, such continuous intensity of treatment, or such frequent achievement of what was obviously worked for, however distasteful or misguided I think it."[3]

That was the verdict of somebody unsympathetic to Catholic ideals and romantic photography. Yet *The Fugitive* was Ford's gift of gratitude to his God and his Church. At the end of the war, he was trying to impose his concept of faith and family on the film industry as well as on the Field Photo Farm and at home. Used to command in combat, he believed his will might match his desire.

To show his faith, he did make *The Fugitive* and present two huge bronze doors to his place of worship in Hollywood, the Blessed Sacrament Church on Sunset Boulevard. He also had his confessor, Father Stagg, to dinner each week at his home in Odin Street. If his Catholicism was hurt by his daughter Barbara's divorce after a brief marriage to the actor Robert Walker, he tried to remain close to her and to his son Patrick as the patriarch of his household, together in the faith. Despite his long absences at war, his marriage with his wife Mary had endured because of their belief in its true place within the Church.

Yet he was all too conscious of the strains within his own household and the disintegration of many of his friends' homes in the postwar world. He even planned to make for Argosy a feature called *The Family* about some White Russians exiled to China after the Bolshevik Revolution. The strains of expatriation were to destroy the close links of blood and kin. In Ford's own words it was to be "the story of the disintegration of a family after it has been unrooted."[4]

Until he was faced with the explosive effect of the postwar years on the home Ford had presented the family as the most coherent group in society. When they had lost their land, the Joads tried to keep together in *The Grapes of Wrath,* as the Morgans did until near the end of *How Green Was My Valley.* Ford had even wanted Wyatt Earp to settle with his brothers in Tombstone and put down roots there. But the pressures of peace seemed to undermine what even war could not sunder, the ties and rituals of the home.

Ford tried to restore his way of life aboard *The Araner,* which he had leased to the navy for the duration of the war for a symbolic dollar a year. "We never got the dollar," Mary Ford commented. Most of the private yachts leased by the fleet for coastal defense were returned filthy to their owners. But Ford had been canny enough to leave one of his stuntmen, Frankie McGrath, assigned to the boat. McGrath stopped the ratings from carving it to pieces, even on one long voyage hunting submarines all the way to the Galapagos Islands and back again. When the ketch was restored to Ford in San Pedro Harbor, he had it blessed by a priest to fit it for the purposes of peace once more.

Ford had now paid his dues to the war and to his faith by creating *They Were Expendable,* the Field Photo Farm, and *The Fugitive.* His first production for Argosy was a financial disaster and ended his long collaboration with Dudley Nichols, who had always encouraged Ford in overt symbolism and meaningful unpopular movies. Ford's single most salutary act with Nichols had been his heaving the overlong script through the porthole of *The Araner.* Now faced with keeping his new Argosy and his expensive ketch afloat, Ford had to make money by doing what he did best. He prepared to shoot five Westerns in a row for Argosy.

14:   The Holding of the West

Occasionally you get some luck in pictures. More occasionally you have bad luck. If something happens that wasn't premeditated, photograph it.
—John Ford

"You build a legend," Ford once said, "and it becomes a fact."[1] He himself had been occupied in building legends from the facts of the Second World War. On the soundtrack of *The Battle of Midway,* he had played "The Star-Spangled Banner" while the film showed the sailors really raising the flag under fire, and he had deliberately glorified General MacArthur and Bulkeley in *They Were Expendable.* He knew that a nation and its military needed legends to inspire groups of men under pressure and to bind them in a common purpose.

"It's good for the country," he said, "to have heroes to look up to."[2] He was himself an expert at forging universal myths from the bravado of little actions. He understood how memory hallows the past in need as much as nostalgia. For him the ritual of remembrance was the best answer to anarchy. The continuity of society depended on Memorial Day, as the Church did on the Cross at Easter.

His recent war experience gave Ford a new perspective on the settling of the Great Plains. In his early Westerns he had concentrated on bandits and rebels, making heroes of his badmen, and sometimes sheriffs. His chief concern had been the conflict between rules and freedom. He knew the paradox that the lawman and the outlaw are the reverse image of each other, and that the oath taken by the pursuing posse is much the same as the thieves' honor that holds together the fleeing bandits. In the only film he made for Argosy in memory of Harry Carey and the old tradition, *Three Godfathers,* he had one outlaw rage to the other two, "Why didn't someone stop me afore I promised that mother!" Yet the outlaw had promised the dying woman and so was bound unto death to keep his word.

The power of honor—the duty of the oath—these are the concepts that Ford transferred from his legendary badmen to the United States Cavalry in the trilogy he made for Argosy between 1948 and 1950, *Fort Apache* and *She Wore a Yellow Ribbon* and *Rio Grande.* If he remained a rebel at heart, he had been a captain, had been wounded in combat, and would soon become a rear admiral. He had seen how a sense of duty could hold together the competitive and quirky Hollywood technicians who had made up the Field Photographic Branch. He applied this insight to the history of the West and created another legend.

The mounted Indians of the Plains were naturally shown as tribes. They were born Sioux or Comanche, Cheyenne or Apache. They inherited their fierce way of life or death. Yet Ford had the penetration to examine the artificial tribalism of the United States Cavalry, of vagrants who enlisted in a military community and were initiated into its ceremonies and habits. In *The Iron Horse* and *Stagecoach* the cavalry had only been shown by Ford as a horde of avengers, a charge through the dust against Indian intruders. Yet now Ford was imbued with the spirit of the forced and tight-knit society of men at war. So he chose to examine the artificial tribe of the cavalry regiment, set like his lawmen to enforce the order necessary for progress on the anarchic and archaic world of the outlaw band and the Indian braves.

In each of Ford's three cavalry films on this period, all of them based on stories by James Warner Bellah, the same characters appear in fact or memory at different stages in the pacification of the West. If many of the cavalrymen seem to be Irish-American regulars recruited from the Ford stock company, the truth was that many Irish immigrants and debtors had joined the horse soldiers after the Civil War in order to escape the law or the demands of social life. The first film, *Fort Apache,* deals with the reasons for the disaster at Little Big Horn and the myth made out of the commander's mistaken strategy. "We have legends about people like General Custer," Ford once said. "He's one of our great heroes. He did a very stupid thing." Then he added, for that is what he showed in his film about the defeat, "A legend is more interesting than the actual facts."[3]

The legend told in *Fort Apache* is of a solitary Eastern career officer, Owen Thursday, who is disgusted at being posted to a squalid fortified camp in the West to hunt down Apache warriors, who he thinks are ignorant savages. He curses an ungrateful war department that has shunted him aside after his service as a general in the Civil War and on missions to Europe. Henry Fonda plays Colonel Thursday with arrogance and disdain, but his anger seems directed less against his posting than the fact that his daughter Philadelphia is played by Shirley Temple. For once Fonda fails to suggest the reserves of compassion and strength which had made him Ford's favorite actor. John Wayne, indeed, growing in stature with every performance for Ford, takes the picture away from Fonda in the role of the experienced Indian fighter, Captain Kirby York, grown old and wise in "the dirtiest job in the army . . . fighting the best light cavalry the world has ever known—or ever will—the American Indian."[4]

Thursday sets a trap for an Apache raiding party by using his daughter's suitor and a wagon as bait. In the arid landscape of Monument Valley one superb overhead shot shows the connection between military tactics and the dry ground, with the escaping wagon breaking free from the cloud of dust that the charging cavalrymen make in their attack on the pursuing Indians.

This easy victory makes Thursday despise the Apaches even more and tempts him into a fatal error. York bravely goes on a mission to Cochise, the Apache leader who has taken his main force across the Mexican border, and persuades him to return to American soil to negotiate with Thursday and renew his treaty with the government in Washington. But Thursday tells York that the honor of an American officer does not apply to a promise given to a savage—and later he insults Cochise at the parley and condemns the regiment to death and glory.

"They're recalcitrant swine," he says to the interpreter. "Tell them I find them without honor." Although he is surrounded by a superior force of mounted Indians, Thursday threatens Cochise with an attack at dawn. While he is preparing to lead his men into a false cloud of dust York tells him that he is committing suicide. He calls York a coward and orders him back to the wagons, refusing to fight a duel there and then. The last charge of the doomed cavalry regiment is as futile as the charge of the Light Brigade in the Crimea. They are picked off by Indian sharpshooters almost to a man. Cochise, whom York has called a decent man, spares him and the last few survivors to ride back and report the defeat.

Fort Apache would be a simple story of catastrophic pride if it did not lovingly explore the hierarchy and habits of the old cavalry regiments. The romance between the sergeant major's son, now a commissioned lieutenant, and Philadelphia Thursday is an acid and comic commentary on the class differences between the ranks. One magnificent scene recalls *How Green Was My Valley* and the mine-owner's visit to Mr. Morgan to ask permission for his son to court the miner's daughter. The intruding

Colonel Thursday, chasing after his daughter, is told by the Irish sergeant major to respect his house. "This is *my* home, Colonel Owen Thursday," he says, "and in my home I will say who is to get out, and who to stay." So Ford reasserts the sanctity of each man's house against any assault of privilege.

Again in the Grand March sequence at the non-commissioned officers' dance class differences are sketched by Thursday's stiff parade movements as he leads off with the sergeant major's wife, followed by his daughter bouncing merrily with the sergeant major. In every scene, from the comic drunkenness of the sergeants to the men currying their horses, the routine of the cavalryman is shown as carefully as in a military print of the time. As a stickler for detail, Ford outdid even Colonel Thursday. "The Grand March in *Fort Apache* is typical of the period," Ford said. "It's a ritual, part of their tradition. I try to make it true to life."[5]

The folly of Thursday's charge gives the ending of *Fort Apache* significance. York has become commander of the regiment and is speaking to some newspapermen. Behind him hangs a portrait of Colonel Thursday, whom York now imitates in stiffness and correct uniform. The reporters are asking about Thursday's charge—like Custer, he has become a national hero for his splendid folly. York deceives through his silence about Thursday's stupidity. He merely says, "No man died more gallantly nor won more honor for his regiment."

Both these statements are technically correct. Thursday did die gallantly, returning to the massacre on York's horse and redeeming himself in his rival's eyes. The legend of his courage has also improved the morale of the cavalry, making the new recruits proud to serve after such an example of noble self-sacrifice. York then delivers to the press a hymn of praise to the horse soldiers while his dead comrades ride to glory as reflections in a window through which he is looking aside. The full speech in the revised screenplay by Lawrence Stallings and Frank Nugent also reflected Ford's philosophy that the brave dead live in the memory of their comrades and the pride of their uniforms:

> "They'll keep on living as long as the regiment lives . . . Their pay is thirteen dollars a month and their diet is beans and hay . . . and they may be eating horsemeat before this campaign is over . . . They'll fight over cards or a bottle of rotgut, but they'll share the last drop in their canteens . . . Their names may change and their faces change . . . but they're the regiment and the regular army . . . now and fifty years from now . . . They're better men than they used to be. Thursday did that. He made it a command to be proud of . . . and I'm proud to command it."

After this speech York rides out at the head of his regiment to fight a larger threat, Geronimo and his Apache braves. He has supported the lie and the legend of Thursday's charge because it is good for the regiment and the nation to look up to a hero figure. The legend is not only more interesting than the facts; it is the fabric of the regimental flag fluttering above the advance troop. Ford even repeats the same camera angles and music, "The Girl I Left Behind Me," that he used in the earlier scene of Thursday leading out the regiment to the massacre. His signals are obvious. The rebellious York has become the martinet Thursday, noble folly is necessary, orders are orders, regiment without end, amen.

The next film in the cavalry trilogy, *She Wore a Yellow Ribbon,* deals with the regular soldier who fights long campaigns and may win quiet victories, living without glory and doing his job. John Wayne had just finished playing for Howard Hawks in *Red River,* a film so beholden to Ford's Western inventions that he was often thought to have made it and sometimes said he had, since he had created the legend that justified his lie. Wayne's performance for Hawks as an aging rancher persuaded Ford that his discovery on *Stagecoach* had learned to act well, so he asked Wayne to play Captain Nathan Brittles, an aging cavalry officer on the eve of retirement after forty-three years of service. "I finally arrived," Wayne said after Ford had given him a birthday cake with one candle to mark his first year of maturity as an actor. "And I think it's the best thing I've ever done."[6]

She Wore a Yellow Ribbon begins with Custer's defeat. Over a shot of torn and bloody cavalry banners a voice says: "Custer is dead and around the bloody guidons of the Seventh Cavalry lie the two hundred and twelve officers and men he led." Captain Brittles and the remnants of the cavalry have to stop the Indian victory from becoming a massacre of the pioneers moving into that territory. The film shows the slow and thoughtful campaign of Brittles with his horse soldiers, culminating in a peace parley between the old cavalry officer and an aged Indian friend, Pony-That-Walks, who cannot restrain the belligerence of his young warriors, led by a fanatic with the significant name of Red Shirt. He tells Brittles that neither of them can stop the attack of the young.

PONY-THAT-WALKS:
Too late, Nathan. Young men do not listen to me. They listen to big medicine. Yellow-haired Custer dead. Buffalo come back. Bad sign. Too late, Nathan. You come with me. Hunt buffalo together. Smoke many pipes. We are too old for war.

NATHAN BRITTLES:
Yes, we are too old for war. But old men should stop wars.

Brittles stops the war. His parley has also been his reconnaissance of the enemy camp. On the night before his retirement he leads a sortie against the enemy's ponies and stampedes them through the Indian tents. Without shedding a drop of blood he disperses the Indian warriors with their own best weapon. Their riderless ponies charge them and scatter, leaving them to the long humiliation of walking back to their homelands.

So Brittles's trickery is shown as superior to Thursday's bravery. Intelligence outdoes folly, but it is not recorded. In a happy ending Brittles is not paid off but instead sent out as chief scout to use his wisdom and experience in the final settling of the West. Yet this film must be the only witness of men such as him. As Bellah's original screen treatment declares, "Nobody saw his works, nobody wrote of his service, nobody realized that it was always the thousands of Nathan Brittles—that really *made* the United States . . . Where ten or twenty of them in dirty shirt blue were gathered together—that place became the United States."

The film appears luminous in its beauty. Ford was shooting in color and was trying to copy the look of the western artist Frederic Remington, and he thought he had partly succeeded. His cameraman was Winton Hoch, who had worked for him once before on *Three Godfathers.* In the most memorable sequence in the film the cavalry troop rides through thunder and lightning and storm clouds towards their duty. Hoch shot the scene unwillingly. "Then we finished it up in the studio," Ford commented later. "He put 'Under Protest' on it and won the Academy Award."[7]

Fonda had noticed Ford's inspired use of bad weather during the shooting of *Fort Apache.* Clouds and drizzle had appeared as the seven hundred Mormon extras playing the United States Cavalry were getting into position to jog down the hill into Monument Valley. Ford had said, "Roll 'em." The cameraman, Archie Stout, had looked more unhappy than his father before D-Day and had not moved. "Do I have to roll 'em myself?" Ford had asked, and soon the seven hundred were jogging downhill through the drizzle and the cloudburst. "Of course," Fonda said, "it's one of the all-time great shots. I mean, you could see the moisture on the leather. It had a little glisten to it. It had a quality, a feeling, it wouldn't have had with the sun. Now he didn't know it was going to happen like that. It happened and he used it. And it's so right."[8]

If Ford knew how to turn an occasion to his advantage, he would only do so within the tight structure of the film already conceived in his mind.

"You don't compose a film on the set," he told one French critic. "You put a predesigned composition on film. It is wrong to liken a director to an author. He is more like an architect, if he is creative. An architect conceives his plan from given premises—the purpose of the building, its size, its terrain. If he is clever, he can do something within these limitations."[9]

So it was when he asked John Wayne to repeat a favorite scene, that of the survivor speaking to the graves of those he has loved. Captain Brittles has lost his wife and his two daughters. Their graves are much of his reason for staying on as a horse soldier in Indian country. Yet the army is now retiring him. He must leave the beloved dead. He will not desert them by going east, he tells the tombstone of his wife. He will go west to California. "That way, I'll be out ahead . . . waiting . . . for everybody . . . to catch up with me. Mary, you'll know where I am?"

Such a scene is almost impossible to play without falling into bathos. Yet Wayne had now acquired the authority that Ford had achieved twenty years earlier. He only needed Ford to explain to him that he is not talking to his dead wife in her grave, "but he happens to go to the grave because that's where she last was." So Ford told him the exact line between the sentimental and the maudlin.

"He's not afraid of those kind of scenes," Wayne said of Ford. "As a matter of fact, one of the things that he told me early in my career was, 'Duke, you're going to get a lot of scenes during your life. They're going to seem corny to you.' And he said, 'Play 'em. Play 'em to the hilt. If it's East Lynne, play it.' And he says, 'You'll get by with it, but if you start trying to play it with your tongue in your cheek and getting cute, you'll lose sight of yourself . . . and the scene will be lost.' "[10]

Such nice judgment and control made Ford the folk artist that he was. He could depict simply and essentially the passions and faith of humanity. "He would introduce religion to show his belief in the hereafter," declared one of the character actors from *She Wore a Yellow Ribbon*, "but he didn't hit you over the head with it."[11] When Ford exaggerated his creed in his pictures, as in *The Fugitive* and *Three Godfathers*, his films were not popular. But when he was discreet with his beliefs and symbols, as in the third part of the cavalry trilogy, *Rio Grande*, he achieved that balance between genius and sentiment that is the art of the common, the grace of the popular.

Rio Grande ends in a shoot-out in a Mexican Catholic church, with Ford's usual trinity of heroes firing through a cross-shaped opening at the attacking Apaches. At their backs the children of the regiment huddle

behind the altar after summoning salvation by ringing the church bell to
signal the enemy attack to the waiting, hidden cavalry. Such a contrived
ending would be mawkish and mechanical if the whole of the film before
had not dealt again with the rituals and sufferings of the horse soldiers
on their dirty, dangerous duty, spread thin along the Mexican frontier,
resisting a ruthless enemy to protect an empty land for future settlers.

The insignificance of the job is pointed out by the cavalry commander's
estranged wife, played by Maureen O'Hara in the first of her romantic
roles opposite John Wayne. "All this danger to serve people as yet un-
born," she complains, "—and probably not worth serving." She is a
Southern aristocrat; her husband was ordered to burn down her planta-
tion house during Sheridan's advance into the Shenandoah Valley in the
Civil War. She has never forgiven him for that necessary arson. "Ramrod,
wreckage, and ruin—still the same old Kirby," she says, to which he
replies, "Special privilege for the special-born. Still the same old Kathleen."

So Ford and his screenwriter—in this case James Kevin McGuinness—
replay his favorite antagonisms: home against the army, privilege against
duty, private good against public order, mercy against the law, in the
framework of the memory of the Civil War. If there is a suspicious soft-
ness in *Rio Grande* which is absent from the earlier cavalry films, it is due
to the strange intrusion of a Roy Rogers-style singing group, The Sons
of the Pioneers, who provide the obligatory folksong interludes, and to
the contrived grand finale in which the wounded Wayne salutes the flag
and the cavalry with his good hand, set as the dominant father figure over
the children of the regiment, the future horse soldiers and their heroic
wives.

Outside of the role of Chief Natchez, who is captured early in the film
and escapes, the Indians are treated crudely in *Rio Grande* as if they were
still the savage figures from children's nightmares of *Drums Along the
Mohawk.* Scenes of rape and torture are sketched or suggested in the
trilogy, setting Indian brutality against the clean sabers of the cavalry. If
Cochise is made more decent and merciful than Colonel Thursday in *Fort
Apache,* Natchez's warriors in *Rio Grande* are sadistic killers.

So Ford understood the two faces of the Indians of North America.
They were the faces, after all, which the first European fur traders had
seen in the eighteenth century. As Henry Hastings Sibley wrote after
trading in Minnesota, the truth lay somewhere between the Indian as "the
impersonation of the chivalry of olden times, proud, hospitable and gallant" and the Indian as "revengeful, implacable and bloody minded."

Edwin Denig supported him, recognizing two sets of pictures both equally wrong, "one setting forth the Indians as a noble, generous, and chivalrous race far above the standards of Europeans, the others representing them below the level of brute creation." And another early fur trader, Henry Boller, gave the dual impression of the Plains Indians that Ford always sought to show:

> I could "paint you" two pictures:
> The One would represent the bright side of Indian Life, with its feathers, lances, gaily dressed and mounted "banneries," fights, buffalo hunting, etc.
> The Other, the dark side, showing the filth, vermin, poverty, nakedness, suffering, starvation, superstition, etc. Both would be equally true—neither exaggerated, or distorted; both totally dissimilar![12]

Only someone of the confidence and purpose of Ford would dare to present the double-faced truth of the Plains tribes, neither falling into a sentimental whitewashing of the redmen nor into the bigoted condemnation of those who sought to dispossess them. In the opinion of the leading Sioux writer, Vine Deloria, Ford's presentation of his Indian characters was always correct, even if they sometimes appeared incredible. Deloria admires his comprehensive vision of braves and horse soldiers, the tension and the dialectic he shows in both the Indian camps and the cavalry forts, the differences between old and young, experience and fury, between Thursday and York, or Pony-That-Walks and Red Shirt.

Deloria admits that the Northern Sioux, for instance, did use terror tactics, leaving the scalped and castrated bodies of the first white intruders on the borders of their territory to discourage further interlopers. To deny the Indians' brutality or to exaggerate it was simply false. Ford depicted both sides of their life, yet presented them as the true children of the landscape, with the United States Cavalry lumbering in blue and out of place in the red and hostile sandstone bluffs of Monument Valley.[13]

"The Indians are very near to my heart," Ford said himself. "There is truth in the accusation that the Indian has not been painted with justice in the Western, but that is false as a generalization. The Indian did not like the white man, and he was no diplomat. We were enemies and we fought each other. The struggle against the Indian was fundamental in the history of the Far West. There was a lot of prejudice, and there still is. The Indian has a much more civilized understanding of us than we have of him."[14]

So Ford saw his treatment of the Indians as the truth. And now that he and Merian C. Cooper controlled their own production company, in association first with RKO-Radio Studios and then with Republic, Ford could present the truth much as he saw it or the legend as he wished it. With such power his habits became commandments. He applied his professionalism and his sense of economy to everything. First, he would spend months with his writers over each script, which ended in their expression of his desires. He would make them write and rewrite the drafts until the final draft represented a whole film in his mind before he would allow the shooting with its improvisations to begin.

When the writers exceeded their brief and tried to insist on a beautiful and unnecessary shot, he took his revenge. In *She Wore a Yellow Ribbon* he gave Nugent and Stallings what they wanted, a shot of gunslingers riding down the street of a cowtown, but he only used it for a short clip in the credit titles, printing their names over the rumps of horses when they turned their tails to the camera eye.

He worked fast, as his second unit cameraman noticed on *Fort Apache*. He would not arrive on set until nine o'clock in the morning and go early in the afternoon after completing all the shots he needed to take. In fact he brought in the film for three-quarters of its budget of $2,800,000 three weeks early. He despised the close shot, knowing that somebody would try to cut it in if it were shot and that it was not needed. "And we wouldn't shoot it," his cameraman said. "Ford was one of the old school. Everything he shot was put in the picture. So we didn't shoot a lot of setups, but we shot a lot of picture."[15] Ford even used to say that the Eastman Kodak company complained that he used too little film stock in shooting a movie. He was bad for their business.

Ford's precision and sense of structure did not make him too rigid during the making of the film. Although he had the complete picture in his head, he would change his mind if the mood or the weather were wrong, as long as he could stay strictly within his preconceived framework. "You can change a cue," he once said, "modify an incident, but the movement of the camera, like its position, is determined in advance. A director who changes his mind is a director who loses time. You should make your decisions before, not during the shooting."[16]

Within this framework Ford could be ruthless with his original script, his own intentions, and his chosen actors. "He is the cruelest man I know with his own work," John Wayne once said. "He won't often shoot a scene that he doesn't intend to use, but he'll discard one ruthlessly if it won't play right after filming, just as he'll discard a juicy scene in the script that doesn't fit the nature of the players when he has them in front of camera."[17]

His economy extended to his communications with his actors. He hardly talked to them, since he had chosen them for the quality of their performances. If they were his regulars, he would have already broken them into his style. They would sense what he wanted them to do. "Ford is a director who doesn't talk very much," Fonda said of him. "In fact, he shies away from it. If an actor comes to him and wants to talk about a scene, he will change the subject or tell him to shut up. He doesn't even talk to his assistants or his script supervisors. They never know what he's going to do next. But back inside, Ford is working all the time. He likes to be mysterious, he likes to be surprised . . . he does it his own way."[18]

Faced with new actors and technicians, Ford could be very hard until they understood some of his thought processes and could sense what he wanted. John Agar and Harry "Dobie" Carey, Jr. were mercilessly worked over by Ford in front of the camera until both of them were ready to walk off the set forever. John Wayne saved them both, explaining that Ford's selection of them as the scapegoats was the ordeal of every Ford regular. If they broke down under the sweating, then they would never work for him again. "If you didn't cut the mustard," Mark Armistead recalled, "he'd have nothing to do with you. If you did cut the mustard, you became an unhappy man. He'd sit on your back, making you do a bit better. He was a perfectionist."[19]

Now that Ford had control of the cutting process after leaving Zanuck and Twentieth Century-Fox, he did spend some time in the cutting room, often with Jack Murray, one of his regular editors after the Second World War. Murray claimed that Ford did not cut his later pictures entirely in the camera but left him plenty of footage. For the first cut Murray would try to use all the shots. If he did not, Ford would say, "I shot a scene that cost several thousands of dollars and you leave it out." Ford might then omit the scene itself if it did not play well; but in Murray's long experience with him, he never dropped more than twenty minutes of screen time on the cutting room floor.[20]

Ford now began to use his family in his film-making as he used the sons of his friends. His Irish and combat sense of loyalty drew the circle round him even tighter. His daughter Barbara became his assistant editor, trained by Darryl Zanuck, and her father's adviser and confidante. "Barbara and Jack were two peas out of the same pod," Mary Ford said. "They looked alike, thought alike, and sometimes drank alike. She knew the business about as well as he, and he adored her."[21] He could never deny her anything, and so she learned the ways of the film industry.

With his son Patrick he was different. In the old tradition he wanted his boy to work his passage without favor. The fact that Patrick was his flesh and blood made him appear hard. He hid his pride and hounded his son to excel. Patrick was given scripts to polish and then graduated to assistant researcher and producer, preparing to take over the roles of Ford's other relatives, Wingate Smith and Edward O'Fearna. Thus, the generations would replace each other and the family continue in its work.

Ford was also loyal to the sons of his friends, and hard on them. In a nostalgic tribute to the dead Harry Carey he decided to remake his favorite early western, *Marked Men.* He starred and bullied a good performance out of Carey's son Dobie, who was helped by John Wayne, Pedro Armendariz, and Ward Bond. The script was rewritten by Stallings and Nugent, who fell too much under the influence of Ford's religious symbolism and feeling for his dead cowboy friend. They forgot their usual realism and sparse prose to produce a screenplay that makes Dudley Nichols's excesses on *The Fugitive* seem no more obtrusive than saints' bones buried in a crypt.

The script and film, now called *Three Godfathers,* are a blatant replaying of the biblical story of the Three Magi coming to the Christ Child in the manger at Bethlehem. The dying Abilene Kid's Bible falls open at a passage directing the three fleeing bandits to the town of New Jerusalem with the baby whose life they have pledged its expiring mother to protect. Two of them die, but Wayne plods through Death Valley with his frail bundle of future life, laying it finally on a saloon bar on Christmas Day with the words: "Set 'em up, Mister. Milk for the infant—an' a cold beer for me."

Ward Bond and the furnace salt flats of Death Valley save the film from suffocating in Hail Marys. Bond plays Sheriff Perley "Buck" Sweet with a dogged professionalism, hunting down the bandits with his deputies by shipping their horses ahead on railroad cars. After many worthy performances for Ford, Bond stars at last because Wayne's role has been drowned in sacred molasses. Winton Hoch's photography also turns the long stagger of the outlaws with the infant into the most parched and desperate Death Valley sequence since the closing scenes of *Greed.*

Ford's chief flaw as a film-maker was obvious on the rare occasion when his religious faith overcame his cinematic sense. His tribute to Harry Carey developed into an incongruous ceremonial in cactus and desert of the Christian symbols of death and resurrection, at odds with the earthy

vigor and unassuming habits of the old cowboy star. It was out of propor-
tion to equate the Star of Bethlehem with Carey's life, as the opening
credit states:

To the Memory of
HARRY CAREY
"Bright star of the early western sky . . ."

Behind the double meaning of the title played the cowboy lament "Empty
Saddles in the Old Corral." But the bandits and the Magi really had
nothing in common. The Old West had not changed from saddles to
prayer cushions, from evil ways to good deeds, even if the script stated
that the chief cowtown had altered its name from Tarantula to Welcome.

Ford lost his other tutor in the cinema in the year of his tribute to Harry
Carey. D. W. Griffith, who had taught him so much in the early days, died
on July 23, 1948, after twenty years of unemployment in the film industry,
even though he had invented much of its visual grammar and composition. Only six people visited his body in the funeral parlor. One was Cecil
B. De Mille, who had begun his career in Hollywood at the same time as
Ford, who himself visited the body of his master with Mae Marsh to pay
their last respects. They remained silent with the dead man for a long
time.[22]

They did not go to the official funeral, where the studio chiefs and
movie celebrities jostled each other to be recognized at the burial of the
genius who had invented their art and lived on to suffer their neglect. If,
as Ford said, Griffith had taken Hollywood from the dark ages to the light,
that light was dying now as his pupils aged and the studio system re-
trenched and cut back the work of Ford and his peers with committees,
indecision, cost accountancy and crap.

15:   Another Peace, Another War

I've led sort of a peculiar life . . . I was never arrested for anything. I haven't committed arson or petty larceny or anything of that sort, but during World War Two, for example, I was in the O.S.S. I've had a checkered career. I've alternated my life between motion pictures and the Navy. I retired as an admiral of the Navy. I think you know that.

—John Ford

The ending of the peace, the coming of the Cold War, and the conflict in Korea gave an ambiguous quality to Ford's films of the period. In the two war comedies he made for Zanuck and Twentieth Century-Fox his unease was apparent. But in his one tribute to the Mormon pioneers, *Wagonmaster,* made for himself and Argosy, his values were clear-cut. The good people outlasted and destroyed the evil ones. Even in a Cold War there were lines to be drawn between virtue and sin—at least in the past. Then, the enemy identified himself and could be resisted.

The screenplay of *Wagonmaster* was again written by Frank Nugent, but was polished by Ford's son Patrick in close cooperation with his father. Ford had become attached to the Mormons when they were serving as his cavalry in *She Wore a Yellow Ribbon.* He admired the way they would rise at six o'clock in the morning and work hard until sundown. It was their religion and their pride. So, he wanted to make a film which explained how such people came to be. He found a true story about their coming to the West.

Shot without stars and without fanfare, *Wagonmaster* was Ford's response to a world of increasing complexity and a tribute to the abiding values of courage and endurance, loyalty, and faith in troubled times. The plot resembles *Stagecoach,* with a group of people traveling toward a promised land through a series of dangers. In both films there is a whore with a heart of gold named after a Western city—Denver takes over from

Dallas—and a tough-gentle guardian, with Ben Johnson as Travis Blue playing John Wayne's old character of the Ringo Kid. But *Wagon Master* is more episodic and relaxed, its unity the moving picture of the wagons rolling or straining across the continent in sequences of continuous effort, not the mere device of a single Concord coach pulling the protagonists from conflict to climax to conclusion.

The wagons are, indeed, the film; their master is John Ford. For once his images approach those of his only rival, Eisenstein. The screen is filled with moving lines that climb it or slash it, curve away or strain down it, change direction or criss-cross over it. The dialectic of movement that was the invention of the early Russian cinema appears in *Wagon Master.* Ford is at the reins and in the cutting room, working with his daughter and Jack Murray to show in edited pictures the long traverse to the pioneer dream.

Wagonmaster is also a return to the simpler world of Ford's early Westerns, not to the religious symbolism of *Three Godfathers,* but to the sweat and hardship, detail, and dirt of the lives of the settlers and outlaws. When the Navajos appear, they are the rightful guardians of the land, friendly to the Mormons because they seem only petty thieves. But when the bandit Cleggs appear, they are as villainous as Lucifer himself, old Uncle Shiloh with his appalling nephews as irredeemable as any black-masked desperado from a melodrama.

If there is a human hero in the film, it is Ward Bond, playing the Mormon leader, Elder Wiggs, a man of surpassing faith in God and in himself. He likes to interpret what he thinks the wagon train should do as the will of the Lord. When Travis points out to him that he and the Lord seem to think alike, he replies, "Not always, son—sometimes He takes a little persuadin'." He is Ford's essential hero, enduring and tricky, religious and wry, who takes to violence only as the last resort.

Oddly enough, Elder Wiggs is also an outcast, along with his people. They have been outlawed from American society because of plural marriage, as well as other imagined sins. The irony of *Wagonmaster* is that the Mormons, themselves the victims of prejudice, are prejudiced in their turn. They fear Travis and his friend as Gentiles, and they despise Denver and her traveling stage companions as sinners. Like *Stagecoach,* the film is also a comedy of social prejudice as well as a hymn of praise of community in adversity, bound together by folksongs that seem to flow as easily as the sequences and the wagon wheels rolling across the wasteland. When the Mormon caravan finally reaches the last stretch of water before the promised land and the music swells in triumph to the tune of "Shall

We Gather at the River?" the confusion of the actions of men and the hope of God is perfect, and the earthly way seems to become the heavenly purpose. As Ward Bond has already said in Elder Wiggs's crafty words, "The way I see it, the Lord went to an awful lot of trouble to put these people in our way . . . and if I was *Him,* I wouldn't want anybody messin' up *my* plans."

Like Travis Blue in *Wagonmaster,* John Ford was eventually forced to stand up and be counted as a man of peace against a group who wished to cause conflict within the community. All had been coming to the boil since the foundation of the Motion Picture Alliance in 1944 to combat Communist influence in Hollywood, and since the House Un-American Activities Committee had questioned many film people in 1947 about their connections with the Communist party. Lists of friends and enemies were being drawn up, blacklists and white lists and red lists. Respected professionals were being denied jobs because they were merely accused of being Communist sympathizers. The right wing was in the saddle, following the rising stars of Richard Nixon and Joseph McCarthy, and they were driving the herd before them.

On the film set Ford had been able to control such excesses with his usual curtness. Dobie Carey remembers all of Ford's regular players complaining during the shooting of *She Wore a Yellow Ribbon* that Roosevelt and Truman were Communist fellow travelers who wanted to take away everything a man earned and hand it over to the state. Ford happened to overhear the conversation. "I don't know what you guys are talking about," he said. "You all became millionaires off Roosevelt." There was a silence while this truth sank in, and Ford walked off.[1]

Yet actors were actors, while the Screen Directors' Guild was a more serious affair. Cecil B. De Mille had set up a Foundation for Americanism —its chief function was to pass information about Communist "sympathizers" to the head of the California Un-American Activities Committee, which passed it on to Congress. Joe Mankiewicz, the maker of *All About Eve,* was then the president of the Screen Directors' Guild, of which De Mille was a charter member. De Mille and his backers wanted every American director to sign a loyalty oath and provide information on the political beliefs of all the actors and technicians they employed on the set as a condition of working in Hollywood.

So, a petition was started to recall Mankiewicz in order that De Mille and his supporters on the board of directors could take power in the guild. The liberal opposition rallied just in time, signing a counter-petition demanding an open meeting of the guild to vote on the recall of the president. At the packed meeting De Mille accused the signatories of the counter-petition of being affiliated with un-American or subversive organizations, or of being foreign-born. This led to a storm of protest. One director said that he was fighting at Bastogne while De Mille was defending his capital gains at home, and William Wyler threatened to punch the next man who suggested he was a Communist because he disagreed with De Mille. The debate was full of heat, and the only light came from George Stevens, who asked De Mille to withdraw his recall motion. De Mille refused to do so.

During the four hours the meeting had lasted, John Ford had not spoken. Because of the company he kept among actors he was presumed to be a supporter of the right wing. When he rose, chewing on his dirty handkerchief, with his old baseball cap on his head, there was a silence. The other directors knew something definitive would be said to stop the quarreling.

"My name's John Ford," he said. "I make Westerns. I don't think there is anyone in this room who knows more about what the American public wants than Cecil B. De Mille—and he certainly knows how to give it to them. In that respect I admire him." Then he stared at De Mille and said, "But I don't like you, C.B. I don't like what you stand for and I don't like what you've been saying here tonight." He demanded an apology from De Mille for Mankiewicz and did not get one. So he moved that De Mille and his men resign from the board of directors, and that Mankiewicz be given a vote of thanks. The two votes were immediately carried by the members of the guild, and the meeting was over.[2]

It was a demonstration of Ford's authority and integrity. It also confirmed what his close friends knew. He would go to great lengths not to embroil himself in politics. He did not mind being damned as a reactionary because of the company he chose to keep. Yet if a man's beliefs were questioned or his job was threatened, then Ford would speak. He believed in privacy and liberty under the law. These were American activities to him, and that was the end of the matter.

To fund Argosy and the Field Photo Farm, Ford had to continue making commercial pictures for people like Darryl Zanuck and Twentieth Century-Fox. He had been about to make *Pinky,* an attack on racial prejudice that dealt with a black girl who passed for white; but there was trouble over the casting and the playing of the roles which he could not solve. He fell ill and passed on directing the film, working out his commitments later by making two war comedies, *When Willie Comes Marching Home* and *What Price Glory*. In these his mastery was in conflict with his material, his patriotism with their message of pacifism.

For this was the time of his tribute to the United States Cavalry, *Rio Grande*, in which the professional horse soldiers were the heroes, outnumbered and unsung. Now modern cavalry units were preparing to go into Korea in their tanks, and Ford would go with them to war again, photographing their advance towards Seoul. In this confusion of the real and the contrived, of combat and celluloid, Ford seemed to give only his professionalism to the films that were not his own and his commitment to his country's conflict overseas. His documentary for the navy, *This Is Korea!*, showed none of the glory of *The Battle of Midway*, only the necessary duty of a man at war. As General Sheridan says in *Rio Grande*, "That's the policy—and soldiers don't make policy. We merely carry it out." Ford himself was more practical, saying, "It's just too bad we couldn't photograph the charges of the Chinese at night. But there was nothing glorious about it. It was not the last of the chivalrous wars."[3]

In his two war comedies for Fox, Ford was out of touch. His sense of humor was more physical than verbal, based on the stunt and the pratfall more than the wisecrack. As he once said, he could not look at a dramatic scene without hoping to see the female star sit on a cactus.[4] He made his fight scenes into his best comedy sequences, but not his love scenes, which he admitted were not his forte. He always knew his weakness for knockabout and sentiment, although he once said, "I've never had a cowboy kiss his horse good-bye."[5]

The first of the Fox comedies, *When Willie Comes Marching Home*, was an effort to remake Preston Sturges's success of 1944, *Hail the Conquering Hero*. Sturges had achieved exactly the right mixture of hat in hand and tongue in cheek in his story of a soldier returning to small town life. But the techniques of farce which Ford had used for his comedies with Buck Jones and Will Rogers were too broad for the story of Sergeant Kluggs, posted back to his home town, then sent on a secret mission to France, only to find that nobody believed he had ever left.

The song-and-dance man Dan Dailey played the first of three lead roles for Ford and gave the film an amiable quality without making it uproarious. He had to yell away his own delicate sense of humor in long shouting matches with William Demarest which he was to echo with James Cagney in *What Price Glory*. The film amuses without engaging attention until Dailey's fond farewell to the French Resistance heroine, Corinne Calvet, which is as romantic as any Irish adolescent fantasy. The war sequences, however, are shot with Ford's bleak realism. With the army going back into Korea he saw nothing funny about them.

What Price Glory was made after Ford's return from active duty in Asia. It could not have been a less suitable vehicle for him at that stage. It had already been well made by Raoul Walsh, with Victor McLaglen and Dolores Del Rio playing lead roles for the first time. It was a script that debunked war, showing the folly of the sacrifice of the men in the trenches of France. Ford had actually produced the play on stage in Hollywood in 1949, using it to make money for the Military Order of the Purple Heart. John Wayne and Pat O'Brien, Gregory Peck and Maureen O'Hara, Ward Bond and Robert Montgomery had all played brief engagements when the play went on tour in California in order to raise more money for Ford's military charity. And now that Fox wanted to make it into a motion picture, Ford felt obliged to agree to be the director.

His Korean experience, however, had made him unhappy with the message of the play. He was also out of temper because Cagney was given the lead role instead of Wayne, who had played for him on stage. He quarreled with the screenwriters, Phoebe and Henry Ephron, because they did not know his values or understand his rough sense of humor. On the set of the French village on the Fox back lot Phoebe Ephron remarked that there were a lot of Catholic churches for one small French village. "Don't you think there are a lot of synagogues in a Jewish village?" Ford replied, sending off both screenwriters forever, deeply insulted.[6] They were too green and thin-skinned to survive Ford's normal testing of a newcomer's responses, and they presumed bigotry when they were only enduring his trial by their error.

As he could not work on the screenplay with his usual trained writers, Ford barely consulted it when he shot the picture. The opening had nothing to do with the play or Walsh's film, in which the beaten American soldiers slouch defeated into the village and its bar. Ford makes his ragged and muddy men catch sight of some spit-and-polish French troops watching them, so they stiffen and form ranks and march in as if on parade, with drum and fife playing martial music. So he sets a mood of military pride and competition, the levers which must be used after a defeat to put a group of soldiers back into the field as a fighting force.

The play is famous for its ritual battles between Captain Flagg and Sergeant Quirt, which Ford was to restage in *Donovan's Reef*. The two rivals, played by Cagney and Dailey, both love the same French bargirl, Corinne Calvet, and they fight it out in a ceremonious *commedia dell' arte*. There are even unspoken rules in their interminable combats. When Quirt first sees Flagg, they both have to chalk a cross on the floor before

Quirt can be knocked down, only to rise and report himself ready for duty and a transfer. Their battles are amusing rehearsals for the most comic and epic bare-knuckle fight ever staged, Wayne versus McLaglen in *The Quiet Man.*

Although the screenplay was too wordy, Ford managed to show his dialectic of war in his contrasts between the muddy camaraderie of the front line that even forces old enemies to face danger together, and the ferocious discipline of the rear area where men are whipped into shape again. In one long moving overhead shot that seems to be a homage to *All Quiet on the Western Front* Ford repeats his obsession about the chain of duty that binds the living and the dead by showing the ranked graves of the fallen soldiers standing on guard until, with a sudden whistle blast, Cagney rises with his men out of the long grasses nearby to go on the attack. Yet in the end Ford's uneasiness with his material is not resolved by the knockabout fury of his characters or the careful counterpoint of his images until he can make his American soldiers march purposefully back to war again on Cagney's last words to the bargirl: "There's something about the profession of arms, some kind of religion you can't shake . . . You'll never see me again."

Ford's ambivalence about the messages of his two films for Fox was matched by his country's hesitation about the need to intervene in Korea at all. President Truman's original decision to send the armed forces there was never wholly popular. There was no feeling of fighting a crusade for democracy, as there had been in the war against the Axis powers. There might be a strategic reason, the need to stop Communism from overrunning the whole of Asia. But only patriots who believed they should serve their country, right or wrong, would become involved in a struggle that could be called an imperial war if it were not sanctioned by a resolution from the United Nations.

Ford was such a patriot. He knew that Mark Armistead, his trusted aide in England for the Field Photographic Branch, had to spend two weeks on reserve duty in 1950. So he sent him off to see Admiral Radford, then Chief of Naval Intelligence, and find out what was happening during the initial triumphant North Korean attack. "Why don't you go and take a look for yourself," Radford asked Armistead, "and report to Ford?" So Armistead took himself off to Korea on a preliminary reconnaissance mission during the sad days of the first retreat to the coast.

Returning to Hollywood and his camera rental business, he did not call Ford for a week. Finally Ford called him and asked for a report. "Pretty rugged out there," Armistead told his old commander. "We're being pushed off." Ford thought for a moment and replied, "I can walk up and down any hill you can walk up and down. When do we leave?" He was fifty-five years old and paunchy and his sight was failing.

It took Armistead two days to select the necessary film equipment and leave with Ford to serve for eight months as combat cameramen with the First Marines and Seventh Fleet in the American counterattack. Once again Ford disappeared on his own, sharing a tent with the most ferocious Marine officer he could find, "Chesty" Puller, whose decorations outnumbered even Admiral John Bulkeley's. Armistead was not unhappy to see Ford go. It was no joke traveling with the man.

"His night shirts were like battle honors, scarred with cigar burns, dirty with old tobacco and dropped chocolate bars and spilled drinks—just filthy." He had only one pair of pants and no laundry. His idea of changing clothes was to transfer his lucky rabbit's foot, jackknife, dirty handkerchief, leaky tobacco pouch, and chewed pipe from one ruined pocket to another. And he always wanted to be one of the boys in blue. "One drink was too many," Armistead said, "and a thousand were not enough. But he always remembered everything."

Armistead did not worry about Ford looking after himself. "His genius was his ability to talk and argue with Koreans, Japanese, black people, Germans—within three minutes, they would talk to him at their level. He never was a linguist, but he always had a few words in any language at that level. So when he made a film, he would get the smallest detail accurate. He was always right, the pictures were always authentic—not the dialect, but he knew how the people really thought and felt in their hearts."

Armistead was used to being abandoned by his commander. It had happened to him in London during the previous war. This time Ford left him on an aircraft carrier of the Seventh Fleet with the words, "Stay here and do a good job with the navy." Armistead followed these instructions and flew ten combat missions over Korea photographing the pilots and the planes. He even had himself strapped into the basket for the wounded on the side of a helicopter to get an aerial shot. For his aide's efforts Ford earned an air medal and another citation from the Secretary of the Navy, which read:

> For meritorious achievement in aerial flight as Officer-in-Charge of Pacific Fleet Photographic Team ABLE during operations against enemy aggressor forces in Korea from January 4 to February 2, 1951. Completing

ten missions during this period, Captain Ford carried out daring photographic flights over active combat areas. By his courage, skilled airmanship and unswerving devotion to duty in the face of grave hazards, he contributed materially to the success achieved by his unit and upheld the highest traditions of the United States Naval Service.[7]

Ford himself was actually inland with "Chesty" Puller and the Marines, photographing more material for the documentary, *This Is Korea!* Soon he returned to the fleet, and Armistead decided to play on Ford one of the practical jokes usually inflicted upon his subordinates. He cabled his commander: "URGENT SECRET MISSION—ONLY YOU CAN DO IT." Then he arranged for Ford to be transferred from the aircraft carrier to the battleship *Missouri* in a breeches buoy that dunked the director deep into the ocean before hauling him dripping on board. There a band was ready to pipe him below for his birthday dinner.

Ford had his revenge on the vice admiral in command of the *Missouri.* He persuaded him that the documentary needed a spectacular climax. Then he asked whether the *Missouri*, "Mighty Mo," had ever fired all of her sixteen-inch guns in one broadside and in one direction. The vice-admiral replied that no American battleship had ever done that, for fear that the recoil would make the ship turn turtle.

"How much longer have you got in the navy before you retire?" Ford asked. When the answer was a mere six months, he said, "Wouldn't you like to know anyway?"

"We'll try it," the vice admiral said.

The next day a target was selected somewhere on the mainland of Asia, and all the huge guns of the "Mighty Mo" were trained on it. Ford and Armistead wisely rose from the battleship in a helicopter and turned their cameras on the target below. "Roll 'em," Ford said on the radio.

The *Missouri* fired her thundering broadside into Korea. The battleship rocked sideways on the recoil, heeling nearly halfway over, until her starboard decks were awash. Then she righted herself, shaking off the water like the leviathan she was. Armistead got the shot, Ford had a climax for his film, the vice admiral settled a navy puzzle, and somewhere in Asia there was a series of vast explosions.[8]

So Ford staged a finale for what he had seen beginning as a boy in Casco Bay. Then he had stood on his high tower on Munjoy Hill to watch Teddy Roosevelt's battle cruisers come into the deepwater harbor after their voyage round the world had first displayed American power on the high seas. The British fleet was mostly in mothballs now, and the American navy ruled the waves from Portland to Beirut, from Long Beach to Taiwan and Inchon.

From his high observatory, as a child, Ford had seen the coming of the American dreadnought. From his helicopter, as an aging man, he saw one of the last few battleships in the navy firing randomly towards Asia. Soon they would prove useless and be scrapped or retired, the last one returning from mothballs to serve vainly off Vietnam. They were no longer needed in a naval age which would prefer guided missiles to *Missouris* and smart bombs to big broadsides.

16:   Repose and Unsettling

*"It's a fine soft night, so I think I'll go join me comrades and talk a
little treason."*

MICHAELEEN OGE FLYNN in *The Quiet Man*

*"It's one country. And one flag. Teddy Roosevelt's our president. . . . I
shall be happy to serve as a guard of honor for our flag, Mr. Habersham.
There are times when politics should be forgotten."*

JUDGE PRIEST in *The Sun Shines Bright*

After the conflict in Korea and during the making of *What Price Glory*, Ford
had earned the right of reflection and repose. For thirty years he had lived
with his beloved wife and helped to rear their two children in the gray
house on Odin Street over the rise from the Hollywood Bowl. Both
children were now married, Barbara for the second time to the charming
young singer and actor Ken Curtis. His son Patrick and his wife had
produced two grandchildren, Timothy and Daniel, who were often taken
by their grandparents to the children's parties at the Field Photo Farm.
The family was coherent again, and both Barbara and Patrick now worked
with their father in making his films.

These thirty years of family life had seen Hollywood change from a
small California town into the center of the world's richest film industry.
The free-for-all of the original small producers and directors and distributors had given way to the system of large studios and linked chains
of cinemas looking for a certain product. But the studios had been legally
forced to divest themselves of their theaters, and television had now come
on the scene, taking small screens into most American homes and remov-
ing much of the audience from the cinemas. Members of the family were
no longer going out once or twice a week to see pictures about them-

selves. They were staying by their television sets to watch talk shows or soap operas or situation comedies, interspersed with only the occasional old movie to show what people had once seen.

So the values that Ford had preached with such feeling and art in his films were now being presented on television in a cheap and vulgar way. The declining cinema audiences had begun to hurt the confidence and profits of the old studio chiefs, who had themselves risen to power when the first Hollywood tycoons had collapsed after the Great Crash. Now they were being replaced in their turn by younger men who were seeking to change the image of the Hollywood cinema in order to compete with the threat of the small screen in the home.

Ford worked on through the third cataclysm that had struck Holly- wood. He found equally irrelevant the scandals of 1922, the crash of 1929, and the rise of television, a medium in which he would work. In fact, while the new studio chiefs began to maneuver their policies towards epic and shock, tit and violence, the last survivors of the days of independence were left free, especially when they had the friendship of the new power- brokers, the leading stars. Ford had discovered many of them, and now John Wayne was significant enough to make a film bankable for his old friend and teacher, and he was not a man ever to forget a debt.

So in 1952 and 1953 Ford could make the two films of his wisdom and his repose, *The Quiet Man* and *The Sun Shines Bright.* The first was his tribute to the Irish country people who had bred his father and his mother, and had given him a love of the poor and the proud. As George O'Brien once said, "Ford, myself, John Wayne, we started from humble beginnings, and when we realized we were up against it, we went to work."[1]

Ford was no longer up against it, but he still worked because he did not know what else to do. The second film of his golden maturity was a homage to his other mentor, D.W. Griffith, and to the southern society which had given his wife her values. If *The Quiet Man* was for his family, *The Sun Shines Bright* was for his teacher and for her. In a time of division in Hollywood and of increasing bigotry he wanted to recreate a town where the values of family and friendship, courage and honor, could bind the wounds of a society long divided by the Civil War. It was his favorite picture, for it explained so beautifully how an Irish-American boy from Maine had come to admire many of the values of the Protestant South. "In what other country," the Confederate veteran Judge Priest asks the Union veterans who have borrowed his Stars and Stripes, "could a man who fought against you be permitted to serve as a judge over you?" The

Irish rebel had become the healer of wounds, the minstrel boy turned Good Samaritan.

The making of *The Quiet Man* in Connemara was an affair of family and friends. Never had Ford gathered around him so many he knew and loved. His co-producer was his old wartime friend, Merian C. Cooper. The screenwriter was Frank Nugent, whom Ford had taught when Nugent came to Hollywood after a career as a leading film critic. The two cameramen were his combat and postwar friends, Winton Hoch and Archie Stout. His daughter was assisting Jack Murray in the cutting room. Her husband Ken Curtis was playing a character part beside Ford's elder brother Francis. His son Patrick was one of the second unit directors along with John Wayne, who was also playing the lead and had his three children acting in the film.

The Irish family relationships continued. Maureen O'Hara was starring opposite Wayne, so she included her young brother Charles Fitzsimmons in the cast. Victor McLaglen was also playing, so his son Andrew became Ford's assistant director on his way to directing Westerns himself. Ward Bond led the rest of the Ford regulars and Barry Fitzgerald led the Abbey Players, some of whom had performed for Ford in *The Plough and the Stars*. Ford even mocked himself by giving Jack McGowran the surname of Feeney and the role of McLaglen's errand boy, while Wayne took Ford's Irish Christian name of Sean and his rebel cousin's name of Thornton.

Even Mark Armistead, the comrade from Korea, was not forgotten— nor the ducking he had given Captain Ford on the breeches buoy. Ford had just been ducked again by Wayne in Galway Bay when the news came that he had been promoted to rear admiral. Armistead was summoned across the Atlantic to have a cup of coffee and then was thrown fully clothed into the sea in front of the cast. He was baptised officially with epaulettes of clothesline and Ford's hand on his soaked scalp. "I officially appoint you aide to the admiral," Ford said and admitted him to the company of the elect. Ford had even brought across his local Hollywood priest, Father Stagg, to bless the film—a technical adviser who knew how to get the nod from God.

The script of *The Quiet Man* was based on a screen treatment by the nostalgic Irish writer Maurice Walsh. It showed a Galway village through the eyes of an American ex-boxer, Sean Thornton, come home to the land of his fathers and surprised by its rough, warm ways. The part was a difficult one for Wayne to act. "That was a goddam hard script," he said. "For nine weeks I was just playing a straight man to those wonderful

characters, and that's really hard."[2] Yet in his explosive love scenes with
Maureen O'Hara, which culminate in his wrecking their marriage bed by
hurling her down on it, he earns Barry Fitzgerald's comment, "Impetu-
ous—Homeric!"

He also earns an award for valor in his final fight sequence with Victor
McLaglen, playing his wife's brother, Red Will Danaher. They punch
each other for a whole reel of film through field and stream, haystack and
door, street and bar, all the time belting and smashing, toppling and
rising, until laughter gives the watchers ribs sorer than the fighters'. "If
I do a fight scene," Ford once said, "I try to make it as humorous as
possible."[3] For once Ford's broad blows are heroically funny. There is
Homer in the humor of *The Quiet Man*.

Of course Ford was using his roguery to provoke his actors into their
great performances. Although an ex-heavyweight army champion boxer,
Victor McLaglen was the mildest of men. So on the eve of the fight
sequence Ford set up the scene in which Danaher throws his sister's
dowry on the floor. In front of McLaglen's son Ford cursed him for a poor
performance and said it was useless to go on shooting that day. McLaglen
fumed all night and came out next morning, raging and humiliated, a man
of violence choking on his own emotions. He kept on trying to hit at Ford
through Wayne's face, tricked into the wrath Ford wanted him to show.

Even with his friends and family around him Ford used his ill-temper
and secretiveness for the good of the players, economical in what he said,
in control of all that happened. "You become so tuned to him," Maureen
O'Hara said, "one word of his becomes a volume. You become aware that
he understands the story and knows how to get it out of you. It's a frame
of mind he creates. He puts you at ease and sets you free to think, and
you can move easily." Although there was tension on set, there was also
understanding, with Ford changing the mood to suit the shooting and
allowing the actors to speak the sense of their speeches, not the exact
words. "Consequently we can concentrate on playing, not remembering," Maureen O'Hara added. "You are able to invent, improvise, and
use your body; then he spots things you do without thinking, and uses
them."[4]

What makes *The Quiet Man* the most agreeable film ever shot about
village life is the relaxed mastery of its making. Nothing could be better
done in the best of all possible film worlds. There is no sense of contrivance, no thrust for effect. The camera seems exactly placed to be the eye
of the casual observer. When Charles Fitzsimmons suggested a trick shot
from a railroad bridge to show the arrival of the train at the local station,

Ford told him that the setup would be from the point of view of a passenger waiting on the platform. "That's how I shoot movies," Ford said. "Right between the eyes."[5]

The only criticism of his little masterpiece that ever angered Ford was the assertion of one Irish critic that Galway had never looked so green as in *The Quiet Man,* and must have been shot through a green filter. Wayne claimed that Ford was so sensitive to colors that he would even relate them to an actor. "You're like a color to him. And he knows how he's going to use you. He always uses blue where blue should be and red where red should be. That's why it's wonderful to work with him. You never feel displaced."[6]

Ford had engaged his heart in tribute to his homeland. "I was all choked up at leaving our beloved Ireland," he wrote to Lady Killanin on October 2, 1951. "I was afraid I would burst into tears—(which I did on reaching my berth and thereupon fell fast asleep and awoke in New York!) I don't recollect anything at all hardly—it seemed like the finish of an epoch in my somewhat troubled life. . . . Galway is in my blood and the only place I have found peace." Yet he knew he had recorded what he wanted. As he told Lady Killanin, he even liked *The Quiet Man* himself for its "strange humorous quality and the mature romance."

Ford was to win the last of his six Oscars for the *The Quiet Man,* beating Fred Zinnemann's *High Noon* for the Academy Award. It seemed a fair tribute from the Academy to a director who sought to heal the differences of Hollywood, not to fight out its battles on screen like Gary Cooper's sheriff in a film that scriptwriter Carl Foreman contrived to mirror local politics at that time. Although John Wayne himself had recently been serving as the president of the right-wing Motion Picture Alliance, his playing in *The Quiet Man* for the upright, and nostalgic Ford seemed to make it a good time to call a truce in Hollywood's civil war.

Ford continued his plea for unity and tolerance in his next film, *The Sun Shines Bright.* As McCarthyism reared its ugly head in American politics and anyone accused of Communist sympathies found it difficult to find work in the studios or in the State Department or in some universities, Ford remade his turn-of-the-century film *Judge Priest* about a southern official coming up for reelection who is honorable enough to stand up and be counted on the side of whores and bastards, black youths accused of rape, and old veterans accused of drunkenness. The setting may be a southern town trying to forget the divisions of the Civil War, but the message is contemporary.

Ford's courtly and humorous hero is played by Charles Winninger, the polished Captain Andy from *Showboat*. He is both a merciful judge and a priest to his society, even delivering a sermon on forgiveness in a black church over the white coffin of a whore who has returned to see her lost daughter and died in the local brothel. He emulates the young Mr. Lincoln by stopping a lynch mob from hanging a black youth tracked down by bloodhounds. "Hear 'em white gemmuns?" his servant and companion Stepin Fetchit complains. "Hear dat white trash? Scuse me, Judge." The judge faces down the white trash with his old horse pistol and older horse sense. "All you got is a fool dog's word for it." The leader of the mob turns out to be the rapist and the thwarted lynchers end up carrying the election for the judge, parading round with a banner stating HE SAVED US FROM OURSELVES.

That was what Ford was trying to do for Hollywood and the political wars in which he would not join until he felt he had to fight. By recreating a time of healing sentiment and bygone grace, he hoped to remind the quarreling factions of the need for tolerance against a tide of bigotry. The flow of the film is as slow as the Mississippi River, its humor as broad as the Delta. There is time to stand and stare at the fond details of Southern small-town life from the right method of drinking a jug of corn liquor to the way of holding a jazz session in court to the music of "Dixie."

If Stepin Fetchit's performance as the judge's shadow is all Marse and molasses, it parodies the subservience which the victims of that society feigned in order to preserve themselves. Fetchit is no more a comic caricature than Ford's drunken Irishmen or golden-hearted whore, which the master director always created to play against the stereotype. He burlesques the double face which some people have to wear to live at all. In fact the whole Southern town is double-faced, caught between convention and common decency. The masks are only dropped at the climax of the film, in which the judge starts off walking alone in his white suit behind the ornate hearse carrying the dead whore, shaming and willing the good-hearted into joining him in an act of public generosity of spirit.

The faults of the film lie in Ford's self-indulgence. He loves to dwell on his favorite effects, the little rituals of the Confederate veterans, the promenade and dance of the cadets of the Stonewall Jackson Academy, the holy black faces of church choirs singing spirituals. Yet as Henry Fonda said, Ford steals from himself, and as Lindsay Anderson wrote, you might as well criticize Niagara.[7] To him *The Sun Shines Bright* has all the mellowness and familiarity of Ford's most personal signals and messages. As he wrote at the time of the film's release:

> It is impossible not to wonder at the way Ford has managed to preserve so freshly, all these years, this power to move and to delight, this *poésie du coeur.* This phrase is Cocteau's; it evokes precisely the kind of positive poetry, full of faith and love of life, which Ford continues to create, alone.[8]

Yet Ford was not allowed to rest or escape into the past. The bloodhounds of change were at his heels, even if they were "the foolishest dogs." A committee recut *The Sun Shines Bright*—"these people who know nothing about nothing," Ford complained later. "They cut out the best parts of it" including his trademark, Judge Priest's chat to the portraits of the dead.[9] Then another committee working for the City of Los Angeles decided to enlarge the Hollywood Bowl and tear down most of the houses in Odin Street to make another parking lot. Once, during the age of enclosures and dispossession in Tudor England, it was said that sheep ate men. Now it was the age when cars ate people.

Mary Ford was heartbroken and expected her husband to fight; but he would not. He knew he had to lose. Sam Goldwyn had tried to fight the city and had just failed. He advised his old friend, "Get out gracefully— there is nothing you can do." So Ford took the compensation and sailed south to Mexico on *The Araner* and got drunk for two weeks. Then he returned to buy up a "director's house" on Copa de Oro Road among the smart suburban ranches of Bel Air. It had belonged to Frank Lloyd, who had made *Mutiny on the Bounty,* and then William Wyler, and now it belonged to John Ford.

The Field Photo Farm had to go as well. Ford was older now and worked slower. He shot fewer pictures each year and earned less. Taxes were rising and the city struck at him again. It wanted the land on the farm, which was suddenly assessed for twenty-five years' back taxes, even though the veterans' organization had been tax-exempt for the ten years of its existence. Ford did not have three hundred thousand dollars to give and could not raise it. The veterans were becoming older, as he was, the ceremonies around the flag more like Judge Priest's meetings with the last few who still remembered and cared. So the farm was appraised and sold. The money was given to the Motion Picture Relief Home along with the furnishings of the Tavern and Chapel Rooms, also the portrait of Captain John Ford that billowed from the canvas and directed all attention to it.[10]

To add to his sufferings, Ford was forced to have an operation on his eyes, which were temporarily bandaged, leaving him totally blind for some weeks. "Himself has great courage and hope," his secretary wrote to Lord Killanin. "The Eye Specialist is delighted with his progress and promises vistas of sight beyond any dreams." In fact, one eye became worse and useless for reading, so that he wore his black patch most of the time.

He was offered an inconsequential picture to make in equatorial Africa. So he set off to film *Mogambo,* a jungle triangle involving Clark Gable and Ava Gardner and Grace Kelly. The story had been made before with Jean Harlow under the title of *Red Dust.* Now it could have been called *Green Hell,* but in his unsettling Ford preferred a brief exile to living near Hollywood and his memories. The company of the Wagenia and Bahaya, Samburu and M'Beti tribesmen seemed to bother him less than the committees of studio bosses and city planners at home. And he would bring to heel even Frank Sinatra, who appeared on location in pursuit of Ava Gardner, and was commanded to cook them all a spaghetti dinner, if he wanted to stay around the set.

17: Old Concerns, New Times

"If it isn't the family, it's nothing."
—Spig Wead in *The Wings of Eagles*

Like the Supreme Court, Hollywood could follow the election returns, which did suggest how the mass market was thinking. When Senator McCarthy was destroyed by the media that had created him—the press and television—and when the new President thawed the Cold War and brought about a truce in Korea, Harry Cohn of Columbia Pictures decided to show his appreciation for a leader whose aim was to restore tranquillity at home and abroad. He bought the film rights to a best-selling book, *Bringing Up the Brass,* which described the fifty-year career of a beloved gym instructor at West Point. The script also happened to feature Dwight D. Eisenhower, as a cadet and in the White House.

Ford was chosen as the director of the project, now called *The Long Gray Line.* He seemed the logical choice for military subjects. He had not worked for a year because of moving house and the serious operation on his eyes that further affected his failing sight. He was asked to shoot in CinemaScope for the first time, which gave him the opportunity to fill the screen with long gray lines of cadets, even though he hated the screen size. "You've never seen a painter use that kind of composition," he said. "Even in the great murals, it still wasn't this huge tennis court."[1] But he did enjoy the chance of filming at West Point as he had once at Annapolis, and he loved military ritual. When he was told by the commandant that every detail had to be correct, he took pleasure in pointing out that the statue of General Patton was packing a non-regulation pistol and that the flag in the Old Chapel was displayed like a distress signal.[2]

If Ford depicted West Point exactly with its plebes and Honor Code and special traditions, he was guilty of two excesses. He made it an Irish

enclosure, as if the Academy was situated on the west point of the Ould
Sod. Also his restraint on his passion for the chain of the living and the
dead was broken. In *Fort Apache* the dead cavalrymen are only seen in a
windowpane; in *The Long Gray Line* the hero's buried family and lost
cadets come out as ghosts on the parade ground. It may be true of
professional soldiers, as the gym instructor says, that "some die young
and some die old, but they all give their lives to their country." Yet to
show the long gray line as a march of Irish phantoms is to take military
duty into mysticism and nonsense.

As the legendary West Point coach and his wife, Tyrone Power and
Maureen O'Hara struggle with their material, while Harry Carey, Jr.,
plays the young Eisenhower with an uncanny bland resemblance. The
script's effort to bolster the new President's rightful authority over mere
politicians is blatant. At one point Power is made to explode in front of
a party of visiting governors and senators and congressmen who dare to
question the traditions and uniforms of West Point during the Second
World War.

> And who d'you think's leading our men in battle? I mean, leading 'em
> —standing up under fire, saying 'Follow me!' Where else would the West
> Pointers be, when there's dying to be done? And who d'you think's making
> the plans, directing the war? Eisenhower, say, and MacArthur—Joe Stilwell
> and Omar Bradley and Georgie Patton. D'you think generals like that just
> happen? They do not! They're made, Mister Alderman or Tax Collector or
> whatever you are! They're made—made right here at West Point! The silly
> Corps of Cadets with their silly uniforms and silly traditions! Look at their
> records! They're the hard core of your army. They're the steel in the bullet,
> and you can thank your God for them!

Such was Ford's statement, through his screenwriter, after he had
met MacArthur during the Korean War and had been made a rear admiral in the Naval Reserve as a reward for his part in that war. He was
counting on Eisenhower to continue respect for the old ways, even
though a new generation was growing up that did not remember the
war against Fascism and did not see the need to intervene in Asia at all.
Ford's love of tradition and discipline was becoming unfashionable, and
Eisenhower himself in the White House played down his military background.

The Long Gray Line was not a success at the box office, and in his new
home Ford began to make a museum of his film awards and military
decorations, as though his career was nearly finished. He had told Lind-

say Anderson that he never wanted to make another film after *The Quiet Man,* but he found that he could not stop making them, even if he felt increasingly isolated in a world of changing values.

His next assignment led to a disaster. Henry Fonda had been playing the lead role in *Mister Roberts,* a Broadway comedy about a supply ship in the Pacific during the war against the Japanese. Fonda loved the part so much that he stayed with the show for more than three years and insisted on starring in the film version, although Jack Warner and the studio wanted Marlon Brando. Fonda also insisted on playing the character his own way and had quarreled with the stage director, Joshua Logan, who was then replaced by Ford on the film project. Ford was known as a director who could secure the navy's cooperation and was thought to be able to control Fonda's performance.

Actually Fonda had begun to rebel against Ford's tutoring during their last film together, *The Fugitive.* "If you do have a disagreement with Ford," he said, "it becomes an all-out fight. No half measures."[3] In one scene Fonda had insisted on playing the priest his way as well as Ford's way. Ford had agreed, shooting it his way first, then he had walked away and Fonda never could get him to shoot the alternative version.

So the battle lines were drawn before *Mister Roberts,* and Fonda thought he knew the character far better than Ford ever could. He wanted Ford to film the play, the whole play, and nothing but the play, while Ford wanted to add scenes of broad humor. The result was that Ford soon shouted at Fonda, "Don't you tell me how to direct," and knocked his star down.[4] He then began to drink, which he never did during shooting, and fell ill with a gall-bladder complication. He was replaced on the film by Mervyn LeRoy, who continued shooting in the way that Fonda wanted, simply using the camera to record the stage play. The discrepancy between Ford's humorous and warm exterior sequences and LeRoy's mechanical staged interiors was so great that the producer had to recall Joshua Logan to complete the shooting and help edit a final version of the film.

Ford never spoke about what had really happened on *Mister Roberts,* any more than he spoke about his intelligence activities. The film was a commercial success, although only the producer and LeRoy found much pleasure in that. LeRoy claimed that he had made nine-tenths of the picture and had accepted a split credit with Ford as "a nice gesture."[5] Fonda took his side, maintaining that the film was terrible because of Ford's efforts to add to the play. "I despised that film,"

Fonda said. "It was ruined by its co-director, John Ford."[6]

Ford took time recovering from his gall-bladder condition and convalesced by directing two television plays, "The Bamboo Cross" and "Rookie of the Year." The first was a story of two Catholic nuns terrorized by a Communist warlord in China. It was only interesting as a prototype for Ford's last feature, *Seven Women*. The second was a baseball story written by Frank Nugent and starring John Wayne's son Pat and Ward Bond. It was a sentimental tale of a reporter who gives up his scoop in order to protect a family's reputation and was reminiscent of the two-reelers that Ford used to turn out in the Hollywood of thirty years before.

By 1955 he seemed to be at the end of his career. Then a film critic before becoming a leading British director, Lindsay Anderson wrote a monograph summing up Ford's contribution to the cinema. First he dealt with Ford's signals and style. Were they his or those of his screenwriters?

> Ford's films had all to be written before they could be directed; this truth is not too elementary to deserve stating. Working with him in varying degrees of collaboration—sometimes very closely, sometimes hardly at all —his writers must have their credit. But it remains none the less fundamental that the peculiar distinction of these films is—their greatness, where that word is applicable, rests in their style. Poetry, declared Housman, is not the thing said, but the way of saying it. Or perhaps more exactly: poetry is when the way of saying becomes the thing said. In the cinema the only artist with the power to effect this vital fusion is the director.

To Anderson, Ford seemed to be a split personality. There were the magnificent films of restraint when the camerawork was unobtrusive, such as *They Were Expendable* and *The Quiet Man*. Then there were the films of lush symbolism such as *The Informer* and *The Fugitive* which took deliberate aim at significance. Yet Anderson found these last films distinguished failures and preferred the works of formal simplicity. Ford's great period seemed to be from 1939 to 1946 between *Stagecoach* and *My Darling Clementine*. Then he had talked about the things that mattered to him, liberty and justice and democracy. "What the hell else does a man live for?" he had asked.[7]

In point of fact Ford still had another extraordinary decade of filmmaking ahead of him. The rich films of his repose like *The Sun Shines Bright* would give way to the fond astringency and curt wisdom of a man who had lived through much and examined all. As the loneliness of old age and its physical suffering began to close in upon him Ford began to test the ways of surviving, the means of facing slow death bravely. His next two films would show that the aging master was not yet ready to decline, only to appraise anew.

The Searchers was Ford's statement on solitude, based on the haunting novel by Alan LeMay and written with his favorite scribe, Frank Nugent. To him it was "the tragedy of a loner [who] could never really be a part of the family."[8] In the famous opening sequence the hero, Ethan Edwards, is seen through a doorway, appearing from nowhere at the cabin of a western family. His brother's wife Martha loves him, but cannot say so, fondling only his coat and condemning him to his loneliness. There is a Comanche raid, Martha and her husband are scalped and killed, their daughters kidnapped.

Over the following years Ethan hunts down the one daughter who survives, as relentless and vengeful in his grief as his implacable opponent, Chief Scar. Both men are savage in their hate—Ethan is almost ready to kill his niece because she has been defiled by Scar. Both the Comanches and the U.S. Cavalry massacre each other senselessly, returning evil for evil. Finally Ethan scalps the dead Scar and takes Martha's daughter to another western family home, which he cannot enter, going away on his doomed wanderings.

In John Wayne's opinion *The Searchers* was Ford's best Western, "a story of the harsh reality of the West, where you're faced with a real enemy." Wayne particularly admired Ford's double view of the Indians as noble and brutal. "In one film, he made them the heroes trying to get back to their homeland against impossible odds. Then in another film he'd show them as harsh as the land they were living in."[9] Ford's dialectic was clear now to his veteran actors and writers, the confrontation between the opposites in the nature of men, given their societies and their place on earth.

It was filmed at all seasons and on many locations in the West. Ford now seemed as much part of the place as one of the bluffs there. "He is big and burly," a witness wrote of him in dead of winter in Colorado, "with a broad weatherbeaten face topped by a wispy thatch which once was red. Invariably, he wears dark glasses and for some years has covered an ailing eye with a black patch which he lifts to read. One eye or two, he sees a great deal more then he would wish anyone to believe. For a man who spurns Hollywood's fashions and traditions, Ford nonetheless makes a colorful appearance. Traveling to a location, Ford is apt to wear a Navy blue blazer, old gray flannels, scarf about his neck, worn Navy officer's raincoat over his arm and an ancient gray cap jammed low over his eyes. A cigar or pipe is customarily clamped in his determined jaw. At work on the set, he often wears his old combat jacket, an American flag emblazoned on the shoulder. There is no mistaking Ford when you see him.''[10]

As always, his tastes in reading and writing were catholic. At night, long after the last card game was over, his light would burn as he went on reading. On *The Searchers* he browsed in Gibbon's *Decline and Fall of the Roman Empire,* a Gene Fowler biography, some Conan Doyle, and P.G. Wodehouse. Any new book on the Civil War was also his meat and drink. "He vacuumed in things," one of his friends said. "He was a goddam dictionary, an encyclopedia.''[11]

So Ford remained in control of his film set and his full powers, but not of his family, his company, or his popular appeal. His son Patrick, who was the assistant producer on *The Searchers,* decided to go off and work for one of the two producers, Cornelius Vanderbilt Whitney, who was backing the film after his successful investment in *Gone With the Wind.* Ford's son wanted to be independent of his famous father and prove his own worth. The other producer, Merian C. Cooper, also had to work for Whitney on *The Searchers,* because his joint venture with Ford, Argosy Pictures, had never solved its problems of distribution. The big investors and studios and cinema chains had the whip-hand. It was no longer possible to resist the octopus of Hollywood. Economics dictated all now, even more than before.

It was not like the old days of the Westerns. "We did them in two or three weeks," Ford reminisced. "Three weeks was a long schedule. Now, by gosh, they cost millions. If you do it under twelve weeks, you probably come near the budget. In those days, you know, we were making pictures for seventy-five thousand . . .'' Even worse than the shooting costs of the new pictures were their preproduction costs. Gone were the days when a script cost nothing at all. "Now it costs a hundred thousand for a story. But we'd just take any story which was good, and just do it. . . . We'd never pay for them.''[12]

So the Western became expensive and structured and cautious. It had lost its élan, just as Ford seemed to have lost his audience. When *The Searchers* was released, the public stayed away and the critics were hostile. Even Lindsay Anderson found it cold, a triumph of technique. Ford seemed to lack belief and was too proud to simulate a feeling that was not there. "He simply films it, throws it in our faces, saying, 'If this is what you want, take it!' ''[13]

It was not so: later American critics found it Ford's masterwork, the beginning of Ford's last odyssey, his quest with Ethan Edwards for the approach to dying alone. His next film, *The Wings of Eagles,* pursued the

Barbara Curran Feeney, John Ford's mother.

John Ford, then called John Feeney, at the age of five.

John Feeney (back row, right) in the Portland High School football squad.

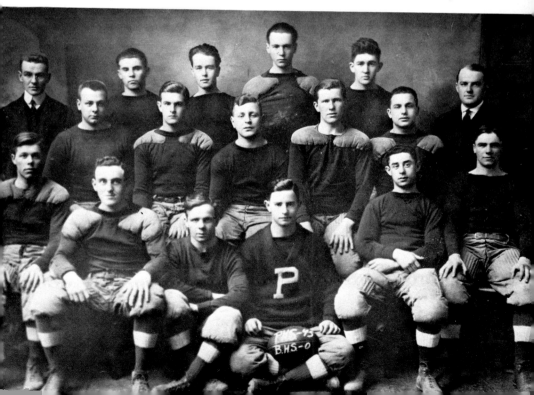

The outlaws by the crevasse in *Straight Shooting* (1917). (*Courtesy of NFI.*)

John Ford (second from left) directs Abraham Lincoln, played by Judge Bull, in signing the railroad legislation in *The Iron Horse* (1924). (*Courtesy of NFI.*)

The railroad sections meet in
The Iron Horse. (Courtesy of NFI.)

John Ford (center) on set with
Tom Mix (center, bottom row),
both wearing white shirts.

The barber, played by Frank Reicher, boasts how he would cut the throat of Napoleon, played by Otto Matiesen, in *Napoleon's Barber* (1928), Ford's first talking picture.
(Courtesy of NFI.)

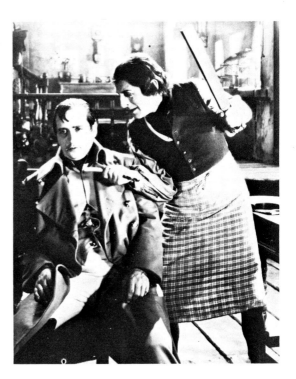

Ronald Colman at his scientific experiments in *Arrowsmith* (1931).
(Courtesy of NFI.)

After the crash in the blizzard in *Air Mail* (1932). (*Courtesy of NFI.*)

Victor McLaglen reviews the swords of his dead comrades in *The Lost Patrol* (1934). (*Courtesy of NFI.*)

The *Araner* under sail.

Will Rogers (left) views the historical
waxworks before he changes their names
in *Steamboat Round the Bend* (1935).
(Courtesy of NFI.)

The race starts in *Steamboat Round the
Bend.* *(Courtesy of NFI.)*

Warner Baxter (second from left), playing Dr. Samuel A. Mudd, is taken to jail in *The Prisoner of Shark Island* (1936). (*Courtesy of NFI.*)

Katharine Hepburn rides to her throne past halberds in the form of crosses in *Mary of Scotland* (1936). (*Courtesy of NFI.*)

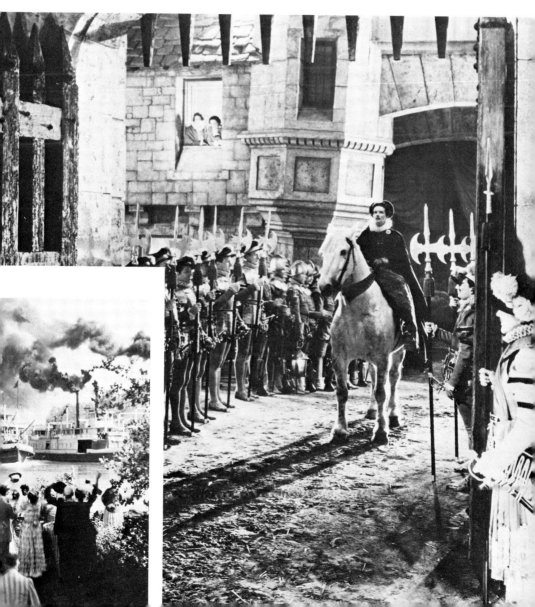

John Ford (second from right) in a white jacket shooting *The Plough and the Stars* (1936) in the sequence of the Easter Rising of the Irish rebels and patriots.

Victor McLaglen teaches British drill to Shirley Temple in *Wee Willie Winkie* (1937). (*Courtesy of NFI.*)

The pagan tree saves the survivors from the Christian church in *The Hurricane* (1937). (*Courtesy of NFI.*)

The hidden gun on the ship in the Splinter Fleet destroys the U-boat in *Submarine Patrol* (1938). (*Courtesy of NFI.*)

John Carradine, playing the gambler Hatfield, discovers the penitential death of the victim of the Apaches in *Stagecoach* (1939).

Pauline Moore as Ann Rutledge meets Henry Fonda in *Young Mr. Lincoln* (1939). The bars of the split-rail fence cross out the possibility of their love.

Young Abe Lincoln kneels by the grave of his first love, his future mapped out by the bars of the fence leading straight away from him.

The farmers clear the land of timber in *Drums Along the Mohawk* (1939).

Claudette Colbert defies the Indians as they burst into the fort in *Drums Along the Mohawk*.

Henry Fonda with Claudette Colbert playing his wife first see the new Stars and Stripes as a detachment of George Washington's army marches into the frontier fort.

Granpa Joad (left) refuses to leave the land he has always known in *The Grapes of Wrath* (1940). (*Courtesy of the Cinema Bookshop.*)

John Ford traps his actors inside confining spaces and bars on the S. S. *Glencairn* and in the London docks in *The Long Voyage Home* (1940).

The Lesters admire their first family car in *Tobacco Road* (1941). *(Courtesy of NFI.)*

Donald Crisp, playing Mr. Morgan, keeps the family peace in his house in *How Green Was My Valley* (1941).

The Pacific fleet is sunk at Pearl Harbor. Footage from the documentary *December 7th.* (*Courtesy of NFI.*)

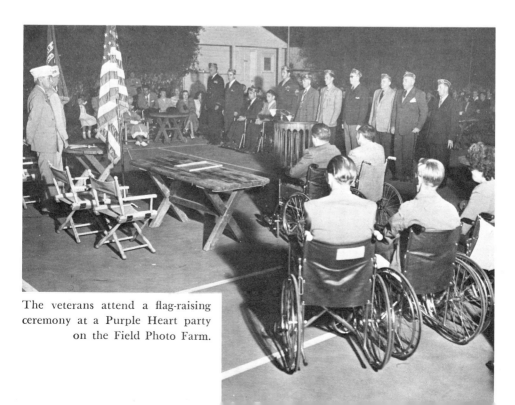

The veterans attend a flag-raising ceremony at a Purple Heart party on the Field Photo Farm.

Ford's iconography was exaggerated in *The Fugitive* (1947). Henry Fonda, playing the priest, opens the door of the empty village church and makes his body into the shape of the cross.

The village women come to mass as if into Christ's tomb.

Ward Bond as "El Gringo" sees the wanted poster just as Victor McLaglen saw one in *The Informer*.

The Mexican mounted police attack the village for harboring a priest, while the church stands serenely above the violence.

The police lieutenant, played by Pedro Armendariz, threatens the villagers who are hiding the priest.

By the symbol of the crucifixion Henry Fonda gives his hand to Dolores del Rio to kiss in *The Fugitive*.

The U.S. Cavalry forms a parade before riding out to disaster in *Fort Apache* (1948).

The Apaches attack a supply wagon after the massacre.

John Wayne, playing the last surviving badman, staggers with the baby through the Mojave Desert in *Three Godfathers* (1948).

The cavalry patrol stampedes the Indians' horses in *She Wore a Yellow Ribbon* (1949).

John Wayne, playing Captain Nathan Brittles, leads the cavalry across Monument Valley in *She Wore a Yellow Ribbon*.

John Wayne takes the salute, the commander and father figure of the regiment in *Rio Grande* (1950).

In *Wagonmaster* (1950) Ford used lines of motion and contours of landscape as boldly as Eisenstein.

John Wayne treats Maureen O'Hara in the good old Irish way in *The Quiet Man* (1952). *(Courtesy of NFI.)*

James Cagney, leading his men, rises out of field beyond the graveyard in *What Price Glory* (1952).

Wayne fights it out with Victor McLaglen in *The Quiet Man. (Courtesy of NFI.)*

John Ford, ready for duty.

Mary and John Ford with their
two grandsons, Timothy and Daniel,
at the Field Photo Farm.

The cadets on parade in *The Long
Gray Line* (1955).

John Ford directs the whip duel in *The Sun Shines Bright* (1953).

The lynchers parade in front of Judge Priest's home in his victory parade.

A goat fails to upset Henry Fonda in *Mister Roberts* (1955).

John Wayne as Ethan Edwards leads the search through Colorado and through Monument Valley in *The Searchers* (1956).

Ward Bond as the Captain Reverend Samuel Clayton (left) gives the oath in *The Searchers.*

Natalie Wood shows how Indian she has become when she drops a lance as a barrier in front of John Wayne and Jeffrey Hunter.

Another goat offends the English couple on the train in the middle episode of *The Rising of the Moon* (1957).

John Ford directs Cyril Cusack and Noel Purcell outside an Irish cottage in *The Rising of the Moon*.

The false nuns come to the rescue of the condemned man and hoodwink the British soldiers in the last episode of *The Rising of the Moon*.

Spencer Tracy, playing Frank Skeffington, runs for reelection in *The Last Hurrah* (1958).

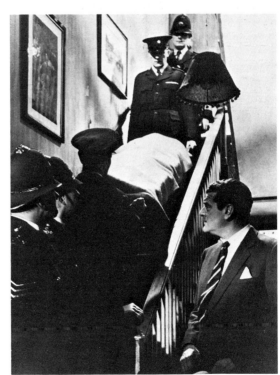

Jack Hawkins (right) watches the murder victim carried down the stairs in *Gideon's Day* (1959). (*Courtesy of NFI.*)

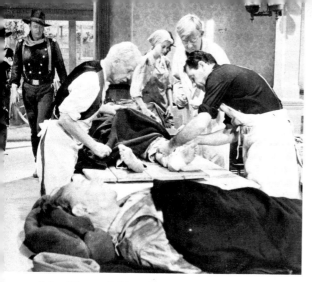

John Wayne (left) strides in to see William Holden (right) about to perform an operation in *The Horse Soldiers* (1959)—one of Ford's many scenes set in a field hospital after a battle.

John Ford on location in the West.

John Ford directs the horse soldiers crossing a swamp.

James Stewart (right) and Richard Widmark (center) trade for the white captives with Henry Brandon in *Two Rode Together* (1961).

The Indian boy is lynched by the pioneers in *Two Rode Together.*

The mocking Lee Marvin (right) shoots at the wounded James Stewart in *The Man Who Shot Liberty Valance* (1962).

John Ford directs, his unlit "Ford Special" cigar butt in his hand.

Lee Marvin and John Wayne in one of their repeated fights in *Donovan's Reef* (1963).

Wayne and Marvin patch up their quarrel in front of the many religious symbols near the island's Catholic church.

The Cheyennes wait for the congressional delegation that never comes to the Oklahoma dustbowl in *Cheyenne Autumn* (1964).

Ford directs Anne Bancroft, playing Dr. Cartwright, in how to swagger in *Seven Women* (1966).

(*Following page*)
John Ford, director.

theme. If its subject was the story of his friend from the navy, Spig Wead, it was also the story of a reckless and aggressive flier, as incapable as Ethan Edwards of living within the family, yet capable of overcoming a crippling spinal injury and developing the pocket aircraft carrier in the Second World War, only to be retired as he is dying.

After his accident had forced Wead to give up flying for the navy, Ford had helped him to become a screenwriter. They had worked together on *Air Mail* and *They Were Expendable,* in which Wayne had starred as part of his war effort. As with Harry Carey, Ford had wanted to pay a tribute to his old friend. So he put together a script, full of stunt flying and slapstick, courage and crassness in love. "Ford cut through the nuance and all that crap," Wayne said, "and got down to the basic story. He put the nuance in with the camera."[14]

That was true of the most remarkable sequence in *The Wings of Eagles,* as the film was finally called. Playing the role of the paralyzed Wead, Wayne is strapped down on his stomach with his sidekick Dan Dailey trying to persuade him to move one toe. Dailey even goes into a song-and-dance routine to encourage his crippled friend to respond, singing:

> *I'm goin' to move that toe,*
> *I'm goin' to move that toe . . .*

Yet when the toe does move, Ford does not show it, only Dailey's great happiness. Such perfect discretion, which refused to display the expected shot, was Ford's nuance in the camera.

In another extraordinary episode Ford allowed a parody of himself as a film director. Ward Bond, who had so often been Ford's mouthpiece in films such as *Wagonmaster* and *The Quiet Man,* now played the man himself. He stole Ford's good hat and pipe and Academy Awards and put them on set for the scene in which the fictional Wead meets the great film director and producer. With relish Bond delivered Ford's own words on screenwriting to Wayne. "I don't want a story just about ships and planes. I want it about the men who run them—how they live and think and talk. I want it from a pen dipped in salt water, not dry martinis. You know what I mean?"

Yet in this most compassionate and personal tribute, Ford did not miss the chance of spreading propaganda for naval flying. As Eisenhower was extending his understanding with the Russians, so the Navy was becoming more worried about its share of the military budget, particularly as Eisenhower himself came from the Army. In the film Spig Wead is given a speech in front of a congressional committee that harks back to Ford's concern between the two world wars—and to his worry about remaining prepared for wars to come:

SPIG WEAD:
We're losing carriers we need and planes to fly from them. And some day we might lose something bigger than that. If you can't develop both services impartially, you're either shirking your duty or you don't know what your duty is.
SENATOR BARTON:
Son, there's a lot of things we don't know. But here's some we do. We got a country yelling "pacifism" at us. "Disarmament, tax reduction—no more wars—and the army and navy is going out of business." Now you maybe fight one war a generation. But we got to fight those voters every blamed two years.

It was not a popular message at a time when President Eisenhower himself became suspicious of the military-industrial complex. But Ford had learned under Donovan how to make films to stimulate a congressional vote for more funds for a forgotten army or navy. He used those techniques in *The Wings of Eagles* to appeal both for more funds for the Navy and more compassion for those who gave their lives to the service. "Stay broke and keep moving," Wayne is made to say at one point to his wife, Maureen O'Hara, "it's the story of our lives." In the story of Wead's life Ford also tried to show his deep feeling for the permanently maimed and the paraplegics, whom he had privately helped on the Field Photo Farm. A bad injury should not be enough to end a man's usefulness, even if *The Wings of Eagles* had to end with Wayne in a breeches buoy, forcibly recalled from duty in a scene recalling the indignities Ford had suffered off Korea.

If Ford's concerns appeared out of date, his craft had exceeded mastery and approached genius. He seemed to be able to make a film shorthand of decades of time, dissolving from Ethan Edward's oath, "We'll find her as sure as the turning of the earth" to the sight of the two searchers returning in spring from another fruitless quest. In the space of a feature he is able to comprehend the fifty years' service of a gym instructor at West Point; the forty years of Spig Wead's heroism and endurance; and the ten years of Ethan Edwards's search for revenge and absolution. He had discovered a fresh film grammar of time. The thing now was—to endure with economy, not to explain.

18: What You Might See Anyplace

It bears no dedication, but it deserves one. "To Ireland, with love."
Sign it: John Ford.

—Frank S. Nugent on *The Rising of the Moon.*

For the time being Ford had had enough of large productions in Hollywood, so he returned to Ireland to work with his claimed cousin, Lord Killanin, for almost nothing in making something dear to his heart. Ford considered Killanin part of his own family and showed him a hidden emotional warmth in a rare correspondence over thirty years. They had intended to make Conan Doyle's *The White Company* together, but the project had failed. "Michael," Ford admonished his cousin, "you must rid yourself of this middle class mind of yours. Show biz is show biz . . . theatre . . . carnival . . . ballet . . . circus . . . radio . . . movies . . . TV and so on down the list. You think it's kidding. I think it is tragic and poignant."

Yet Killanin did arrange the financing of a literary Irish film intended to revive the home film industry. He worked hard on the project, *The Rising of the Moon,* which Ford agreed to direct with Frank Nugent as his screenwriter. "Too bad Mr. Killanin has that coronet," Frank Nugent wrote. "He's a natural location man with a cameraman's eye and a unit manager's sense of logistics. Mr. Ford had to agree that King John's castle in Limerick would do admirably as a prison; that Lord Gort's ruined, dank-walled manse at Lough Cutra had the look, feel and smell of a Tan headquarters."[1]

The film script, like the ill-fated *The Plough and the Stars,* was based on three Irish stories, written this time without a spurious connection between them. The first story, "The Majesty of the Law," was Frank O'Connor's tale of a moonshining patriarch invited by a detective inspector to come to jail for refusing to pay a fine after cracking open his neighbor's head. It was full of the sense of worth and insane pride and warm manners of the Irish. The patriarch's cottage was modeled on Ford's own memory of his family's place in Galway, while the patriarch himself was made to deliver a nostalgic eulogy on the wandering Irish and the passing of the old ways that would have graced Ford's tongue himself:

DAN:
Ever since things became what they are, the liquor is not what it used to be.
DILLON:
In what way now?
DAN:
Liquor is a thing that takes time. There was never a good job done in a hurry. For there's art in it—and secrets. Every art has its secret and the secrets of distilling are being lost the way the old songs were lost.
When I was a boy, there wasn't a man in the barony but had a hundred songs in his heart . . . but with the people running here, there and everywhere . . . and off to Australia, and America and Canada . . . and the automobiles and the pictures and the radio and this other new thing . . . with it, all the songs were lost—and the secrets were lost.

The second episode, "A Minute's Wait," is an extended joke about a train's stopping at a small halt and staying there for an hour, what with one thing and another. It is a broad and uproarious farce, which Ford shot straight between the eyes. The station bar fills and empties and fills again, a goat is pulled into the compartment of the stuffy English pair, and finally a triumphant hurley team climbs aboard and the train puffs away, leaving only the English behind, estranged from this Celtic merry-go-round. "Charles," the English lady asks, "is this another one of their rebellions?" No, it is another one of their director's Rabelaisian moods.

The final episode, loosely based on Lady Gregory's "The Rising of the Moon," revives the Ford of *The Informer* with a wink and a nod. Just as the first episode shows him at his simplest and the second at his most farcical, the third catches him in his symbolic style. The camera tilts, walls loom, protesting crowds march silently in mourning arcs like the damned in a Doré engraving. But his humor redeems the heaviness of the camera angles, including one shot of a false nun showing a flash of high heel and silk stocking as she steps out of a cab.

Human decency also pervades this tale of British oppression and a doomed man waiting to be dropped on a noose in the morning. The British officer in command complains, "Four years of war and I end up as a hangman. How much longer are they going to keep us here?" And the Irish policeman serving the British echoes Michaeleen Oge Flynn in *The Quiet Man*. Hearing the street balladeer singing "The Rising of the Moon" as the escaped condemned man rows away from the dockside, he turns a blind eye to the sight and says, "I used to sing it myself, though there was a bit of treason in it. But there's a bit of treason in us all."

Ford's thoughts of treason against the British had become a fond treason, almost a joke of a treason. The girl in the nun's habit who substitutes for the escaped prisoner produces her American passport with a smile when she is discovered. Like Ford himself in 1921, she cannot be prosecuted, for the bearing of the American eagle on her papers. The doings of the Second World War had made Ford respect the British Empire—as long as it kept out of Ireland. So when Killanin suggested another project to be shot in London itself, Ford accepted, once he had finished another tribute—this time to his father's breed of Irish-American politicians, who had once ruled city politics on the East Coast and now were fighting their last campaigns in the old style that few seemed to want any more.

Frank Nugent changed Edwin O'Connor's novel, *The Last Hurrah,* to suit Ford's perception. In the original book Mayor Frank Skeffington loses his fifth campaign for reelection because of the new techniques of his witless but well-advised opponent. In Ford's film Skeffington has become irrelevant, using old-fashioned devices and torchlight parades to kindle loyalty among new voters who do not know how they are meant to respond. Even though the bishop says he prefers an engaging rogue like Skeffington to a complete fool, Skeffington loses and walks out of politics along with the old ward bosses. "There is an air of defeat here," an announcer says, "but it was not shared by the candidate. There's only one way to describe him, and that is that he was victorious in defeat."

Spencer Tracy's playing of Skeffington gives the part an authority and charm which undercuts some of the bitterness of the conflicts in the script. Ford had not forgotten the discrimination against Catholics which he had known in his boyhood in Maine. Two years before John Fitzgerald Kennedy finally laid the ghost of political anti-Catholicism by reaching the White House. Ford recalled its importance in Skeffington's last campaign. One of the mayor's chief opponents is an ex-Ku Klux Klansman, so stingy that he only quit when he had to buy his own white sheet. The Protestant elite is shown as privileged and exclusive, with its kind never liking or meeting Skeffington's kind.

Yet the old campaigner must lose. There can be no happy ending, as for Judge Priest. Skeffington is out of touch with his own constituency, and nostalgia is no substitute for the media. Like the southern judge, Skeffington may also meditate under the portrait of his dead wife instead of talking on the television screen, but the torchlight parade cannot restore his fortunes. Ford recreates that scene lovingly and expensively in a requiem for a lost world of his youth, never to be seen again. The federal government had taken over the charities and patronage and voting blocs of the old ward heelers and saloon bosses, and the generation of the box and Coca-Cola had replaced the Feeneys' beer picnics and the Skeffingtons' marching bands.

Once Ford had delivered *The Last Hurrah,* he returned to Europe to make his second film for Killanin, the odd film out in his late career. It was a police thriller about Scotland Yard, dealing with one day in the life of a chief inspector of the Flying Squad, played by Jack Hawkins. Ford's distance from his subject in *Gideon's Day,* his mockery of the genre with its unlikely incidents and routine action sequences are amusing without being compromising. Ford's vigor and enjoyment make the piece a kind burlesque of the English detective story, Sherlock Homes in satire and blue, entertaining and unmalicious. One of Gideon's criminals is even called Feeney, "a wicked-looking" razorman who is worked over and made into a hospital case by the large Reverend Small. Despite an effort by some critics to elevate the film into some sort of significance because of the conflict between the chief inspector's private and public life, it remains a minor work performed with professional skill.[2]

Ford showed how much he now felt at home in England by shooting for the Free Cinema and the British Film Institute a short film about two street singers walking through the Wapping docks. It was called *So Alone* and its title seemed to mock Ford's increasing isolation in the cinema world. George O'Brien had recruited him to join a patriotic group of reserve officers in Hollywood that included Frank Capra, George Sidney, and Glenn Ford. They were meant to help make short films for the Armed Forces Radio and Television Service. These would be designed to teach American military personnel something of the customs of the Asian countries they were sent to defend.

The projects were funded by the Department of Defense. John Ford agreed to direct one of them, to be called *Korea—Land of the Morning Calm.* He went with George O'Brien to Seoul in 1959 to shoot near the capital of South Korea. It was nearly thirty years since the two men had set off on another intelligence mission across the Far East, pretending to film background shots for *Seas Beneath* while actually recording Asian harbor approaches and defenses. In that interval, the American armed forces had extended their protective perimeter across the Pacific from the Philippines to the mainland. They would not be caught napping at Pearl Harbor again.

Ford also advised O'Brien's Hollywood group on two other projects dealing with Taiwan and Vietnam. His admiration for General MacArthur made him accept the Korean war hero's grand strategy, which Glenn Ford explained in *Taiwan—The Island Fortress:* "If this line is held, we may have peace; lose it, and war is inevitable." The theory of the United States as an Asian power containing Communism and maintaining military facilities all across the Pacific was a far cry from the sparse cavalry forts on the old western frontiers of the homeland.

Yet Ford was too much the patriot to question the Pentagon's or the White House's strategy. His films always showed soldiers and sailors obeying orders, even if they were suicidal. Ford also advised on the script of *Vietnam—The New Republic,* which was intended to tell the arriving Military Assistance Advisory Groups why they were going there. The script had to admit that Vietnam was "a long way from home base," although it should be defended to save it for the free world. The values of the Second World War still dominated men like Ford, who did not want to see the change in the nature of the new American commitments in Asia.

He also wanted to keep in touch with the navy, so he arranged to teach naval camera crews how to film the fleets in action. When he was gone, after all, where would they find another director who was a rear admiral and could produce free Hollywood technicians at the drop of a peaked cap? As a pilot film he recreated off Hawaii the true story of a submarine commander who had won the Medal of Honor for ordering his crew, "Take her down" while he was lying wounded on deck. The only trouble was that Ford's technical adviser, another admiral, kept interrupting to demand a training manual instead of a heroic tale. "Oh," Ford asked, "have you ever directed a *whole* picture?"[3]

So Ford was marking time until his last late statements on the legends of the West which he had done much to create and soon would spell out. He had enjoyed himself in Ireland and England, and he had done his duty again, always on call as the rear admiral with the camera crew. If he had fallen out of favor with the critics, he did not care overmuch. Although a competent professional like Sam Fuller might now be preferred in Europe, Ford had always had difficulty hiding his contempt for critics who could not make films themselves. Now he hid his commitment to his art completely, saying that he was only in the trade for the money and fooling only the foolish.

Even in the films of Ford's relaxation there is an abiding sense of people and place together. As Robert Flaherty once said, every good story is "the theme of the location." That story Ford always told. While he was filming *The Rising of the Moon,* a small Irishman approached him to ask if he was what they called the director. Ford confessed he was. The small Irishman looked disapproving.

"Y'know," he said, "I wouldn't go about it this way at all. Now if I was to make a fillum, I'd have men in red coats riding their fine horses and I'd have women in those fancy costumes . . . This isn't anything at all, but what you might see anyplace."[4]

So he paid Ford a fine compliment for his sense of geography and his understanding. For Ford did try to film what you might see anyplace, as long as the place was his.

19: Last Word on the West

I hope I haven't been abrupt with you. I hope I haven't been rude. You see, people have been asking me these questions for more than fifty years, and no one's yet come up with an original question.
You say someone's called me the greatest poet of the Western saga. I am not a poet, and I don't know what a Western saga is. I would say that is horseshit. I'm just a hard-nosed, hardworking, run-of-the-mill director.
—John Ford

He sees more out of one good eye than two producers see out of four.
—Martin Rackin on John Ford

"Hollywood today is a market for sex and horror," John Ford said in 1959. "I don't want any part of that." He was then making *Sergeant Rutledge,* the story of a black cavalryman accused of murder and worse. "Now we'll have to see about raping that girl," he said to an assistant without smiling at the interviewer. The new preoccupations of the film industry had affected even his choice of subject, making his features richer, subtler, and more complex. If the first of the films of his Indian summer was an epic, *The Horse Soldiers,* his subjects shrank in size and grew in resonance. "I don't want to make great sprawling pictures," he said. "I want to make films in a kitchen . . . The old enthusiasm has gone, maybe. But don't quote that—oh hell, you can quote it."[1]

The Horse Soldiers reflected the change in economics and values of the new Hollywood, growing again like a hydra after television seemed to have chopped off all its heads. The production was an expensive independent picture made by a pair of producer-writers, John Lee Mahin and Martin Rackin. The big stars were no longer bound by long-standing studio contracts, so that they could demand large fees for each film. Their dominance was reflected in the budget of *The Horse Soldiers.* John Wayne and William Holden each received $750,000 from the budget of $5,-000,000 and twenty percent of the profits. John Ford only received $200,-000 and ten percent of the producers' share of the profits for directing the ex-propman whom he had made a star in *Stagecoach*.[2] In Hollywood the money was now put on the actors who could draw audiences.

The film was Ford's first feature about the Civil War, a subject which had obsessed him all his life. His favorite reading was the three-volume historical work *Lee's Lieutenants,* while he possessed at home a huge library on the war. Portraits of Lincoln and Lee and Grant hung in his living room. He himself could not take sides in a Civil War that had once divided his family from his wife's.

The Horse Soldiers was a true story, based on a Union cavalry raid into the Deep South in 1863. In sixteen days Colonel Benjamin Grierson had led his troops across Mississippi and much of Louisiana, proving the logic of a thrust into the heart of Confederate territory. Grierson also cut the Vicksburg railroad and played hell with Southern morale. General Grant considered it one of the more brilliant feats of military history, even though it was at the expense of other Americans.

Such a subject gave full rein to Ford's ambivalence about the Civil War, his loyalty to the Union and military discipline, his love of Southern panache and rebels and losers. John Wayne played Colonel Grierson under the name of Colonel John Marlowe, while William Holden played a doctor, Major Hank Kendall. Their conflict between military and medical values was the dialectic of the script, on which Ford kept his writers working during the shooting. He would not speak to Rackin as a producer, only as a writer. "Go and sit under that tree," he would say, "and do something better with it."

Rackin had to obey the old director's commands as everybody else did. In private, Ford might complain to Lord Killanin, "Here come my producers . . . and there goes my ulcer again!" Yet in public he might have been Lee himself directing his lieutenants. "He used to run the unit like a military operation," Rackin said. "Everyone had to be on hand even when not directly needed." When his son Patrick broke a leg during a shot, Ford completed it before looking after his own.[3] Wet or dry, work went on because Ford wanted his horse soldiers to look weary and suffering, part of the elements as well as playing a part. In this confusion of location tactics and military history Ford managed to recapture the fatigue and obedience to discipline of the old horse soldiers. His art lay in turning acting into the actual, the chance of nature into the contrivance of celluloid. "There's no problem," he would say to the producers. "It's an opportunity to do it differently."[4] Only when an elderly stuntman, Frank McGrath, was accidently killed near the end of shooting did Ford suddenly wrap up the picture and return to Hollywood to mourn.

In Ford's opinion the Civil War was the last gallant war. Two memorable sequences in *The Horse Soldiers* examine that gallantry. The first is the massacre at Newton Station, when the Confederate soldiers charge vainly into an ambush set by the norse soldiers, who have had dirt thrown on them by the townswomen and want to set fire to the place in revenge. The rebel carrying the Dixie flag is shot and falls. A second rebel picks up the standard and is shot down. Another scoops it up and falls again. Then the Southern colonel-in-command himself raises the banner, only to be dropped and rescued by the Northern doctor, Major Kendall, who has to operate on the wounded man in a characteristic Fordian scene, while Wayne gets drunk, remembering how his wife died under the surgeon's knife.

The second display of gallantry is the marching out of the cadets from the Jefferson Military Academy to delay the horse soldiers until the arrival of regular troops. Mere boys, they parade behind the old commandant while the mother of one of them rushes out to pull her kicking son back to safety. The commandant allows the mother to save her child, then leads the rest of them to attack the Union soldiers. Historically the cadets were massacred, but in the film Wayne refuses to fight them, even when they open fire and kill two of his men. When a drummer boy is captured, he will not take the child prisoner. "Spank him!" he orders.

If Ford gives the glory of failure to the Southerners, he also praises his Union cavalrymen for their strategy of success. They ride the crests of the hills like Indian avengers, they plunge through swampland like predatory alligators. Although the story line is weak, with its incredible conflict between Wayne and Holden and its unlikely love affair between Wayne and a Southern woman hostage, Ford's sense of military duty and guerrilla tactics is superb. The values of the flag transcend the artifices of the script, as they also do in Ford's next Civil War drama, an episode in the *Wagon Train* television series based on his own film *Wagonmaster*.

"The Colter Craven Story" once again features a drunken doctor, unable to give up the bottle after witnessing the horrors of the Battle of Shiloh. Yet, like Doc Holliday in *My Darling Clementine*, he sobers up enough to perform an operation. Craven's inspiration is the memory of General Ulysses S. Grant, whose story is told by Ward Bond. Grant was dismissed from the service for alcoholism, then reinstated allowing him to lead the Union armies to victory and later reach the White House. "It's one of the great American stories," Ford once said, "but you can't do it. You can't show him as a drunkard, getting kicked out of the Army."[5] So Ford did it in a way that turned a disgrace into an inspiration, making Grant's weakness the cowardly doctor's opportunity.

Ford's next film, however, was a personal project, both an explanation and an expiation. He had long resented his unjust reputation as a bigot, although Stepin Fetchit, Woody Strode, and the Navajo Indians could have revealed the untruth of it. Ever since he had fallen ill while shooting *Pinky,* rumors had started that he treated black people like caricatures or Aunt Jemimas.[6] So when James Warner Bellah, the original writer of the stories in Ford's cavalry trilogy, suggested a film on the black Ninth Cavalry in the West, Ford took the chance. Stimulated by a Frederic Remington painting of the black cavalrymen, Ford and Bellah and Willis Goldbeck hammered out a hybrid story, both Western and courtroom drama, a cross between *Fort Apache* and the closing sequences of *Young Mr. Lincoln.* The working title of the picture was *Captain Buffalo,* the theme song of the film, which the cavalrymen sing to inspire themselves with the vision of a mighty black ideal soldier:

> *He'll march all night and he'll march all day*
> *And he'll wear out a twenty mule team along the way*
> *With a hoot and a holler and a ring-a-dang do*
> *Hup-two-three-fo'—Captain Buffalo!*

Yet if the first word in the final title, *Sergeant Rutledge,* hymns the devotion to duty of the Ninth Cavalry, the second word of the title relates the black hero to young Abe Lincoln's lost love, Ann Rutledge. The character of the sergeant, played by Woody Strode, emphasizes the spirit of the president who had freed the slaves. He comes from Fort Lincoln to the west, he carries his freedom papers, yet he knows that one act of liberation does not solve the problems of black people. "It was fine for Mr. Lincoln," he tells his defender, the white Lieutenant Cantrell, "to tell us we're free Americans, same as any man. But that don't make it so. Not yet. Maybe some day—but not yet."

In *Sergeant Rutledge* Ford ruthlessly examines the sexual fears and hypocrisies of white people faced with black strength. He introduces Rutledge in a flashback as an apparent rapist and murderer, putting a huge hand over a white girl's mouth in a deserted railroad station, as gloomy with shadow and menace as any haunted house. (In fact Rutledge is saving the girl from some Apache marauders—to hallow the black soldiers in the film, Ford shows the dark side of the red men.) The sergeant is then put under arrest for the murder and violation of a major's daughter in the camp. He appears guilty, and the military wives gloat at the prospect of a hanging. Yet his defender and ex-commander, Lieutenant Cantrell, believes in his innocence because of Rutledge's bravery in saving a cavalry patrol from an Apache ambush. The key to the accused's final acquittal is a gold cross wrenched off the neck of the murdered girl, "a symbol of the purity" the rapist has destroyed.

If the courtroom sequences end, as in *Young Mr. Lincoln,* with a melodramatic confession by the real, white rapist, the film survives such crudities and ennobles its subject through its dignity and concern. The character of Sergeant Rutledge is a monument of self-respect, the good soldier who values his regiment because his own values are so admirable. Rutledge obeys orders only because they enhance his pride as a man. When the false accusation of rape makes him finally rebel, he tries to get himself shot rather than stand trial, and when he escapes, he returns to save his comrades from an Apache assault. Even when a friend dies in his arms, complaining about fighting the white man's wars, Rutledge replies, "We're fightin' for us!" Someday blacks also will come to live in Indian country. And when he explains why he gave up his liberty to save the patrol, he is given a courtroom speech worthy of Henry B. Walthall.

"It's because the Ninth Cavalry was my home. My real freedom. And my self-respect. And the way I was desertin' it, I wasn't nothin' but a swamp-runnin' nigger. And I ain't that! Do you hear me? I'm a *man!*"

It was one of the first times that the word "nigger" had been used on the Hollywood screen, but Ford and Strode got away with it because a black man had used the word about himself. Ford's films had often been censored under the Hollywood Code, particularly the scenes with prostitutes in *The Informer* and his Westerns, but in *Sergeant Rutledge* he won a victory for explicit vocabulary and black pride in the cinema. Woody Strode himself, a personal friend of long standing, regarded his final elevation by Ford to the role of hero as an accolade for his service in the stock company. "I've never gotten over *Sergeant Rutledge,*" he said late in his career. "It had dignity. John Ford put classic words in my mouth . . . You never seen a Negro come off a mountain like John Wayne before. I had the greatest Glory Hallelujah ride across the Pecos River that any black man ever had on the screen. And I did it myself. I carried the whole black race across that river."[7]

If *Sergeant Rutledge* could be criticized for setting the blacks under their white officers against the Indians, it was historically true. Ford had also not completed his final restatement of his Western values. His next film would deal with the problem of sexual hypocrisy in the relations between Indians and whites, and the film after that with the meaning of the legendary West. Only then would he turn his attention to the Indians themselves, paying them his tribute in *Cheyenne Autumn,* which he shot in the fall of his own life. If any one of his films seemed to tip the balance towards prejudice, the others were sure to tilt the scales the opposite way. Ford always knew that one film could only show a partial truth, while the body of a man's work might suggest his beliefs and his vision of his country's history.

Two Rode Together, released in 1961, was not a personal project, but a film for Columbia and Harry Cohn, a man Ford said he admired like "a large, brilliant serpent." Frank Nugent, however, worked closely with Ford on the script, which tells the story of a corrupt sheriff, played by James Stewart, who rides out with a cavalry officer to redeem some white captives from the Indians. Yet the prisoners have been seized so long ago that they have become Indians, and they do not wish to return. The Indian chief, however, is being challenged by an ambitious warrior, Stone Calf (played by Woody Strode), whose wife is a captured Spanish aristocrat. Stewart rides back with her and a white boy, now become an Indian brave. He kills Stone Calf with ease as the black Indian rushes into the Spanish woman's campfire confession to Stewart. She mourns her warrior husband in the Indian way, then switches her nature and transfers her love to the sheriff.

Back among the pioneers, the boy brought up among the Indians tries to escape, commits a murder, and is lynched. The Spanish woman is snubbed and humiliated for having had sexual relations with Stone Calf. Ford uses his habitual dance sequence to attack hypocrisy, not to praise community of feeling. Stewart ends by raging at the pioneers in defense of the Spanish woman: "She was treated better by the Comanches than by some of you." Dallas had said much the same thing in *Stagecoach* when she found the wives of Tonto worse than the Apaches.

Finally, however, the script evades the issue of a white woman's pollution by Indians. The Spanish aristocrat is a Catholic and says that she could not kill herself after her violation by Stone Calf because of her religion. (The script infers that suicide may be an option for a good Protestant after a savage assault.) The purity of Catholic women was still an obsession with Ford, which he resolved by making Stone Calf's woman end up with the corrupt sheriff, himself tainted by the company of local whores. Both lovers have lost their innocence, the woman through force, the man through choice. They are now fit for one another.

Such a conclusion is offensive to feminists. In her passivity Stone Calf's woman resembles most of Ford's women, not a human being in her own right but an adjunct of her men.[8] Such women may be shown as nobler than men and even halfway between men and God, but they do not follow their own destinies. They run homes, are victims of violence, expose social hypocrisy, sacrifice themselves for their children or their religion. Yet they do not make things happen. They continue the human race without changing its course. Their duty is to the men who do their duty.

So it had always been in Ford's own marriage, a mutual love that lasted for fifty years between a man and a woman who both accepted their traditional places in the Catholic scheme of things which set the family near to God. Ford had his own son working with him again, preparing scripts and helping him as a producer. His daughter, too, was part of his professional and home life. It was justly so, and should not change.

By now, Ford himself was so professional that he began to use a short-hand of the film vocabulary which he had invented. In the famous shot in *Two Rode Together* of the long conversation between James Stewart and Richard Widmark beside a riverbank, he displayed his casual command over a sequence everybody would remember. "It was early in the morning," Stewart recalled of Ford, "and he was sort of grouchy." So he walked out into the middle of the river and insisted on setting up the camera there "because that meant that all the crew had to walk out up to their waists in the river, he's like that, and it was terribly cold."[9] Stewart and Widmark then went through their long talk to each other, trying to make their voices carry above the noise of the running water. When the sound man complained, Ford pretended to be deaf. And when the studio wanted the sequence looped with new voices on the soundtrack, Ford said, "Looping? What does that mean?" Indeed, when the film was released, the voices were totally natural, backed by the noise of the river.[10]

This casual control became a method of shooting in Ford's next feature. Widmark had already noticed the director's increasing spareness and declining enthusiasm for what he could do so efficiently. "Ford usually gets bored with a picture before the end and takes off," Widmark said at this time. "And as he makes a film in such a complicated way that nobody else can put it together, this can create problems."[11]

In point of fact, what were problems to the actors were opportunities to Ford. He wanted the scripts and the images pared down to the bare bone. Like Hitchcock, Ford had no respect for the spoken word, upon which the actors thought they depended. "He loves to tear pages out of scripts," Stewart noticed. "He likes to cut sentences down to phrases, and phrases to words. He'll spend an hour getting the wind at the right force, so that it blows the sand in the background just right. But if you don't have the dialogue right immediately he is ready, he is completely impatient."[12]

That impatience, that shorthand, that total control, allowed Ford to make in a studio on a small budget his final statement on the whole history of the American West. Working once more with Bellah and Goldbeck, he made *The Man Who Shot Liberty Valance.* It was his epitaph for the Western, as fundamental and cursory as the writing on a pioneer grave. Ford no longer called his basic western town Tonto or Tombstone or New Jerusalem but merely Shinbone, as though he had reduced his lifelong experience to one dry bone, which would serve to tell the full story of the anatomy of a new society and its connections, shinbone to kneebone to thighbone to pelvis to backbone—the whole skeleton of the settling of the legendary West.

The film opens with a mocking credit sequence—the names of John Wayne and James Stewart and John Ford and the film title are set on broken wooden crosses, as if they had been abandoned in some forgotten desert cemetery. The first shot is another Fordian epigram—an old train puffs past cactus and sand through the desert. When it arrives at Shinbone, James Stewart descends with his wife in the ceremonial black of a senator come to a funeral. The dead man is Tom Doniphon, a local rancher, and the press wants the story of why the senator has traveled so far for him. Stewart is reluctant to tell, but the editor insists that the press has a *right* to know. Stewart accepts this argument and leaves his friend's body in its coffin to stand by an old Concord coach covered with dust in the town museum. So Ford quickly sets out his icons from *The Iron Horse* to *Stagecoach* before Stewart begins to describe how Horace Greeley had made him "Go West, Young Man" long ago, when the stage (and a flashback) first carried him to Shinbone.

Ward Bond had died during the making of *Two Rode Together.* Ford had grieved for him and gone on shooting. His place as Ford's favorite bully was taken by Lee Marvin, in a command performance as the most evil man ever to appear in a Ford western. He first appears as a masked figure in black, shouting the old highwayman's line, "Stand and deliver!" When Stewart, playing the young lawyer Ransom Stoddard, threatens him with the law, Marvin beats him to a pulp with his quirt to prove that the law of the West is still a man's strong arm. The coach is no longer set in

Monument Valley but filmed close on a sound stage, as if the wide open spaces had contracted into a box around the last survivors of those times, replaying the legends of their lives.

John Wayne soon dismounts in Shinbone and strides into the restaurant, where Stewart is nursed and taken to work as a dishwasher, as there is no pressing need for lawyers yet in town. Deliberately and symbolically, Wayne calls Stewart by the name of "Pilgrim." He plays the archetype of the tough, free rancher, just as Marvin represents the archetype of the badman for hire, while Stewart tries to mediate between them and prevent their inevitable confrontation.

"What a name for a heavy!" Marvin said of Liberty Valance. "I never got over it! Liberty is a dangerous dangerous thing. It requires more discipline than anything else."[13] When Stewart, armed only with his law books, tries to deal with Marvin, armed with quirt and gun and gang, only Wayne and his devoted companion Pompey, played by Woody Strode, can save his life by the threat of Wayne's rifle. If Liberty is anarchy, Valance is also valiance. These are brave men, even if they risk their lives in bad causes. Stewart himself finally has to pick up a gun and face Liberty Valance because "when force threatens, talk's no good anymore." Temporarily he has to accept Wayne's dictum, "Out here a man settles his own problems."

Interspersed with the action leading to the final shoot-out between Stewart and Marvin and Wayne, Ford places five lectures on American history, which put in capsules his version of the settling of the West—the distillation of nearly a hundred Westerns. It is the epilogue of a complete artist. The first lesson is formally set in a schoolroom, where Stewart is teaching children and illiterate adults. When they have chanted their ABC's, Stewart talks about the local newspaper's article defending the small homesteaders from the attack of the cattlemen. This is true democracy.

A Mexican-Indian girl then repeats her lesson. "The United States is a Republic and the Republic is a State. In this, the people is the boss. And if the big folks in Washington don't do what we want we don't vote for 'em." After that, Woody Strode repeats his lesson from the Gettysburg Address, "We hold these truths to be self-evident . . . that all men are created equal . . ." Such is Ford's shorthand that Lincoln's portrait hangs behind the black man as he speaks, while Washington's hangs behind Stewart, the teacher of them all.

It is a short and sweet definition of democracy which is instantly put into practice. To keep the range open and the homesteaders out, the cattlemen want the area to remain a territory. Stewart and the local editor, Peabody, call a town meeting to elect two delegates to the forthcoming territorial convention. The two men then give a second lesson on frontier history, calling for statehood so that dams and fences and towns and schools and churches can be built for the new immigrants and small farmers. Liberty Valance and his gang try to terrorize the meeting, with Valance shouting, "You sodbusters are brave in a bunch, but alone—" Yet the sodbusters elect Stewart and the editor to represent them and end the reign of terror of the cattle barons.

The third lesson takes place during a scene of calculated brutality. Liberty Valance and his thugs march into Peabody's newspaper office and smash up his presses. Peabody tries to joke. "Liberty Valance taking liberties with the liberty of the press?" But he is literally made to eat the words he has printed, then whipped savagely with Liberty's quirt. When he is revived, he mutters proudly, "I sure told that Liberty Valance about the freedom of the press."

Before the final lessons in western democracy the shoot-out takes place. Stewart is wearing his apron as he creeps towards the drunken and dominant Marvin, who shoots the gun out of his hand and shames him into picking it up to meet a certain death. Yet as Stewart fires, Marvin falls, a bullet in his head. Justice seems to have directed Stewart's fluke shot. In fact the bullet comes from the unseen John Wayne's rifle, thrown to him by Woody Strode. "Liberty had to be stopped," Marvin commented later. "It was the only time John Wayne ever shot anybody in the back of the head."

So cold-blooded murder ends the legend of the bold rancher and the badman. Yet Stewart does not know that the fatal bullet is not his. He becomes the hero of the sodbusters, and Peabody delivers the fourth history lesson while nominating Stewart for Congress in opposition to "the cattlemen's mouthpiece, the lowing herd." That lesson traces the westward march of the pioneers, the rule of law taking over from the rule of the gun, the coming of the railroads and the people. He asks the delegates not to confuse the winning of the West with the settling of the West, which demands a different set of values. He finally nominates Stewart, "a man who came to us not packing a gun, but carrying a bag of law books." So young Abe Lincoln had come once to Springfield, Illinois, when that was a frontier town in the new Midwest.

Stewart is about to refuse the nomination because he knows that he has not been chosen for his qualities but for his reputation as the man who shot Liberty Valance. When the drunken Wayne bursts in on him, he asks,

"Isn't it enough to kill a man without having to build a life on it?" Then Wayne tells him to take the nomination because Wayne himself is the killer. A flashback shows Liberty's death from Wayne's point of view as he deliberately guns the badman down. "Cold-blooded murder," Wayne says, "but I can live with it."

That is the reason why the distinguished senator has come to pay his last respects to Wayne in his coffin. He has also incidentally taken Wayne's girl for his wife, although she shows her lasting love by leaving a cactus rose by the coffin. The confession, however, does not make the Shinbone editor print the truth. He cannot destroy the basis of the senator's career, a man who has done so much for his state. "This is the West, sir," the editor says. "When the legend becomes fact, print the legend."

A train whistle sounds. Stewart and his wife are next seen in a compartment, stating Ford's final lesson about the West. Stewart says he will leave Washington and come back to settle in his wife's home state, but only after he has seen through a vital irrigation bill. His wife then states the theme from the Bible and Henry Nash Smith's masterpiece, *Virgin Land.* "Look at it. It was once a wilderness. It is now a garden. Aren't you proud?" Stewart is proud for a moment, until the train conductor appears to remind him of the lie behind his public life. "Nothing's too good for the man who shot Liberty Valance."

Yet if the last words of the film are ironic, the last shot explains Ford's ultimate message. As the train rounds a curve in the line, going away, it is surrounded by wheatfields. Grain grows where the desert was. The film needs no analysis, because it has expressed all of the statements that Ford had spent forty-five years in making, the themes of the law against the outlaw, the town against the wilderness, the civilized man against the savage, the farmer against the rancher, the family against the loner, the church against wicked liberty. Everything was pared down to the bone, only the necessary was shown. "He shot them bare," Lee Marvin said. "If it ain't out there, you ain't going to have it at all . . . He really knew the binoculars he was looking through—in specifics."[14]

To the new generation of film critics *The Man Who Shot Liberty Valance* confirmed Ford's reputation as the master of his genre and range. His supremacy overcame their suspicions about his politics and his militarism. To one critic the film "achieves greatness as a unified work of art with the emotional and intellectual resonance of a personal testament"; to another critic it was "an old man's reverie on the glory of a vanished wildness."[15] If it could never become a popular film, because Ford's rigor had cut all the flesh and amiable detail out of the work, he had ordered the cemetery of his career, laid out the burial plots, and prepared the funeral speeches on the legends of the West.

He had one last act of absolution to perform. He worked on the project with his son Patrick in Hawaii, where he had sailed *The Araner*. It was inspired by Mari Sandoz's book on the long flight in 1878 of the exiled Cheyennes from their arid reservation in Oklahoma back to their sacred grounds near the Yellowstone. In the planning stages Dudley Nichols had worked with Patrick Ford, but later Ford worked on it alone with his son, who noted down his father's intentions to send back to the new screen-writer, James R. Webb. The notes on the project are worth quoting because they prove that Ford himself dictated what he wanted on screen, as long as he was in control before a screenplay was written:

> The Cheyennes are not to be heavies, nor are they to be ignorant, mis-guided savages without plan or purpose to their warmaking. Their motives must be clearly expressed in the beginning of the picture. If there is to be a heavy, it must be the distant United States government, a government blind to the plight of the Indians. The Army is to be portrayed as an underpaid, undermanned force, all but forgotten on a distant frontier, a group of dedicated men trying to maintain a virtually impossible peace despite Washington's mismanagement. The "Penny Dreadful" press of the period is no help with its stories of "savage red men" and of buckskin knights-errant to inflame the imaginations of a semi-literate public. . . .
>
> My father and I are agreed that the Cheyenne should not speak English in the picture. They should serve, in his words, as a "Greek Chorus." Since lack of communication was one of their chief causes of trouble, it would be ridiculous to show them speaking the national language . . . The Indians, as a people, are to be portrayed as Indians . . . unable to speak English or to communicate their thoughts to the Whites, but magnificent in their stoical dignity.
>
> We talked in detail about cast. My father expressed a desire to have Little Wolf and Dull Knife played by honest to God Indians—Navajos probably. I admit that there is something in an Indian face that no actor can hope to have, but it isn't good box-office to have such important roles handled by non-professionals. For that matter, I doubt if the bankers would entertain such radical notions . . .

Ford's outline of the film he wanted was continued for another twenty pages. To attract star names in cameo roles, it was deliberately planned to be a hybrid movie like *Sergeant Rutledge*. The first and third acts would deal with the Cheyennes' long flight from the Oklahoma dustbowl, pre-cursors of the Okies in *The Grapes of Wrath* as they escape a " 'Hooverville' cluster of shanties, dusty, miserable, unfit for human habitation."[16] The second act would be a Western comedy set in Dodge City with James Stewart and Arthur Kennedy playing the archetypal roles of Wyatt Earp and Doc Holliday in a protracted saloon gambling session. This interlude was meant to break up the film, and did it only too well, interfering with the drive and purpose of the whole for box-office reasons.

The other failure in the final version of *Cheyenne Autumn* was the commercial decision to cast the chief Indian roles with non-Indian actors like Sal Mineo and Ricardo Montalban. Ford could not get his producer to accept his wishes, although even Navajo players would have offended the Cheyennes, who would recognize the Navajos in the minor roles and complain that it was "not like our mother told us".[17] Ford himself, though, always insisted that he did capture the essence of all the Plains tribes in the picture and had told something of the truth about them.

"I've killed more Indians," he said, "than Custer, Beecher and Chivington put together, and people in Europe always want to know about the Indians. There are two sides to every story, but I wanted to show their point of view for a change. Let's face it, we've treated them very badly —it's a blot on our shield; we've cheated and robbed, killed, murdered, massacred and everything else, but they kill one white man and, God, out come the troops."[18]

Yet expiation was not enough to save *Cheyenne Autumn,* given the compromises made for commercial reasons. Visually gorgeous and sympathetic to its subject, the film could not survive the miscasting and an unlikely love affair between a Quaker schoolteacher, played by Carroll Baker, and a cavalry officer, played by Richard Widmark. None of the actors distinguished themselves except for Edward G. Robinson, who took over from Spencer Tracy at the last moment to play the role of the Secretary of the Interior, Carl Schurz. He gave nobility to the part of the peacemaker and binder of wounds, although Ford once again felt obliged to pose him by a portrait of Lincoln.

Even if *Cheyenne Autumn* is more an act of penance than a film production, Ford's sense of geography has rarely been bettered. He did not spare himself in capturing the sense of the ground. As he wrote to Lord Killanin, he had to endure deserts, mountains, ice and snow, and glaciers for more than two months on location. "For a guy pushing seventy it sounds like a tough physical task. But Thank God I am THE Irish peasant of the peasants . . . and they never stop working until past ninety." As a result of this dedication, the splendors and powers of Monument and Moab Valleys and the Gunnison Canyon have never so nobly shown figures in landscape.

Ford also showed his sense of mass action. James Stewart remembers playing in a scene of six hundred people in the "Battle of Dodge City," later cut out arbitrarily by the studio. Ford's only instruction to his star was to "move out kind of fast" once he got into the battle.

"The horses were frightened to death," Stewart recalls. "Everybody was shooting. Move out kind of fast! There was nothing I could do. I have never gone so fast with horses in my life . . . Throwing it up for grabs is the thing I think is very amazing about Ford and makes sense really. It's a very good idea. It makes you nervous and it gets you concerned about what's going to happen. And it sort of sets the stage for something good happening, and it's not really spontaneity. It's not really 'get it on the first take' because he's prepared and everybody pretty much is prepared, but nobody's stale on the thing. What he's trying to do is get everybody to act as though it were happening the first time. And this is a very difficult thing."[19]

So Ford completed his last Western and his history of the place, although his son claimed that the old man would still be making Westerns a couple of years after he was dead.[20] He had created the world-wide vocabulary and the legend and the dialectic, so that they could even be imitated by "spaghetti Westerns" in Italy. Now he had wound up the genre with an epilogue and funeral rites, so that he might present a summary of his work and balance those matters in which he had been harsh or unfair. The five historical films between *The Horse Soldiers* and *Cheyenne Autumn* were his last will and testament to the cavalry and the Indians, the winning and the losing of the West.

One project Ford never filmed. It was called *Comanche Stallion* and was also set in 1878. It was intended to elevate the Western to the mystical level of *Moby Dick*. The stallion was to have trampled to death the only son of a drunken cavalry colonel. The father's megalomania would be "to capture the Comanche stallion alive, to torture and to kill it." Southern cavalrymen would "form a Greek Chorus to the Colonel's mania." The stallion would also be a stolen Apache god, five thousand years old. "When it is returned the Apaches will become a great nation." The colonel would import four Kentucky thoroughbreds to catch the stallion—and fail, just as Ford would fail to make the film.

Comanche Stallion might well have been the greatest of Ford's Westerns, the one in which he could publicly admit to seeking myths as profound as Melville's or O'Neill's. In his presentation of the project he wrote that he would film it all in Monument Valley and that the total budget would be no more than four hundred thousand dollars. Then he added: "I, John Ford, am putting myself on a limb working for no salary. I guarantee that it will be great. That is all."

He did not get the money, and that was all.

20: The End of a Time

Oh, you can't do a picture for yourself anymore—it's impossible. You've got to go through a series of committees now and you never know who the hell reads the scripts anymore. You can't get an O.K. here in Hollywood for a script—it's got to go back to New York, and through a president and a board of directors and bankers and everybody else. What I used to do was try and make a big picture, a smash, and then I could palm off a little one on them. You can't do it anymore.

—John Ford in 1965.

Ford was enough of a Californian to believe that his body should go on for ever. He never took to old age gracefully. He remained what he had always been—tough, stoical, terse, professional. Only to young people would he assume the role of teacher, trying to pass on his love of learning that he hid from the world of cinema.

When George O'Brien took his son to visit Ford in the large Spanish-style house in Copa de Oro, the boy saw a frail old man, lively in intellect, casually dressed, with one eye hooded by a black patch, the other by a thick dark lens. He told the boy to read Swift, Dr. Johnson, Fielding, and Sterne. The greatest of these was Swift, except for Joyce, who could write circles around anyone. So the old man discoursed on literature for more than an hour, filling up his coffee cup with whiskey. Then a dark mood came upon him, and he spoke of the Irish famine, saying that the English had behaved worse to the Irish than the Germans had to the Jews. Then he dozed off and the O'Briens left.

"He's got a lot of bitterness in him," George O'Brien said to his son. "He's one of these guys, no matter what he does, he always wants something he doesn't think he has."

"He's an artist," the young O'Brien replied.[1]

He was an artist and a thinker, who would rarely disclose himself. And he hardly worked now, because cancer was beginning to attack his body in the last ten years of his life. He did not have the strength anymore to do what he could not do easily. Other than *Cheyenne Autumn* the films of his later years were indulgences, the Civil War section in *How the West Was Won,* the Hawaiian holiday of *Donovan's Reef,* his sequences in *Young Cassidy,* the tolerant and mocking *Seven Women,* and the final salute to his military past, documentaries on Chesty Puller and Vietnam, where one of his grandsons was fighting.

The first short project was an experiment, designed to exploit the possibilities of a new process, Cinerama. Ford thought the largest screen of all had little to do with showing how the West was won. He was meant to direct three segments of a six-part spectacle, but he ended up only directing one of them. He did not like composing pictures to make use of three converging screens that split action like the charge of an army on the left wing, the center, and the right. "The ends curl on moving shots," he said, "and the audience moves instead of the picture. You have to hold onto your chair. I didn't care for it."[2]

Yet his segment has no concessions to the tricks of the new process. It is made so simply that it might be the work of D.W. Griffith. It does not share in the sentimental crudities of the rest of the epic, through which Henry Fonda wanders with many other stars looking vainly among trainwrecks and buffalo stampedes and whitewater rapids for the niceties and humanity of *My Darling Clementine.* Ford's segment is merely the work of an expert who is not very interested in what he is doing well.

The episode tells the story of the Rawlings family on an Ohio farm, with an interlude played at the Battle of Shiloh. The father has gone to war and the mother, well played by Carroll Baker, is torn about allowing her elder son to volunteer. He does so, but is so horrified by the bloodshed at Shiloh that he is nearly persuaded to desert, only to save General Grant and General Sherman from being assassinated by a renegade Texan. He returns to his farm to find both his mother and his father dead before setting off to join the United States Cavalry in the West.

Although the opening and the ending are shot with the full Fordian vocabulary, the Civil War interlude is as packed with melodramatic action as one of his early two-reelers. All the memorable touches of the episode are repeated from other Ford films. Once again Carroll Baker kneels in the family graveyard to ask the dead for advice. Once again the horrors of war are shown by John Wayne, now playing General Sherman, as he comes onto an amputation scene with a drunken surgeon about to saw off the limbs of the wounded. Once again Ford puts his camera in a river to show a long dialogue between the wounded farm boy from Ohio and the Texas deserter. Only one commanding shot of a line of guns firing a rolling barrage into the night, soon counterpointed by a line of men filling a mass grave with puffs of quicklime, has the ultimate touch of the master director.

Donovan's Reef was not so much a film as a farewell to *The Araner* and a way of life that Ford could not longer support. The yacht had been sailed out to Hawaii in 1954 through a storm to serve as a houseboat and holiday home, but its upkeep was ruinous. So Ford wanted a project which would commemorate his yacht on film and reunite his friends around him. "It was summer fun," Lee Marvin said, "his last return to paradise."[3] Until Frank Nugent went to work, there was not even a script, merely an outline of ten pages about the interminable fights between "Guns" Donovan and "Boats" Gilhooley, replaying the roles of Flagg and Quirt in a South Seas *What Price Nostalgia?*

So John Ford took his family and his friends on a last Pacific trip along with John Wayne and his children, Lee Marvin and his children, and Anna Lee's children, to make a fond picture about bar fights and Christmas, forgotten wars and omnipresent nuns, fists and seawater and rituals, Christian and pagan and masculine. No hurricane batters and destroys the island church—its roof only leaks a little in the downpour. There is no apocalypse, only an adieu. As one leading critic put it:

> "*Donovan's Reef* is John Ford's *Picnic on the Grass* just as *Picnic on the Grass* is Jean Renoir's *The Tempest*, the ultimate distillation of an old artist's serenity and wisdom. The delicate brush strokes of characterization have now been blurred over by the buoyant mists of a personal vision, and, consequently, a psychological analysis of the characters in *Donovan's Reef* would have as much point as a case history of Caliban.
>
> There are directors who discover the world and directors who invent it. Ford and most of his Hollywood colleagues belong in the second category, where the cinema has always been more a dream than a document . . . [Yet] the blissful world of *Donovan's Reef* is not the anarchic world of the Noble Savage. The lines of responsibility cut deep into the sun-baked flesh. Whether it is Church, State, Community, Army or simply remembered service, the characters of John Ford acknowledge certain limits to their power and discretion in the form of a superior authority . . . [in] a beautiful example of cinematic art."[4]

After the shooting was over, *The Araner* was sold for a song and became a tourist cruise boat under the name of *The Windjammer*. Relinquishing his Western dream, Ford himself was persuaded to travel to the eastern pole of his nostalgia, back to Ireland. He had not forgiven himself for failing with Sean O'Casey's *The Plough and the Stars,* and given the chance of filming the first four volumes of O'Casey's autobiography, scripted by John Whiting, he accepted. *Young Cassidy* was to be his commemoration of every young Irishman who survived his native land and set off for his great opportunity. If on the way the hero met Lady Gregory and W.B. Yeats and the players of the Abbey Theater, so much the better. He even accepted one-fifth of his usual director's fee of a quarter of a million dollars in an effort to propitiate O'Casey for his failure in filming *The Plough and the Stars.*

While he was shooting the picture in Dublin, Ford used all of his tricks to keep people on their toes. He told the cameraman Ted Scaife to choose any setup he liked, stunning that veteran. Was this the director Orson Welles had studied before deciding how to shoot *Citizen Kane?* Then the associate producer, Lord Killanin, revealed the secret of one of Ford's devices. "He uses irritation," Killanin said, "as a race track fixer uses amphetamines, to extract a superior achievement."

Yet as he was shooting Ford was falling sick. He lost thirty pounds in three weeks and only his willpower kept him going. His behavior was benign, as the co-producer Robert Emmett Ginna noted—if a trifle bawdy. He would hold a levée, not upon rising in the royal manner, but after going to bed at the end of the day's work.

> Then the mahatma, wreathed in tobacco smoke and wearing a white silk sleeping coat, received various members of the unit who presented matters for his approval, while a few regulars kept him company. His bedding, as usual, looked like he was at war with it . . . The conversation in Ford's lair was lively and uninhibited. A feature of the entertainment was Ford's attempts to shock the ladies, and their denial of that satisfaction. It was his custom to relieve himself into the wastebasket with the panache of Louis Seize, often in the full flight of some story.[5]

Yet ill and bed-ridden though he was, he still took the time to teach the producers and technicians and actors the hard-earned tricks of the trade, passing them on to those who would work after him.

One sequence he did complete before he fell too ill to continue denied the legend that he was a puritan about sex on the screen. "Hell," he exploded, *"The Quiet Man* was entirely about a man trying to get a girl into bed." He filmed a love scene between the young Julie Christie and Rod Taylor. She stood against the wall in her chemise, while her lover slid below screen and her left breast popped out of its silk. "It was for its time a scene of smoking sensuality," Ginna wrote, yet in the final version of the film, completed by Jack Cardiff, the love scene was altered by the new director and finally censored in Hollywood as too sexual. Ford himself always refused to sign Catholic petitions against 'dirty' pictures. "I make pictures for my grandchildren," he said.

At the age of seventy-two, almost as a disproof of the consensus that he could not direct women, Ford decided to make his last feature about seven women and their relationships under siege and under stress. He assembled a distinguished cast including Flora Robson, Margaret Leighton, Sue Lyon (from *Lolita*), Anna Lee, and Anne Bancroft, who took over from Patricia Neal after she had a succession of strokes at the beginning of shooting. According to Anna Lee, bets were widely taken that Ford would hate *Seven Women* and be in a continual rage. Instead he could not have been more charming and tolerant, giving the ladies tea every afternoon from a silver tea service, and only picking on the sole leading man, Eddie Albert, to play the role of the necessary scapegoat.

He worked his usual magic to bring out good performances from the actors. "You could never really analyze what he did as a director to get the results he got," Anna Lee said. "He'd never talk to you about the scene, but about anything else. Then he'd say, 'Start working!' And you never played it in the way you thought you would. It was almost as though he was implanting something without your knowing it. It was a very uncanny way, which was almost a psychic thing."[6]

The film, completely reconstructed by Ford during the shooting, is a swansong to part of his dialectic, particularly the confrontation of the civilized with the savage, humanity with hypocrisy, and the way to live and to prepare to die. Ironically, he gives Anne Bancroft his favorite role of the drunken doctor, bringing her on set swaggering in jodhpurs, a cigarette loose in her mouth as a symbol of defiance to the missionary group she has come to help on the frontiers of China. Replaying *"Boule de Suif,"* she dresses finally in the robes of a Chinese prostitute and sacrifices herself to the warlord, Tungha Khan, in the role of a Genghis. So she saves the lives of the other women—and is damned for her sacrifice by their inhuman godliness.

"Ye are of your father the devil," the mission leader accuses her, "the lusts of your father ye will do."

"Never mind my lusts," the doctor replies, observing the mission leader's suppressed love of Sue Lyon. "You keep your hands off Emma."

Better, Ford says, to be open than hidden, a frank sinner than a secret

lesbian. If *Seven Women* is a raw and sketchy film, set in an incredible China
no more real than von Sternberg's Shanghai, it is still a frontier story with
women acting out independent roles usually given to men. Bancroft's
performance as the doctor is memorable, tough-talking and hard-drink-
ing, compassionate without self-pity, a disbeliever who looks after people
on earth more than any believer in heaven can.

"I spent years in slum hospitals," she says. "New York, Chicago—
hellholes some of 'em. I never saw God come down and take care of
anyone."

So Ford wrapped up his last feature, proving that he could make a film
about the relationships of women, as long as he put them in an isolated
group near a conflict, where they would be forced into the moral choices
faced by men in danger. If the film ultimately does not work, it is because
the situation is artificial and out-of-date—and it was released in the time
of Mao's long control of the mainland. It seemed to be a reactionary and
racist picture of China, although it was no more than the re-creation of
a historical context for playing a frontier drama—an ironical Eastern with
women rather than the usual Western with men.

Yet Communism in Asia, indeed, was calling Ford back to duty. He was
persuaded to make a dramatized documentary of the life of his friend,
Lieutenant General Lewis Puller, called *Chesty: A Tribute to a Legend.*
Shooting began in Puller's Virginia home in 1968 and ended two years
later on the set of Howard Hawks's *Rio Lobo,* the night John Wayne had
won his Oscar for his performance in a movie that mocked the western
legend, *True Grit.* "We need more heroes like this," Wayne said of Puller,
"in this country today. Good luck, Chesty."

Such a message to a hero of the Korean War was untimely when
American armies were being committed in Vietnam to a war that was
dividing the nation behind them. Ford's extreme loyalty to his old military friends seemed both blind and misplaced, especially when he also
agreed to be the executive producer of *Vietnam! Vietnam!,* a documentary of the fighting made for the United States Information Agency. If
he was true to his belief that a soldier in combat must obey orders
without question, he was untrue to his feeling for rebels against Big
Government and misgovernment, be they Okies or Cheyennes or even
Asian peasants.

He was only in the Naval Reserve and could have chosen to sit out the
dubious conflict. "The Navy wants me to do a temporary tour of duty,"
he wrote to Lord Killanin on May 2, 1966, "and they gave me my choice

between a place called Vietnam and the Mediterranean. They can request me back but they cannot order me back. Under the circumstances, I think I'd prefer the Mediterranean. I am tired of foxholes." And so Rear-Admiral Ford left on a "long arduous duty with my avocation—the Navy," which took him around the world to Manila.

Yet he could not stay out of Vietnam. His elder grandson was serving in the Merchant Marine and received a decoration. His younger grandson was serving in the army and was promoted on the battlefield. "Of course, their grandmother is proud," Ford wrote to Lord Killanin, "but I shiver in my boots." All the same, he arranged to visit Vietnam to find out why documentary footage was not getting back to America. He wanted to go to the front line to visit his grandson Daniel, but instead the young soldier was flown back to see his grandfather in Saigon. The high command would no longer risk its most distinguished rear admiral in front of enemy bullets. Korea was his last front-line engagement.

In between wars he also worked on other projects dealing with combat, which were never produced. One was a comedy set in England during the Second World War called *The Miracle of Merriford;* another was Wild Bill Donovan's story in *O.S.S.;* while the one closest to his heart was the alpha and the omega of his long course in American history—*April Morning,* the story of a blacksmith and his son before the Battle of Lexington, to be completed in time for the Bicentennial ceremonies.

Lee Marvin, asked to play a part in *April Morning,* never replied to Ford because he thought the script would hardly work. In his opinion the Americans were, after all, English before the Revolution. Everyone was torn between the two sides, rather like the way the nation was torn over Vietnam. Simple patriotism could only come during and after a revolutionary war. Ford seemed to agree with Marvin, and the film was never made.[7] Only once did Ford tell his daughter that a group of Italians were prepared to back him totally on his last picture. He went to a meeting with them and told his daughter that it had gone well. "Only I can't see," he said, "Sophia Loren as a blacksmith."[8]

With cancer eating at his body, Ford was unable to move about much now. The stairs in the Copa de Oro house became impossible for him, so he sent out his wife and daughter to find him a bungalow in the desert for his last few years. They found a large ranch-style home in Palm Desert on the Old Prospector Trail. "I'll buy it," Ford said. "I make Westerns, don't I? Anyway, you're never stepping down when you go to Palm Springs."[9]

There he was installed on a medical bed in a room overlooking the low hills of the Indian reservation to the south. He was only a short drive away from the Eisenhower Hospital, where he could take therapy. He waited for visits from his old friends, only leaving his bed rarely for great occasions. His wife and his daughter, who was on her own again, looked after him with the help of nurses, while his business managers managed his assets in the way that business managers do.

He was noble and gentle in his slow dying. He gave his nurses as little trouble as possible in their unpleasant chores. He was too proud to complain. "A very remarkable man," his old friend Katharine Hepburn said. She found him, like Bogart, a man who met his death "like a gentleman. With great distinction."[10] Once again the living room of his last house was prepared as a museum of his career, with photographs of cardinals now hanging beside Lincoln and Lee. He grew even closer to the Church as Catholics often do in their dying, remembering his friends like Cardinal Spellman and his one audience with the Pope.

In 1964 he had voted Republican for the first time—in memory of Abraham Lincoln, he said. In fact, he thought Lyndon Johnson little better than a scalawag, while he had become friendly with Barry Goldwater and his son, joining the Goldwater Associates with such luminaries as Bob Hope. It was not so much an apostasy as a hardening of his patriotism as he lay dying. He liked a forthright man like Goldwater, who raised the Stars and Stripes in front of his house every day, rather than a Texan wheeler-dealer who seemed to have no style.

In 1972 he voted for Richard Nixon for the second time and struck up a last, odd political friendship. When the American Film Institute honored Ford with their first award banquet, the President of the United States himself appeared to help the sick man up to the podium in a rare act of compassion. He also completed Ford's dream, in his capacity as Commander-in-Chief of the Armed Forces, by giving Ford the braided cap of a full admiral, the crowning glory of a double life. The photograph of Nixon with Ford and his wife still hangs by her bed. She calls it "The Last Supper."

Tormented by the souring of America on the war in Vietnam, Nixon may have felt the need of Ford's public support. More likely he recognized a great man dying, lonely in his fame, and he suspected his own greatness and wanted an association with such lifelong integrity. He was also hoping still to be leading the nation for the Bicentennial of 1976. So he wished to honor the American who had done more than any other to teach his people the history and values of their country's steadfast democracy.

Nixon also gave Ford the presidential Medal of Freedom, the nation's highest civilian honor. The commendation was a fit memorial to a man of great influence:

> In the annals of American film, no name shines more brightly than that of John Ford. Director and film-maker for more than half a century, he stands pre-eminent in his craft—not only as a creator of individual films of surpassing excellence, but as a master among those who transformed the early motion pictures into a compelling new art form that developed in America and swept the world. As an interpreter of the Nation's heritage, he left his personal stamp indelibly printed on the consciousness of whole generations both here and abroad. In his life and in his work, John Ford represents the best in American films and the best in America.[11]

Many went to pay tribute to the old man dying at the age of seventy-eight, who refused to admit his condition and talked of making three more films. The visitors included Frank Capra and George Stevens, John Wayne and Robert Parrish, Howard Hawks and Peter Bogdanovich, who had filmed the tribute *Directed by John Ford* for the American Film Institute. They would sit by his bedside near the statute of the Virgin Mary and the lighted candles and the silver-mounted saddle at the end of the room. Ford would search among a collection of old cigar butts in a plastic bucket and select one to chew and talk for the five minutes each visitor was allowed by his nurses. Around his neck he wore a lucky string with his navy identification tag, a St. Christopher's medal, a Star of David, a ring of rhinoceros hair, an elk's tooth, and other, unidentifiable objects.[12] He wanted to be ready for anyone who came to visit him or take him away.

When Wayne arrived, he was greeted with the remark, "Come for the deathwatch, Duke?"

"Hell, no, Jack," Wayne replied. "You're the anchor—you'll bury us all."

"Oh, well," Ford said, "maybe I'll stick around a while longer, then."

He stuck around until August 31, 1973, then he died peacefully in his sleep. The funeral, as Bogdanovich noted, could well have used Ford's touch. He knew how to bury the dead.[13] Yet all the same he was laid simply to rest in a green valley by the side of his dead brothers Francis and Edward, who had worked on his films with him. A rifle squad from the navy fired a last salute, and a bugler blew taps. His grandson Daniel, in full military uniform, took from the coffin the American flag that the

Marines had hoisted in the Battle of Midway and gave it to Mary before the body was lowered into the grave.

Most of the old working directors and stars and technicians were at the funeral, paying their respects to the greatest of them all. Yet two small tributes were the most fitting for the man. The Stuntmen's Association took a page in *Variety* to say, "One of us and we'll miss him." Then Woody Strode said: "He should be buried in Monument Valley."[14]

21: Print the Legend

*No American director has ranged so far across the landscape of the
American past, the worlds of Lincoln, Lee, Twain, O'Neill, the three great
wars, the western and trans-Atlantic migrations, the horseless Indians of
the Mohawk Valley and the Sioux and Comanche cavalries of the West,
the Irish and Spanish incursions, and the delicately balanced politics of
polyglot cities and border states.*

—Andrew Sarris on John Ford

*Those goddam scholars—they're difficult to work with. They take all
that knowledge, put it together, then disguise it.*

—Lee Marvin on John Ford

What Ford sought in his films was the tragic moment, the situation which
forced men to reveal themselves and become aware of what they truly
were. "The device allows me," he said in a rare philosophical confession,
"to find the exceptional in the commonplace . . . I look, before all else,
for simplicity, for the naked truth in the midst of rapid, even brutal,
action." Then he added, "What interests me are the consequences of a
tragic moment—how the individual acts before a crucial act, or in an
exceptional circumstance. That is everything."[1]

With this declaration in Paris in 1955 Ford allied himself with the
tradition of western tragedy from the *Oresteia* through *King Lear* to *Desire
Under The Elms.* In truth his films were memorable for elevating the
commonplace to the level of myth through the consequences of tragedy,
so that John Wayne is changed into a western Odysseus in his ten-year
quest in *The Searchers,* or Henry Fonda becomes almost a demigod of the
chase in his escape from the Indians in *Drums Along the Mohawk,* running
from night into day. "Like a great poet," Roger Greenspun wrote in a
eulogy, "Ford imbues his work with subtlety, richness, complexity, and

a sense of irony that is very close to the tragic. But like a great poet, Ford pushes none of these qualities upon us."[2]

The fact that he worked in a popular form made his disguise the servant of his purpose. William Shakespeare had done the same thing, giving the public in the Globe Theater the blood and swordplay they wanted in order to tell them the messages and myths he wanted. Ford was also fortunate to work in the medium of his time that was the art of the common people. The theater had become largely a middle-class experience, while vaudeville had declined into burlesque and such great comedians of tragedy as Charles Chaplin had transferred their genius from the stage to the screen. When Ford was in his prime, making the extraordinary series of masterpieces between *Stagecoach* and *How Green Was My Valley,* the cinema was the folk art of the world in that age before television. So he could celebrate the history of the American people and examine the complexities of the human condition in the form that instructed the masses. His craft fitted his age.

He was a man who hated jargon. He used simple words and pictures to make his messages and signs popular. The *auteur* theory meant little to him, for he was a director who did what he could do in the commercial system in which he worked. The *écrivain* theory also meant little to him, for he treated screenwriters like Munro Stahr said he did in *The Last Tycoon:* "I never thought that I had more brains than a writer has. But I always thought that his brains *belonged* to me—because I knew how to use them. Like the Romans—I've heard that they never invented things but they knew what to do with them."[3]

Semiology was equally meaningless to Ford, for he would never consider the signs in his films by a rational or a scientific process. He worked on instinct, profiting from the occasion and from the talents of that traveling community of brief purpose which is a film crew. While he did have a sign language formed from his boyhood memories and his Catholic faith and his love of the old rituals that bind society together, he was too practical and generous about the skills of others to exaggerate his control over the medium at the expense of what he could do in the time with the people he had.

He did not abdicate power in any way, but he knew the terms of his trade. If he aimed for posterity, he usually settled for the studio system. That was the condition of his working for fifty years in the ruthless and competitive society of Hollywood. "Being under contract," he said, "you make pictures that you don't want to make, but you try to steel yourself, to get enthused over them. You get on the set, and you forget everything else. You say these actors are doing the best they can. They also have to make a living. As a director I must help them as much as I can. I think a director can help an actor or an actress, and he can also help the cameraman, the electricians and everybody else. I think he brings a great deal to a film."[4]

These were the words of the true professional, and Ford was that. He mocked those critics who hurled their education at his head and found meanings in his films that he had not intended. Like all working directors, he knew that making a good film was only half skill and hard work, while the other half had to do with weather and budget, time and the river. He measured out his shooting in chewed cigar butts, not in meaningful statements. He wanted his craft and popular art to be appreciated by the many, not translated by the few.

Theories of the cinema will come and go, while Ford's language will abide, the text and the sign, the message and the image. For he believed in the words of Swift and the King James Bible, that common language which the English-speaking peoples had in the nineteenth century and largely forgot during the fifty years of his film-making. As Lindsay Anderson, the critic and working director who understood him best, once wrote:

> His technique is characterized by its extreme simplicity. Seldom indulging in the sophistications of camera movement, his films proceed in a series of visual statements—as sparing in their use of natural sound as of dialogue. Rich in phrasing, simple in structure, it is a style which expresses a sure, affirmative response to life—the equivalent to that Biblical prose which, today, takes greatness of spirit to sustain.[5]

Ford's root language was the language of the human heritage, which lay in the rituals of the family and the community, the military and the tribe. He shared a common tongue with the common people without giving up his judgment of them. One critic found that Ford had a tendency to observe humanity with an impatient sort of pity, while another critic noticed that his films always provided a world in which moral choice meant something and in which people had a function.[6] For all his understanding Ford remained a judge who put human beings in their place on earth under God.

Most people work, most have families, most live in communities, some were pioneers, and all have heard of them—Ford celebrated these most human occupations. He liked to quote Jean Renoir's phrase, "If it doesn't show the glory of man, don't do it!"[7] If the country of his films was often a special country of his own mind that he took out of the stranger places in America, such as Monument Valley, he always located his people within it or set them against it.

"John Ford knows what the earth is made of," Orson Welles once said; he also knew of those who come from the earth.[8] He understood every kind of person and their place in the scheme of human events. "He knows how the woman would react," John Wayne has said. "He knows how the big businessman would react. He knows how the little pedlar would react. He just has a deep instinctive feeling for human nature. And it is such an instinct that, before he decided what their reaction would be, he thinks of all the things that they've been through in their life."[9]

This universal understanding made Ford's films cross the frontiers of language and politics. Even to the Russians under Stalin he was the greatest of the directors with his messages of controlled liberty. Eisenstein praised him, as did Pudovkin and Donskoi, who found everything in Ford's films original, profound, and new, without any rival on the American screen.[10] From the other side of the political divide Darryl Zanuck could say the same, calling Ford the best director in the history of motion pictures, unique in getting a story from a shot simply by putting a camera in the right place and moving his people past it.[11]

Although Ford fell out of fashion at the end of his career because the young and the liberals thought him a reactionary, they did not understand the traditions he upheld. The classics which he read as a boy stated that a man should serve the state as well as himself. Ford believed that and served his country through the navy. Yet his long life covered a span from the easy patriotism of Teddy Roosevelt's days to the moral ambiguities of Nixon's withdrawal from Vietnam. Ford himself was too loyal and too old to alter the structure of his commitments. He would not change his beliefs because the times had changed and the young went with the times. "Our ancestors," he said at the end of his life, "would be bloody ashamed if they could see us today."[12] With the mob presuming him a reactionary instead of a man trying to preserve the best in America, he refused to bow his neck or to explain. In the new Rome he did as the Greeks did.

The young radicals, however, began to understand greatness as they aged. Jane Fonda herself recognized her early misjudgment of her father and his best director. She was recently "just blown away by *The Grapes of Wrath* . . . All my life has been privilege. You can be a privileged movie star, or you can commit yourself to the idea that people can change their lives and can change history. I want to make films that will make people feel stronger, understand more clearly, and make them move forward—women and men."[13]

That is what Ford had done in fifty years of making films. There was no formula in what he did, although those who worked with him were often offered money for the secret of his art as a director. He managed to make most of his sequences seem so natural that the audience had the impression it had already seen them many times before. He wrote the common experience of humanity into a film grammar that becomes a series of clichés in lesser hands than his. He made the basic vocabulary of the cinema as simple and rich as the Bible, and as noble as the New World that he called into existence to redress the traditions of the Old.

His fortune was to be in the right place at the right time, at the beginning of Hollywood before the system could wither and the committees stale his infinite variety. His misfortune was perhaps to live too long into an age when Hollywood debased his vocabulary and his countrymen no longer reckoned on his good service. Yet his language and his images will withstand the passing of time. His films were his Monument Valley, and his pictures are printed permanently in our minds as long as we have eyes. He had the gift of capturing the essential and the eternal quality of the everyday, or of persuading us that his special vision, close and far, is a revelation of our own. In his life, he saw the waning of the Great West, and by the time of his death, he had recorded it for all who wished to see.

Notes

1: The Long Voyage Away

For the information in this chapter, I am grateful for the many good books written on the Irish-Americans, in particular to A. Schrier, *Ireland and the American Emigration: 1850–1900* (Minneapolis, 1958); W. V. Shannon, *The American Irish* (New York, 1963); A. M. Greeley, *That Most Distressful Nation: The Taming of the American Irish* (Chicago, 1972); and N. Glazer and D. P. Moynihan, *Beyond the Melting Pot* (Cambridge, Mass., 1963).

I am also indebted for memories of the Feeney family in Portland, to John Ford's wife, his niece Cecil Maclean de Prida, and to his contemporary Francis J. O'Brien.

1. From "Cousin Joe," a screen treatment by Francis Ford.
2. From an interview with Francis J. O'Brien.
3. See *Beyond the Melting Pot,* p. 226.
4. From an interview with Francis J. O'Brien.

2: The Signs from the Observatory

In addition to the sources mentioned in the previous chapter, I am grateful to the reminiscences of Mrs. George Johnston, and to the staffs of the Portland Public Library and the Maine Historical Society.

1. Quoted in Walter Wanger, *You Must Remember This* (New York, 1975), p. 61.
2. Interview with Peter Bogdanovich on *Tape One* in the Ford Archive, Palm Desert.
3. From an interview with Cecil de Prida.
4. John Ford to his co-producer and backer Cornelius Vanderbilt Whitney during the making of *The Searchers,* quoted in an unpublished article, "John Ford," by Robert Emmett Ginna, Jr.
5. From an interview with Mrs. George Johnston.
6. Raoul Walsh, *Each Man in His Time* (New York, 1974), p. 72.
7. W. Wanger, *You Must Remember This,* p. 57.
8. From an interview with Francis J. O'Brien.

3: Straight Shooting

Of the many essential books written about the American West, I have been particularly informed by the seminal works of Frederick Jackson Turner, Walter Prescott Webb, Henry Nash Smith, and J. B. Frantz and J. E. Choate, Jr., *The American Cowboy: The Myth and the Reality* (Norman, Oklahoma, 1955).

Peter Bogdanovich's important long interview with Ford is essential reading for an understanding of the director's early days in Hollywood —see P. Bogdanovich, *John Ford* (Berkeley, California, 1968). So is his documentary *Directed by John Ford,* which he generously screened especially for me—the transcript is at the American Film Institute, the staff of which was unfailingly helpful.

Also important for an understanding of these early years are the articles by Lindsay Anderson, Frank Nugent, and Richard Schickel quoted in the footnotes.

1. See W. Wanger, *You Must Remember This,* p. 57.
2. John Ford on *Tape One* in the Ford Archive, Palm Desert.
3. Frank S. Nugent, "Hollywood's Favorite Rebel," *Saturday Evening Post,* July 23, 1949.
4. P. Bogdanovich, *John Ford,* p. 38.
5. John Ford in *Directed by John Ford.* Also see Jon Tuska, *The Filming of the West* (New York, 1976), p. 71, whose book is a fascinating collection of stories about Western stars and directors.
6. Richard Schickel, "Good Days, Good Years," *Harper's Magazine,* October 1970.
7. John Ford on *Tape One* in the Ford Archive, Palm Desert.
8. P. Bogdanovich, *John Ford,* p. 39.
9. W. P. Webb, *The Great Plains* (Boston, 1931), p. 496.
10. John Ford on *Tape One* in the Ford Archive, Palm Desert.
11. *New York Times Magazine,* September 20, 1959.
12. John Ford on *Tape One* in the Ford Archive, Palm Desert.
13. *Moving Picture World,* December 22, 1917, review of *Bucking Broadway,* producer and star, Harry Carey; director, Jack Ford.
14. See Axel Madsen, "Rencontre Avec John Ford," *Cahiers du Cinéma,* July 1965.

4:   Directed by John Ford

This chapter is principally based on a series of interviews with Mrs. Mary Ford, whose memory is full of the vigor and excitement of the early days of Hollywood. Both Jon Tuska's book and Kevin Brownlow's *The Parade's Gone By* (London, 1968) are essential reading for an understanding of the flavor of the time.

1. "Stepin Fetchit Talks Back," *Film Quarterly,* summer 1971.
2. John Ford on *Tape One* in the Ford Archive, Palm Desert.
3. Quoted in "John Ford in Person," *Focus on Film,* spring 1971.
4. From an interview with Cecil de Prida.
5. From an interview with Robert Emmett Ginna, Jr.

5:   Old Worlds, New Ways

Mrs. Mary Ford's memories are again most valuable in this chapter, as are Peter Bogdanovich's long interview with John Ford and William K. Everson's "Forgotten Ford," *Focus on Film,* Spring 1971. I am also particularly indebted to William Corson for his thorough knowledge of the American intelligence community between the two world wars.

1. From an interview with Leon Selditz.
2. See Maurice Zolotow, *Shooting Star: A Biography of John Wayne* (New York, 1974), p. 49.
3. From *Directed by John Ford.*
4. Ibid.
5. P. Bogdanovich, *John Ford*, p. 48.
6. M. Zolotow, *Shooting Star*, p. 141.
7. From *Directed by John Ford.*
8. John Ford on *Tape One* in the Ford Archive, Palm Desert.
9. P. Bogdanovich, *John Ford*, p. 50.
10. *Photoplay*, January 1929.
11. P. Bogdanovich, *John Ford*, p. 52.
12. From *Directed by John Ford.*
13. Lindsay Anderson, "John Ford," British Film Institute, 1955, p. 24.
14. P. Bogdanovich, *John Ford*, p. 51.
15. From an interview with Leon Selditz.

6:   Half-Genius, Half-Irish

1. Quoted in Frank S. Nugent, "Hollywood's Favorite Rebel."
2. From an interview with Leon Selditz, whose judgment of Ford was valuable and unerring.
3. From an interview with Harry Carey, Jr.
4. From an interview with Leon Selditz.
5. Quoted in Frank S. Nugent, "Hollywood's Favorite Rebel."
6. Robert Parrish, *Growing Up in Hollywood* (London, 1976), pp. 130–131. Parrish's autobiography is one of the most valuable books about Hollywood and incidentally excellent on the subject of John Ford.
7. Ibid., pp. 134–136.
8. Jean Roy, *Pour John Ford* (Paris, 1977), p. 35.
9. Frank Capra, *The Name Above the Title* (New York, 1971), p. 146.
10. From an interview with Leon Selditz.
11. From an interview with Lee Marvin.
12. Jean-Louis Rieupeyrout, "Recontre Avec John Ford," *Cinéma 61*, February 1961.
13. Quoted in Robert Emmett Ginna, Jr.
14. P. Bogdanovich, *John Ford*, pp. 57–58.
15. Lindsay Anderson, "Éléments pour une Biographie," *Cahiers du Cinéma*, August 1958. Anderson's work on Ford is pioneering and seminal.
16. William K. Everson, *Focus on Film*, Spring 1971, p. 19.
17. P. Bogdanovich, *John Ford*, pp. 59.
18. From an interview with Mary Ford.
19. Andrew Sarris, *The John Ford Movie Mystery* (London, 1976), p. 53. While Sarris has written an admirable and important critical study of Ford's films, he has not attempted to research the director's life.
20. Herman Melville, *The Confidence Man* (New York, 1857), end of chapter two.
21. From an interview with Mary Ford.

22. See Raoul Walsh, *Each Man in His Time,* pp. 233–238.
23. See Richard Schickel, "Good Days, Good Years."
24. From an interview with Barbara Ford, whose help and insights have been invaluable to this work.
25. Arthur C. Miller, *Hollywood Cameramen* (London, 1970).
26. Quoted in Lindsay Anderson, "John Ford."

7:   An Inner Vision

1. See Frank Capra, *The Name Above the Title,* pp. 187–188.
2. John Baxter's limited appraisal, *The Cinema of John Ford* (London, 1971), is particularly good in its comparison of *Mary of Scotland* with *The Fugitive* in terms of their common religious symbolism.
3. Quoted in Robert Emmett Ginna, Jr.
4. See E. Eisenburg, "John Ford: Fighting Irish," *New Theater,* April 1936.
5. P. Bogdanovich, *John Ford,* p. 66.
6. See Thomas N. Moon and Carl F. Eifler, *The Deadliest Colonel* (New York, 1975), *passim.*
7. From an interview with Mary Ford.
8. Commandant J. R. Defrees to Lieutenant Commander John Ford, January 16, 1940, in the Ford Archive, Palm Desert.
9. John Ford on *Tape Two* in the Ford Archive, Palm Desert.
10. See *Memo from David Selznick* (New York, 1972).
11. Quoted in Max Wilk, *The Wit and Wisdom of Hollywood* (New York, 1971), pp. 278–279.
12. P. Bogdanovich, *John Ford,* p. 66.
13. Ibid. *p. 69.*

8:   *Stagecoach:* The Burial and Resurrection of the West

1. From an interview with Mary Ford. See also Jon Tuska, *The Filming of the West,* p. 392.
2. See John Ford and Dudley Nichols, *Stagecoach* (Lorrimer Classic Edn., London, 1971).
3. M. Zolotow, *Shooting Star,* pp. 149–150.
4. P. Bogdanovich, *John Ford,* p. 15.
5. From *Directed by John Ford.*
6. Bob Thomas, quoted in M. Zolotow, *Shooting Star,* p. 156.
7. See *Directors in Action: Selections from Action Magazine, the Official Magazine of the Directors' Guild of America* (Bob Thomas, ed., 1973), p. 146. There are excellent accounts of the making of *Stagecoach* by many of those involved in the picture.
8. John Ford, "How We Made *The Long Voyage Home,*" in *Friday* magazine, undated, 1940.
9. From *Directed by John Ford.*
10. Ibid.

9:   The Semaphore of Democracy

1. See F. Daugherty, "John Ford Wants It Real," *Christian Science Monitor,* June 21, 1941.
2. The leading attempts to analyze *Young Mr. Lincoln* with the new critical

tools of semiology are to be found in *Cahiers du Cinéma,* no. 223, August/September 1970, pp. 29–47, and in Jean Roy, *Pour John Ford,* pp. 71–106.

3. See Walter Wanger, *You Must Remember This,* p. 64.
4. Sergei Eisenstein, *Film Essays and a Lecture,* Jay Leyda, ed. (New York, 1970), p. 145.
5. See *Directed by John Ford.*
6. Sergei Eisenstein, *Film Essays,* pp. 145–146.
7. P. Bogdanovich, *John Ford,* p. 73.
8. See *Directed by John Ford.*
9. Quoted in Robert Emmett Ginna, Jr.
10. See *Directed by John Ford.*
11. See *Cahiers du Cinéma, loc. cit.*
12. See *Directed by John Ford.*
13. Quoted in James Brough, *The Fabulous Fondas* (New York, 1973), p. 93.
14. P. Bogdanovich, *John Ford,* p. 76.
15. Walter Wanger, *You Must Remember This,* p. 61.
16. See Parker Tyler, *Magic and Myth in the Movies* (New York, 1947), pp. 230–247.
17. Margaret Thorp, *America at the Movies* (New York, 1939), pp. 271–272.

10:   Preparations for a Private War

1. John Ford, "How We Made *The Long Voyage Home.*"
2. Jean Renoir, *My Life and My Films* (New York, 1974), p. 193.
3. Parker Tyler, *Magic and Myth in the Movies.*
4. From an interview with Anna Lee.
5. I must confess an unusual distaste for the studio artificiality of *How Green Was My Valley,* having myself made *Under Milk Wood* on location in Wales with a cast that was nearly all Welsh.
6. From an interview with Mark Armistead, whose long account of Ford's activities and his own in combat was invaluable to me.
7. From an interview with Mary Ford.
8. From an interview with Mark Armistead.
9. Quoted in Lindsay Anderson, "John Ford."
10. From an interview with Mary Ford.

11:   Theater of War

1. From an interview with Mark Armistead.
2. From an interview with Leon Selditz.
3. See R. Parrish, *Growing Up in Hollywood.*
4. D. W. Bagley, Rear Admiral, U. S. Navy, 14th Naval District, Pearl Harbor, Hawaii, to Commander John Ford, U. S. Naval Reserve. Original in the Ford Archive, Palm Desert.
5. From an interview with Mary Ford.
6. For a full account of the editing of *The Battle of Midway,* see R. Parrish, *Growing Up in Hollywood.*
7. From an interview with Brick Marquard.
8. See Mel Gussow, *Don't Say Yes Until I Finish Talking: A Biography of Darryl F. Zanuck* (New York, 1971), pp. 108–110.

9. T. Moon and C. F. Eifler, *The Deadliest Colonel.*
10. From an interview with Mark Armistead.
11. From an interview with Brick Marquard.
12. See P. Bogdanovich, *John Ford,* p. 83.
13. From an interview with Mary Ford.
14. From an interview with Brick Marquard.
15. Quoted in Robert Emmett Ginna, Jr.
16. From an interview with Cecil de Prida.
17. *The New York Times,* December 30, 1945.
18. Lindsay Anderson, *"They Were Expendable* and John Ford," *Sequence,* summer 1950.

12: They Were Not Expendable

1. See R. Parrish, *Growing Up in Hollywood,* pp. 155–157.
2. From an interview with Mark Armistead. I am most grateful to him for revealing the secret acts of some of Ford's men at the end of the Second World War.
3. Brigadier General G. Bryan Conrad, O.S.C., to Brigadier General Edwin L. Sibert, June 21, 1945.
4. From an interview with Mark Armistead.
5. From the Ford Archive, Palm Desert.
6. From an interview with Brick Marquard.
7. From an interview with Mrs. Patricia Swain.
8. R. Parrish, *Growing Up in Hollywood,* p. 159.
9. From an interview with Mrs. Patricia Swain.
10. From an interview with William Corson.
11. P. Bogdanovich, *John Ford,* p. 40.
12. See "Ford in Person," *Focus on Film,* spring 1971.
13. From an interview with Leon Selditz.
14. Henry Fonda in *Directed by John Ford.*

13: Faith and the Family

1. P. Bogdanovich, *John Ford,* pp. 85–86.
2. Quoted in Lindsay Anderson, "John Ford."
3. See *The Nation,* January 10, 1948.
4. P. Bogdanovich, *John Ford,* p. 134.

14: The Holding of the West

1. John Ford on *Tape Two* in the Ford Archive, Palm Desert.
2. P. Bogdanovich, *John Ford,* p.86.
3. John Ford on *Tape Two* in the Ford Archive, Palm Desert.
4. General Phil Sheridan to Lt. Col. Kirby Yorke, also played by John Wayne, in the script of *Rio Grande,* by James Kevin McGuinness.
5. P. Bogdanovich, *John Ford,* p. 86.
6. See *Directed by John Ford.*
7. Ibid.
8. Ibid.

9. Quoted in Jean Mitry, *Films in Review,* August-September 1955.
10. See *Directed by John Ford.*
11. From an interview with Hank Worden.
12. See Lewis O. Saum, *The Fur Trader and the Indian* (Univ. of Washington, 1965), *passim.* This important book was the first to collect and analyze accounts of the Indians of the plains and forests when they came into contact with European traders. See also Andrew Sinclair, *The Savage: A History of Misunderstanding* (London, 1977), chapter five.
13. From an interview with Vine Deloria, Jr., who has written four remarkable and illuminating books on the clash of cultures between the Indians and the European settlers.
14. Axel Madsen, "Rencontre avec John Ford."
15. William H. Clothier in *Voices of Film Experience: 1894 to the Present,* Jay Leyda, ed. (New York, 1977), p. 79.
16. John Ford in *Cahiers du Cinéma,* March 1955, translated in *Films in Review,* August-September 1955.
17. Quoted in Robert Emmett Ginna, Jr.
18. See Henry Fonda on John Ford, *Sight and Sound,* Spring 1973.
19. From an interview with Mark Armistead.
20. Quoted in Robert Emmett Ginna, Jr.
21. From an interview with Mary Ford.
22. See Lillian Gish, *The Movies, Mr. Griffith and Me* (New York, 1969), p. 356.

15: Another Peace, Another War
1. From an interview with Harry Carey, Jr.
2. For a full account of this episode, see R. Parrish, *Growing Up in Hollywood,* pp. 201–210.
3. P. Bogdanovich, *John Ford,* p. 90.
4. See Axel Madsen, "Rencontre avec John Ford."
5. John Ford on *Tape One* in the Ford Archive, Palm Desert.
6. See Henry Ephron, *We Thought We Could Do Anything* (New York, 1977), pp. 117–120.
7. The Secretary of the Navy to Captain John Ford, U.S. Naval Reserve, original in the Ford Archive, Palm Desert.
8. Again I am deeply indebted to Mark Armistead's recollections of his months spent serving with Ford off Korea, when they became close friends.

16: Repose and Unsettling
1. See Jon Tuska, *The Filming of the West,* p. 347.
2. See Joe McInery, "John Wayne Talks Tough," *Film Comment,* September 1972.
3. John Ford on *Tape Three* in the Ford Archive, Palm Desert.
4. Quoted in Robert Emmett Ginna, Jr.
5. From an interview with Charles Fitzsimmons.
6. See *Directed by John Ford.*
7. See Henry Fonda in *Sight and Sound,* Spring 1955.

8. Lindsay Anderson, "The Sun Shines Bright," *Sight and Sound,* October-December 1953.
9. John Ford on *Tape One* in the Ford Archive, Palm Desert.
10. From an interview with Mary Ford.

17:   Old Concerns, New Times
1. P. Bogdanovich, *John Ford,* p. 92.
2. See Robert Emmett Ginna, Jr.
3. Henry Fonda in *The Radio Times,* November 2, 1972.
4. From an interview with Jim Heneghan.
5. Mervyn LeRoy, *Take One* (New York, 1974), p. 196.
6. Henry Fonda in the *Sunday Express,* September 13, 1959.
7. Lindsay Anderson, "John Ford."
8. P. Bogdanovich, *John Ford,* pp. 92–93.
9. Joe McInery, "John Wayne Talks Tough."
10. See Robert Emmett Ginna, Jr.
11. From an interview with Leon Selditz.
12. John Ford on *Tape Three* at the Ford Archive, Palm Desert.
13. Lindsay Anderson on *The Searchers, Sight and Sound,* Autumn, 1956.
14. Joe McInery, "John Wayne Talks Tough."

18:   What You Might See Anyplace
1. *The New York Times,* July 14, 1957.
2. See particularly Jean Roy, *Pour John Ford,* pp. 189–199.
3. From an interview with Mark Armistead.
4. *The New York Times,* July 14, 1957.

19:   Last Word on the West
1. See Colin Young, "The Old Dependables," *Film Quarterly,* Fall 1959.
2. Kenneth MacGowan, *Behind the Screen: The History and Techniques of the Motion Picture* (New York, 1965), p. 321.
3. John Gilbert interviews Martin Rackin on *The Horse Soldiers, Sight and Sound,* Winter 1959/1960.
4. See Robert Emmett Ginna, Jr.
5. P. Bogdanovich, *John Ford,* p. 141.
6. See Mel Gussow, *Don't Say Yes Until I Finish Talking,* p. 151.
7. Quoted in J. McBride and M. Wilmington, *John Ford* (London, 1974), p. 169.
8. See Molly Haskell, *From Reverence to Rape: The Treatment of Women in the Movies* (New York, 1974), p. 122.
9. James Stewart in *Films and Filming,* April, 1966.
10. See *Directed by John Ford.*
11. See *Sunday Express,* May 28, 1961.
12. See *Films and Filming,* April, 1966.
13. From an interview with Lee Marvin.

14. Ibid.
15. See Andrew Sarris, "Cactus Rosebud or the Man Who Shot Liberty Valance," *Film Culture,* no. 25, Summer 1962; and William S. Pechter, *Twenty-four Times a Second* (New York, 1972), p. 240.
16. Patrick Ford to Bernard Smith, January 21, 1963.
17. For a critique of *Cheyenne Autumn,* see Ralph and Natasha Friar, *The Only Good Indian—The Hollywood Gospel* (New York, 1972), pp. 168–171.
18. P. Bogdanovich, *John Ford,* p. 104.
19. See *Directed by John Ford.*
20. P. Bogdanovich, *John Ford,* p. 19.

20:   The End of a Time

1. See Darcy O'Brien, *A Way of Life, Like Any Other* (London, 1977), pp. 99–102.
2. P. Bogdanovich, *John Ford,* pp. 102–104.
3. From an interview with Lee Marvin.
4. Andrew Sarris, *The John Ford Movie Mystery,* pp. 153–154.
5. See Robert Emmett Ginna, Jr., "Intimations of John Ford," unpublished manuscript.
6. From an interview with Anna Lee.
7. From an interview with Lee Marvin.
8. From an interview with Barbara Ford.
9. From an interview with Mary Ford.
10. Quoted in Robert Emmett Ginna, Jr.
11. Richard Nixon from the White House, March 31, 1973, original in the Ford Archive, Palm Desert.
12. See Robert Parrish, *Growing Up in Hollywood,* pp. 211–214.
13. See P. Bogdanovich, "Taps for Mr. Ford," *New York* magazine, October 29, 1973.
14. I am indebted to the opening chapter of J. McBride and M. Wilmington in their book *John Ford* (London, 1974) for their account of his funeral.

21:   Print the Legend

1. John Ford to Jean Mitry, reproduced in *Interviews with Film Directors* (Andrew Sarris, ed., New York, 1967), pp. 193–201.
2. Roger Greenspun, "John Ford 1895–1973," *The New York Times,* September 9, 1973.
3. F. Scott Fitzgerald, *The Last Tycoon* (New York, 1941), p. 147.
4. See Walter Wanger, *You Must Remember This,* p. 64.
5. Lindsay Anderson, *"They Were Expendable* and John Ford," *Sequence,* Summer 1950.
6. See Albert Johnson, "The Tenth Muse in San Francisco," *Sight and Sound,* spring 1955, and Roger Greenspun, op. cit.
7. From an interview with Lee Marvin.
8. From P. Bogdanovich, "Taps for Mr. Ford."

9. From *Directed by John Ford.*
10. See P. Haudiquet, *John Ford* (Paris, 1966), p. 140.
11. See Mel Gussow, *Don't Say Yes Until I Finish Talking,* p. 163.
12. Quoted in Jeffrey Richards, "Ford's Lost World," *Focus on Film,* Spring 1971.
13. *Newsweek,* October 19, 1977.

AFTERNOTE

I have depended chiefly on oral history for the writing of this biography, and human memory is full of both riches and errors. Although the responsibility of choosing to set down any errors is entirely my own, I would be grateful for any witness who would take the trouble to write to me with any corrections for a future edition of this book. My address is:

> Andrew Sinclair
> c/o James Wade
> The Dial Press
> 1 Dag Hammarskjold Plaza
> 245 East 47 Street
> New York, N.Y. 10017

Only thus can more of the truth be known.

Filmography

The following filmography is based on the work of Peter Bogdanovich and is reproduced by his kind permission. He has produced the definitive filmography on Ford's films in his revised monograph on Ford, reissued by the University of California Press in 1978.

Films Made with Francis Ford As Director in Which John Ford Participated:

1914 *Lucille Love—The Girl of Mystery*
      The Mysterious Rose

1915 *Three Bad Men and a Girl*
      The Hidden City
      The Doorway of Destruction
      The Broken Coin

1916 *The Lumber Yard Gang*
      Chicken-Hearted Jim
      Peg O' the Ring
      The Bandit's Wager

1917 *The Trail of Hate*

1917 *The Tornado* (Universal-101 Bison)
Director-writer: Jack Ford
Jack Ford . . . . *Jack Dayton, "No-gun Man"*

1917 *The Scrapper* (Universal—101 Bison)
Director-writer: Jack Ford
Jack Ford . . . . *Buck, the scrapper*

1917 *The Soul Herder* (Universal—101 Bison)
Director: Jack Ford
Harry Carey . . . . *Cheyenne Harry*

1917 *Cheyenne's Pal* (Universal-Star Featurette)
Director: Jack Ford
Harry Carey . . . . *Cheyenne Harry*

1917 *Straight Shooting* (Butterfly-Universal)
Director: Jack Ford
Executive Producer: Carl Laemmle
Writer: George Hively
Photographer: George Scott
Harry Carey . . . . *Cheyenne Harry*
Molly Malone . . . . Joan Sims
Duke Lee . . . . "Thunder" Flint
Vester Pegg . . . . "Placer" Fremont
Hoot Gibson . . . . Danny Morgan
George Berrell . . . . Sweetwater Sims
Ted Brooks . . . . Ted Sims
Milt Brown . . . . Black-Eyed Pete

1917 *The Secret Man* (Butterfly-Universal)
Director: Jack Ford
Harry Carey . . . . *Cheyenne Harry*

1917 *A Marked Man* (Butterfly-Universal)
Director: Jack Ford
Harry Carey . . . . *Cheyenne Harry*

1917 *Bucking Broadway* (Butterfly-Universal)
Director: Jack Ford
Harry Carey . . . . *Cheyenne Harry*

1918 *The Phantom Riders* (Universal-Special)
Director: Jack Ford
Harry Carey . . . . *Cheyenne Harry*

1918 *Wild Women* (Universal-Special)
Director: Jack Ford
Harry Carey . . . . *Cheyenne Harry*

1918 *Thieves' Gold* (Universal-Special Feature)
Director: Jack Ford
Harry Carey . . . . *Cheyenne Harry*

1918 *The Scarlet Drop* (Universal-Special)
Director: Jack Ford
Harry Carey . . . . "Kaintuck" Harry Ridge

1918   *Hell Bent* (Universal-Special Attraction)

Director: Jack Ford
Harry Carey   . . . . *Cheyenne Harry*

1918   *A Woman's Fool* (Universal-Special Attraction)

Director: Jack Ford
Harry Carey   . . . . *Lin McLean*

1918   *Three Mounted Men* (Universal-Special Attraction)

Director: Jack Ford
Harry Carey   . . . . *Cheyenne Harry*

1919   *Roped* (Universal-Special)

Director: Jack Ford
Harry Carey   . . . . *Cheyenne Harry*

1919   *The Fighting Brothers* (Universal)

Director: Jack Ford
Pete Morrison   . . . . *Sheriff Pete Larkin*
Hoot Gibson   . . . . Lonnie Larkin

1919   *A Fight for Love* (Universal-Special Attraction)

Director: Jack Ford
Harry Carey   . . . . *Cheyenne Harry*

1919   *By Indian Post* (Universal)

Director: Jack Ford
Pete Morrison   . . . . *Jode McWilliams*

1919   *The Rustlers* (Universal)

Director: Jack Ford
Pete Morrison   . . . . *Ben Clayburn*

1919   *Bare Fists* (Universal-Special)

Director: Jack Ford
Harry Carey   . . . . *Cheyenne Harry*

1919   *Gun Law* (Universal)

Director: Jack Ford
Pete Morrison   . . . . *Dick Allen*
Hoot Gibson   . . . . Bart Stevens, alias Smoke Gublen

1919   *The Gun Packer* (Universal)

Director: Jack Ford
Ed Jones . . . . *Sandy McLoughlin*

1919   *Riders of Vengeance* (Universal-Special)

Director: Jack Ford
Harry Carey . . . . *Cheyenne Harry*

1919   *The Last Outlaw* (Universal)

Director: Jack Ford
Ed "King Fisher" Jones   *Bud Coburn*

1919   *The Outcasts of Poker Flat* (Universal-Special)

Director: Jack Ford
Harry Carey . . . . *"Square Shootin' " Lanyon; John Oakhurst*

1919   *The Ace of the Saddle* (Universal-Special)

Director: Jack Ford
Harry Carey . . . . *Cheyenne Harry Henderson*

1919   *The Rider of the Law* (Universal-Special)

Director: Jack Ford
Harry Carey . . . . *Jim Kyneton*

1919   *A Gun Fightin' Gentleman* (Universal-Special)

Director: Jack Ford
Harry Carey . . . . *Cheyenne Harry*

1919   *Marked Men* (Universal-Special)

Director: Jack Ford
Harry Carey . . . . *Cheyenne Harry*

1920   *The Prince of Avenue A* (Universal-Special)

Director: Jack Ford
James J. "Gentleman Jim" Corbett   . . *Barry O'Conner*

1920   *The Girl in Number 29* (Universal-Special)

Director: Jack Ford
Frank Mayo . . . . *Laurie Devon*

1920   *Hitchin' Posts* (Universal-Special)

Director: Jack Ford
Frank Mayo . . . . *Jefferson Todd*

1920 *Just Pals* (Fox-20th Century Brand)
Director: Jack Ford
Buck Jones . . . . *Bim*

1920 *The Big Punch* (Fox-20th Century Brand)
Director: Jack Ford
Buck Jones . . . . *Buck*

1921 *The Freeze Out* (Universal-Special)
Director: Jack Ford
Harry Carey . . . . *Ohio, the Stranger*

1921 *Desperate Trails* (Universal-Special)
Director: Jack Ford
Harry Carey . . . . *Bart Carson*
Irene Rich . . . . Mrs. Walker

1921 *Action* (Universal-Special)
Director: Jack Ford
Hoot Gibson . . . . *Sandy Brooke*

1921 *Sure Fire* (Universal-Special)
Director: Jack Ford
Hoot Gibson . . . . *Jeff Bransford*

1921 *Jackie* (Fox)
Director: Jack Ford
Shirley Mason . . . . *Jackie*

1922 *The Wallop* (Universal-Special)
Director: Jack Ford
Harry Carey . . . . *John Wesley Pringle*

1922 *Little Miss Smiles* (Fox)
Director: Jack Ford
Shirley Mason . . . . *Esther Aaronson*

1922 *The Village Blacksmith* (Fox)
Director: Jack Ford
William Walling . . . . *John Hammond, blacksmith*

1923   *The Face on the Barroom Floor* (Fox)

Director: Jack Ford
Henry B. Walthall . . . . *Robert Stevens, an artist*

1923   *Three Jumps Ahead* (Fox)

Director-writer: Jack Ford
Tom Mix . . . . *Steve Clancy*

1923   *Cameo Kirby* (Fox)

Director: John Ford
John Gilbert . . . . *Cameo Kirby*

1923   *North of Hudson Bay* (Fox)

Director: John Ford
Tom Mix . . . . *Michael Dane, a rancher*

1923   *Hoodman Blind* (Fox)

Director: John Ford
David Butler . . . . *Jack Yeulette*

1924   *The Iron Horse* (Fox)

Director: John Ford
Scenarist: Charles Kenyon, from story by
                                           Kenyon and John Russell
Photographers: George Schneiderman, Burnett
                                           Guffey
Title-writer   Charles Darnton
Music score: Erno Rapee
George O'Brien . . . . *Davy Brandon*
Madge Bellamy . . . . Miriam Marsh
Judge Charles Edward Bull . . . . . . Abraham Lincoln
William Walling . . . . Thomas Marsh
Fred Kohler . . . . Deroux
Cyril Chadwick . . . . Peter Jesson
Gladys Hulette . . . . Ruby
James Marcus . . . . Judge Haller
Francis Powers . . . . Sergeant Slattery
J. Farrell McDonald . . . . Cpl. Casey
James Welch . . . . Pvt. Schultz
Colin Chase . . . . Tony
Walter Rogers . . . . Gen. Dodge
Jack O'Brien . . . . Dinny
George Waggner . . . . Col. "Buffalo Bill" Cody
John Padjan . . . . Wild Bill Hickok
Charles O'Malley . . . . Maj. North
Charles Newton . . . . Cottis P. Harrington
Delbert Mann . . . . Charles Crocker
Chief Big Tree . . . . Cheyenne chief

Chief White Spear   . . . . Sioux chief
Edward Piel   . . . . Old Chinaman
James Gordon   . . . . David Brandon, Sr.
Winston Miller   . . . . Davy, as child
Peggy Cartwright   . . . . Miriam, as child
Thomas Durant   . . . . Jack Ganzhorn
Stanhope Wheatcroft   . . . . John Hay
Frances Teague   . . . . Polka Dot
Dan Borzage

1924   *Hearts of Oak* (Fox)

Director: John Ford
Scenarist: Charles Kenyon, from play by James
                                   A. Herne
Photographer: George Schneiderman
Hobart Bosworth   . . . . *Terry Dunnivan, a sea captain*
Pauline Starke   . . . . Chrystal
Theodore von Eltz   . . . . Ned Fairweather
James Gordon   . . . . John Owen
Francis Powers   . . . . Grandpa Dunnivan
Jennie Lee   . . . . Grandma Dunnivan
Francis Ford

1925   *Lightnin'* (Fox)

Director: John Ford
Scenarist: Frances Marion, from play by
                                   Winchell Smith and Frank Bacon
Photographer: Joseph H. August
Jay Hunt   . . . . *"Lightnin' " Bill Jones*
Madge Bellamy   . . . . Millie
Edythe Chapman   . . . . Mother Jones
Wallace McDonald   . . . . John Marvin
J. Farrell McDonald   . . . . Judge Townsend
Ethel Clayton   . . . . Margaret Davis
Richard Travers   . . . . Raymond Thomas
James Marcus   . . . . Sheriff
Otis Harlan   . . . . Zeb

1925   *Kentucky Pride* (Fox)

Director: John Ford
Writer: Dorothy Yost
Photographer: George Schneiderman
Henry B. Walthall   . . . . *Mr. Beaumont*
J. Farrell McDonald   . . . . Mike Donovan
Gertrude Astor   . . . . Mrs. Beaumont
Malcolm Waite   . . . . Greve Carter
Belle Stoddard   . . . . Mrs. Donovan
Winston Miller   . . . . Danny Donovan
Peaches Jackson   . . . . Virginia Beaumont

(Kentucky Pride, cont.)
Man O'War, Fair Play, Negofol, The
 Finn, Morvich . . . . The horses

1925   *The Fighting Heart* (Fox)

Director:	John Ford
Scenarist:	Lillie Hayward, from novel by Larry Evans
Photographer:	Joseph H. August
George O'Brien	*Denny Bolton*
Billie Dove	Doris Anderson
J. Farrell McDonald	Jerry
Diana Miller	Helen Van Allen
Victor McLaglen	Soapy Williams
Bert Woodruff	Grandfather Bolton
James Marcus	Judge Maynard
Lynn Cowan	Chub Morehouse
Harvey Clark	Dennison
Hank Mann	His assistant
Francis Ford	The town fool
Francis Powers	John Anderson
Hazel Howell	Oklahoma Kate
Edward Piel	Flash Fogarty

1925   *Thank You* (Fox)

Director:	John Ford
Producer:	John Golden
Scenarist:	Frances Marion, from play by Winchell Smith and Tom Cushing
Photographer:	George Schneiderman
George O'Brien	*Kenneth Jamieson*
Jacqueline Logan	Diana Lee, the mother
Alec Francis	David Lee
J. Farrell McDonald	Andy
Cyril Chadwick	Mr. Jones
Edith Bostwick	Mrs. Jones
Vivian Ogden	Miss Blodgett
James Neill	Dr. Cobb
Billy Rinaldi	Sweet, Jr.
Maurice Murphy	Willie Jones
Robert Milasch	Sweet, Sr.
George Fawcett	Jamieson, Sr.
Marion Harlan	Millie Jones
Ida Moore, Frank Bailey	Gossips

1926   *The Shamrock Handicap* (Fox)

Director:	John Ford
Scenarist:	John Stone, from story by Peter B. Kyne
Photographer:	George Schneiderman

Janet Gaynor . . . . *Sheila Gaffney*
Leslie Fenton . . . . Neil Ross
J. Farrell McDonald . . . . Dennis O'Shea
Louis Payne . . . . Sir Miles Gaffney
Claire McDowell . . . . Molly O'Shea
Willard Louis . . . . Martin Finch
Andy Clark . . . . Chesty Morgan
Georgie Harris . . . . Benny Ginsberg
Ely Reynolds . . . . Puss
Thomas Delmar . . . . Michael
Brandon Hurst . . . . The procurer

1926 *Three Bad Men* (Fox)

Director: John Ford
Scenarists: Ford, John Stone, from the novel,
                                   Over the Border, by Herman
                                   Whitaker
Photographer: George Schneiderman
George O'Brien . . . . *Dan O'Malley*
Olive Borden . . . . Lee Carlton
J. Farrell McDonald . . . . Mike Costigan
Tom Santschi . . . . Bull Stanley
Frank Campeau . . . . Spade Allen
Lou Tellegen . . . . Sheriff Layne Hunter
George Harris . . . . Joe Minsk
Jay Hunt . . . . Old prospector
Priscilla Bonner . . . . Millie Stanley
Otis Harlan . . . . Zack Leslie
Walter Perry . . . . Pat Monahan
Grace Gordon . . . . Millie's friend
Alec B. Francis . . . . Rev. Calvin Benson
George Irving . . . . General Neville
Phyllis Haver . . . . Prairie beauty

1926 *The Blue Eagle* (Fox)

Director: John Ford
Scenarist: L.G. Rigby, from story, "The Lord's
                                   Referee," by Gerald Beaumont
Photographer: George Schneiderman
George O'Brien . . . . *George D'Arcy*
Janet Gaynor . . . . Rose Cooper
William Russell . . . . Big Tim Ryan
Robert Edeson . . . . Father Joe
David Butler . . . . Nick Galvani
Phillip Ford . . . . Limpy D'Arcy
Ralph Sipperly . . . . Slats Mulligan
Margaret Livingston . . . . Mary Rohan
Jerry Madden . . . . Baby Tom
Harry Tenbrook . . . . , , Bascom
Lew Short . . . . Captain McCarthy

1927 *Upstream* (Fox)

Director:	John Ford
Scenarist:	Randall H. Faye, from novel, *The Snake's Wife,* by Wallace Smith
Photographer:	Charles G. Clarke

Nancy Nash . . . . *Gertie King*
Earle Foxe . . . . Brasingham
Grant Withers . . . . Jack LeVelle
Raymond Hitchcock . . . . The star border
Lydia Yeamans Titus . . . . Miss Breckenridge
Emile Chautard . . . . Campbell Mandare
Ted McNamara, Sammy Cohen,
   Lilian Worth, Francis Ford, Jane
   Winton, Harry Bailey, Ely
   Reynolds, Judy King . . . . A dance team

1928 *Mother Machree* (Fox)

Director:	John Ford
Scenarist:	Gertrude Orr, from novel by Rita Johnson Young
Photographer:	Chester Lyons
Editors and title-writers:	Katherine Hilliker, H.H. Caldwell

Belle Bennett . . . . *Ellen McHugh*
Neil Hamilton . . . . Brian McHugh
Philippe De Lacy . . . . Brian, as child
Pat Somerset . . . . Robert De Puyster
Victor McLaglen . . . . Terrence O'Dowd
Ted McNamara . . . . Harpist of Wexford
John MacSweeney . . . . Irish priest
Eulalie Jensen . . . . Rachel van Studdiford
Constance Howard . . . . Edith Cutting
Ethel Clayton . . . . Mrs. Cutting
William Platt . . . . Pips
Jacques Rollens . . . . Signor Bellini
Rodney Hildebrand . . . . Brian McHugh, Sr.
Joyce Wirard . . . . Edith Cutting, as child
Robert Parrish . . . . Child

1928 *Four Sons* (Fox)

Director:	John Ford
Scenarist:	Philip Klein, from novel, *Grandma Bernle Learns Her Letters,* by I.A.R. Wylie
Photographers:	George Schneiderman, Charles G. Clarke
Music arranger:	S. L. Rothafel
Theme:	"Little Mother," by Erno Rapee, Lee Pollack
Editor:	Margaret V. Clancey
Title-writers:	Katherine Hilliker, H. H. Caldwell

Margaret Mann . . . . *Frau Bernle*

James Hall . . . . Joseph Bernle
Charles Morton . . . . Johann Bernle
George Meeker . . . . Andres Bernle
Francis X. Bushman, Jr. . . . . Franz Bernle
June Collyer . . . . Annabelle Bernle
Albert Gran . . . . Postman
Earle Foxe . . . . Maj. Von Stomm
Frank Reicher . . . . Headmaster
Jack Pennick . . . . Joseph's American friend
Archduke Leopold of Austria . . . . . German captain
Hughie Mack . . . . Innkeeper
Wendell Franklin . . . . James Henry
Auguste Tollaire . . . . Mayor
Ruth Mix . . . . Johann's girl
Robert Parrish . . . . Child
Michael Mark . . . . Von Stomm's orderly
L. J. O'Conner . . . . Aubergiste
Ferdinand Schumann-Heink

1928 *Hangman's House* (Fox)

Director: John Ford
Scenarist: Marion Orth, from story by Donn
                                     Byrne, adapted by Philip Klein
Photographer: George Schneiderman
Editor: Margaret V. Clancey
Title-writer: Malcolm Stuart Boylan
Victor McLaglen . . . . *Citizen Hogan*
Hobart Bosworth . . . . James O'Brien, Lord Chief Justice
June Collyer . . . . Connaught O'Brien
Larry Kent . . . . Dermott McDermott
Earle Foxe . . . . John Darcy
Eric Mayne . . . . Legionnaire colonel
Joseph Benke . . . . Neddy Joe
Belle Stoddard . . . . Anne McDermott
John Wayne . . . . Spectator at horse race

1928 *Napoleon's Barber* (Fox-Movietone)

Director: John Ford
Scenarist: Arthur Caesar, from his own play
Photographer: George Schneiderman
Otto Matiesen . . . . *Napoleon*
Frank Reicher . . . . The barber
Natalie Golitzin . . . . Josephine
Helen Ware . . . . Barber's wife
Philippe De Lacy . . . . Barber's son
Russell Powell . . . . Blacksmith
D'Arcy Corrigan . . . . Tailor
Michael Mark . . . . Peasant
Buddy Roosevelt, Ervin Renard, Joe
   Waddell, Youcca-Troubetzkoy . . . French officers
Henry Herbert . . . . Soldier

1928 *Riley the Cop* (Fox)

Director: John Ford
Writers: James Gruen, Fred Stanley
Photographer: Charles G. Clarke
Editor: Alex Troffey
J. Farrell McDonald . . . . *Aloysius Riley*
Louise Fazenda . . . . Lena Krausmeyer
Nancy Drexel . . . . Mary Coronelli
David Rollins . . . . Davy Smith
Harry Schultz . . . . Hans Krausmeyer
Billy Bevan . . . . Paris cabdriver
Tom Wilson . . . . Sergeant
Otto H. Fries . . . . Munich cabdriver
Mildred Boyd . . . . Caroline
Ferdinand Schumann-Heink . . . . . . Julius
Del Henderson . . . . Judge Coronelli
Russell Powell . . . . Kuchendorf
Mike Donlin . . . . Crook
Robert Parrish

1929 *Strong Boy* (Fox)

Director: John Ford
Scenarists: James Kevin McGuiness, Andrew
                                        Bennison, John McLain, from story
                                        by Frederick Hazlett Brennan
Photographer: Joseph H. August
Title-writer: Malcolm Stuart Boylan
Victor McLaglen . . . . *William "Strong Boy" Bloss*
Leatrice Joy . . . . Mary McGregor
Clyde Cook . . . . Pete
Slim Summerville . . . . Slim
Kent Sanderson . . . . Wilbur Watkins
Tom Wilson . . . . Baggage master
Jack Pennick . . . . Baggageman
Eulalie Jensen . . . . The Queen
David Torrence . . . . Railroad president
J. Farrell McDonald . . . . Angus McGregor
Dolores Johnson . . . . Usherette
Douglas Scott . . . . Wobby
Robert Ryan . . . . Porter

1929 *The Black Watch* (Fox)

Directors: John Ford, "staged by" Lumsden
                                        Hare
Scenarists: James Kevin McGuiness, John Stone,
                                        from novel, *King of the Khyber Rifles*,
                                        by Talbot Mundy
Photographer: Joseph H. August
Editor: Alex Troffey

Victor McLaglen	*Capt. Donald King*
Myrna Loy	Yasmani
Roy D'Arcy	Rewa Ghunga
Pat Somerset	Highlanders' officer
David Rollins	Lt. Malcolm King
Mitchell Lewis	Mohammed Kahn
Walter Long	Harem Bey
David Percy	Highlanders' officer
Lumsden Hare	Colonel
Cyril Chadwick	Maj. Twynes
David Torrence	Marechal
Francis Ford	Maj. MacGregor
Claude King	
Frederick Sullivan	
Joseph Diskay	
Joyzelle	
Richard Travers	

1929 *Salute* (Fox)

Director:	John Ford
Scenarist:	John Stone, from story by Tristram Tupper
Dialogue:	James K. McGuiness
Photographer:	Joseph H. August
Editor:	Alex Troffey
George O'Brien	*Cadet John Randall*
Helen Chandler	Nancy Wayne
Stepin' Fetchit	Smoke Screen
William Janney	Midshipman Paul Randall
Frank Albertson	Midshipman Albert Edward Price
Joyce Compton	Marion Wilson
Cliff Dempsey	Maj. Gen. Somers
Lumsden Hare	Rear Adm. Randall
David Butler	Navy coach
Rex Bell	Cadet
John Breeden	Midshipman
Ward Bond, John Wayne	Football players

1930 *Men Without Women* (Fox)

Director:	John Ford
Scenarist:	Dudley Nichols, from story, "Submarine," by Ford, James K. McGuiness
Photographer:	Joseph H. August
Music:	Peter Brunelli, Glen Knight
Editor:	Paul Weatherwax
Kenneth MacKenna	*"Burke"*
Frank Albertson	"Price"
Paul Page	"Handsome"

(*Men Without Women, cont.*)
Pat Somerset . . . . Lt. Digby, R.N.
Walter McGrail . . . . Cobb
Stuart Erwin . . . . Jenkins, radio operator
Warren Hymer . . . . Kaufman
J. Farrell McDonald . . . . Costello
Roy Stewart . . . . Capt. Carson
Warner Richmond . . . . Lt. Comdr. Bridewell
Harry Tenbrook . . . . Winkler
Ben Hendricks, Jr. . . . . Murphy
George Le Guera . . . . Pollock
John Wayne
Robert Parrish

1930   *Born Reckless* (Fox)

Directors: John Ford
Scenarist: Dudley Nichols, from novel, *Louis
                                   Beretti,* by Donald Henderson
                                   Clarke
Photographer: George Schneiderman
Editor: Frank E. Hull
Edmund Lowe . . . . *Louis Beretti*
Catherine Dale Owen . . . . Joan Sheldon
Lee Tracy . . . . Bill O'Brien
Margaret Churchill . . . . Rosa Beretti
Warren Hymer . . . . Big Shot
Pat Somerset . . . . Duke
William Harrigan . . . . Good News Brophy
Frank Albertson . . . . Frank Sheldon
Ferike Boros . . . . Ma Beretti
J. Farrell McDonald . . . . District attorney
Paul Porcasi . . . . Pa Beretti
Eddie Gribbon . . . . Bugs
Mike Donlin . . . . Fingy Moscovitz
Ben Bard . . . . Joe Bergman
Paul Page . . . . Ritzy Reilly
Joe Brown . . . . Needle Beer Grogan
Jack Pennick, Ward Bond, Roy
   Stewart . . . . Soldiers

1930   *Up the River* (Fox)

Director: John Ford
Writer: Maurine Watkins (and uncredited:
                                   Ford, William Collier, Sr.)
Photographer: Joseph H. August
Editor: Frank E. Hull
Spencer Tracy . . . . *St. Louis*
Warren Hymer . . . . Dannemora Dan
Humphrey Bogart . . . . Steve
Claire Luce . . . . Judy

Joan Lawes . . . . Jean
Sharon Lynn . . . . Edith La Verne
George McFarlane . . . . Jessup
Gaylord Pendleton . . . . Morris
Morgan Wallace . . . . Frosby
William Collier, Sr. . . . . Pop
Robert E. O'Conner . . . . Guard
Louise MacIntosh . . . . Mrs. Massey
Edythe Chapman . . . . Mrs. Jordan
Johnny Walker . . . . Happy
Noel Francis . . . . Sophie
Mildred Vincent . . . . Annie
Mack Clark . . . . Whitelay
Goodee Montgomery . . . . Kit
Althea Henley . . . . Cynthia
Carol Wines . . . . Daisy Elmore
Adele Windsor . . . . Minnie
Richard Keene . . . . Dick
Elizabeth and Helen Keating . . . . . May and June
Robert Burns . . . . Slim
John Swor . . . . Clem
Pat Somerset . . . . Beauchamp
Joe Brown . . . . Deputy warden
Harvey Clark . . . . Nash
Black and Blue . . . . Slim and Klem
Robert Parrish

1931 *Seas Beneath* (Fox)

Director: John Ford
Scenarist: Dudley Nichols, from story by James Parker, Jr.
Photographer: Joseph H. August
Editor: Frank E. Hull
George O'Brien . . . . *Comdr. Bob Kingsley, USN*
Marion Lessing . . . . Anna M. Von Steuben
Warren Hymer . . . . "Lug" Kaufman
William Collier, Sr. . . . . "Mugs" O'Flaherty
John Loder . . . . Franz Schilling
Walter C. "Judge" Kelly . . . . Chief Mike Costello
Walter McGrail . . . . Joe Cobb
Henry Victor . . . . Ernst Von Steuben, Commandant, U-boat 172
Mona Maris . . . . Lolita
Larry Kent . . . . Lt. MacGregor
Gaylord Pendleton . . . . Ens. Dick Cabot
Nat Pendleton . . . . "Butch" Wagner
Harry Tenbrook . . . . Winkler
Terry Ray . . . . Reilly
Hans Furberg . . . . Fritz Kampf, second officer, U-172
Ferdinand Schumann-Heink . . . . . Adolph Brucker, engineer, U-172
Francis Ford . . . . Trawler captain

(Seas Beneath, cont.)

Kurt Furberg	Hoffman
Ben Hall	Harrigan
Harry Weil	Jevinsky
Maurice Murphy	Merkel

1931 *The Brat* (Fox)

Director:	John Ford
Scenarists:	Sonya Levien, S. N. Behrman, Maude Fulton, from play by Fulton
Photographer:	Joseph H. August
Editor:	Alex Troffey
Sally O'Neil	*The brat*
Alan Dinehart	MacMillan Forester
Frank Albertson	Stephen Forester
Virginia Cherrill	Angela
June Collyer	Jane
J. Farrell McDonald	Timson, the butler
William Collier, Sr.	Judge
Margaret Mann	Housekeeper
Albert Gran	Bishop
Mary Forbes	Mrs. Forester
Louise MacIntosh	Lena

1931 *Arrowsmith* (Goldwyn-United Artists)

Director:	John Ford
Producer:	Samuel Goldwyn
Scenarist:	Sidney Howard, from novel by Sinclair Lewis
Photographer:	Ray June
Art Director:	Richard Day
Music:	Alfred Newman
Editor:	Hugh Bennett
Ronald Colman	*Dr. Martin Arrowsmith*
Helen Hayes	Leora
A. E. Anson	Prof. Gottlieb
Richard Bennett	Sondelius
Claude King	Dr. Tubbs
Beulah Bondi	Mrs. Tozer
Myrna Loy	Joyce Lanyon
Russell Hopton	Terry Wickett
De Witt Jennings	Mr. Tozer
John Qualen	Henry Novak
Adele Watson	Mrs. Novak
Lumsden Hare	Sir Robert Fairland
Bert Roach	Bert Tozer
Charlotte Henry	A young girl
Clarence Brooks	Oliver Marchand
Walter Downing	City clerk
David Landau	

James Marcus
Alec B. Francis
Sidney McGrey
Florence Britton
Bobby Watson

1932   *Air Mail* (Universal)

Director:	John Ford
Producer:	Carl Laemmle, Jr.
Scenarists:	Dale Van Every, Lt. Comdr. Frank W. Wead, from story by Wead
Photographer:	Karl Freund
Special effects:	John P. Fulton
Aerial stunts:	Paul Mantz

Pat O'Brien . . . . *Duke Talbot*
Ralph Bellamy . . . . Mike Miller
Gloria Stuart . . . . Ruth Barnes
Lillian Bond . . . . Irene Wilkins
Russell Hopton . . . . "Dizzy" Wilkins
Slim Summerville . . . . "Slim" McCune
Frank Albertson . . . . Tommy Bogan
Leslie Fenton . . . . Tony Dressel
David Landau . . . . "Pop"
Tom Corrigan . . . . "Sleepy" Collins
William Daly . . . . "Tex" Lane
Hans Furberg . . . . "Heinie" Kramer
Lew Kelly . . . . Drunkard
Frank Beal, Francis Ford, James
   Donlan, Louise MacIntosh,
   Katherine Perry . . . . Passengers
Beth Milton . . . . Plane attendant
Edmund Burns . . . . Radio announcer
Charles de la Montte, Lt. Pat Davis . . Passenger plane pilots
Jim Thorpe . . . . Indian
Enrico Caruso, Jr.
Billy Thorpe
Alene Carroll
Jack Pennick

1932   *Flesh* (Metro-Goldwyn-Mayer)

Director:	John Ford
Scenarists:	Leonard Praskins, Edgar Allen Woolf, from story by Edmund Goulding
Dialogue:	Moss Hart
Photographer:	Arthur Edeson
Editor:	William S. Gray

Wallace Beery . . . . *Polakai*
Karen Morley . . . . Lora
Ricardo Cortez . . . . Nicky

(Flesh, cont.)

Jean Hersholt	Mr. Herman
John Miljan	Joe Willard
Vince Barnett	Waiter
Herman Bing	Pepi
Greta Meyer	Mrs. Herman
Ed Brophy	Dolan
Ward Bond	
Nat Pendleton	

1933 *Pilgrimage* (Fox)

Director:	John Ford
Scenarists:	Philip Klein, Barry Connors, from story, "Gold Star Mother," by I. A. R. Wylie
Dialogue:	Dudley Nichols
Photographer:	George Schneiderman
Art Director:	William Darling
Music:	R. H. Bassett
Editor:	Louis R. Loeffler
Assistant Director:	Edward O'Fearna
Henrietta Grosman	*Hannah Jessop*
Heather Angel	Suzanne
Norman Foster	Jim Jessop
Marian Nixon	Mary Saunders
Maurice Murphy	Gary Worth
Lucille Laverne	Mrs. Hatfield
Charley Grapewin	Dad Saunders
Hedda Hopper	Mrs. Worth
Robert Warwick	Maj. Albertson
Betty Blythe	Janet Prescot
Francis Ford	Mayor
Louise Carter	Mrs. Rogers
Jay Ward	Jim Saunders
Francis Rich	Nurse
Adele Watson	Mrs. Simms

1933 *Dr. Bull* (Fox)

Director:	John Ford
Scenarist:	Paul Green, from novel, *The Last Adam,* by James Gould Cozzens
Dialogue:	Jane Storm
Photographer:	George Schneiderman
Music:	Samuel Kaylin
Will Rogers	*Dr. Bull*
Marian Nixon	May Tripping
Berton Churchill	Herbert Banning
Louise Dresser	Mrs. Banning
Howard Lally	Joe Tripping
Rochelle Hudson	Virginia Banning

Vera Allen . . . . Janet Carmaker
Tempe Pigotte . . . . Grandma
Elizabeth Patterson . . . . Aunt Patricia
Ralph Morgan . . . . Dr. Verney
Andy Devine . . . . Larry Ward
Nora Cecil . . . . Aunt Emily
Patsy O'Byrne . . . . Susan
Effie Ellsler . . . . Aunt Myra
Veda Buckland . . . . Mary
Helen Freeman . . . . Helen Upjohn
Robert Parrish

1934 *The Lost Patrol* (RKO Radio)

Director: John Ford
Executive Producer: Merian C. Cooper
Associate Producer: Cliff Reid
Scenarists: Dudley Nichols, Garrett Fort, from
                                     story, "Patrol," by Philip
                                     MacDonald
Photographer: Harold Wenstrom
Art Directors: Van Nest Polglase, Sidney Ullman
Music: Max Steiner
Editor: Paul Weatherwax
Victor McLaglen . . . . *The sergeant*
Boris Karloff . . . . Sanders
Wallace Ford . . . . Morelli
Reginald Denny . . . . George Brown
J. M. Kerrigan . . . . Quincannon
Billy Bevan . . . . Herbert Hale
Alan Hale . . . . Cook
Brandon Hurst . . . . Bell
Douglas Walton . . . . Pearson
Sammy Stein . . . . Abelson
Howard Wilson . . . . Flyer
Neville Clark . . . . Lt. Hawkins
Paul Hanson . . . . Jock Mackay
Francis Ford

1934 *The World Moves On* (Fox)

Director: John Ford
Producer: Winfield Sheehan
Writer: Reginald C. Berkeley
Photographer: George Schneiderman
Art Director: William Darling
Set Decorator: Thomas Little
Costumes: Rita Kaufman
Music: Max Steiner, Louis De Francesco,
                                     R. H. Bassett, David Buttolph,
                                     Hugo Friedhofer, George Gersh-
                                     win

(The World Moves On, cont.)

Songs:	"Should She Desire Me Not," by De Francesco, "Ave Maria," by Charles Gounod
Madeleine Carroll	*Mrs. Warburton 1824; Mary Warburton,* 1914
Franchot Tone	Richard Girard, 1924 and 1914
Lumsden Hare	Gabriel Warburton, 1824; Sir John Warburton, 1914
Raul Roulien	Carlos Girard, 1824; Henri Girard, 1914
Reginald Denny	Erik Von Gerhardt
Siegfried Rumann	Baron Von Gerhardt
Louise Dresser	Baroness Von Gerhardt
Stepin' Fetchit	Dixie
Dudley Diggs	Mr. Manning
Frank Melton	John Girard, 1824
Brenda Fowler	Mrs. Girard, 1824
Russell Simpson	Notary public, 1824
Walter McGrail	French duelist, 1824
Marcelle Corday	Miss Girard, 1824
Charles Bastin	Jacques Girard, 1914
Barry Norton	Jacques Girard, 1929
George Irving	Charles Girard, 1914
Ferdinand Schumann-Heink	Fritz Von Gerhardt
Georgette Rhodes	Jeanne Girard, 1914
Claude King	Braithwaite
Ivan Simpson	Clumber
Frank Moran	Culbert
Jack Pennick, Francis Ford	Legionnaires
Torbin Mayer	German chamberlain, 1914

1934 *Judge Priest* (Fox)

Director:	John Ford
Producer:	Sol M. Wurtzel
Scenarists:	Dudley Nichols, Lamar Trotti, from stories by Irvin S. Cobb
Photographer:	George Schneiderman
Music:	Samuel Kaylin
Will Rogers	*Judge William "Billy" Priest*
Henry B. Walthall	Rev. Ashby Brand
Tom Brown	Jerome Priest
Anita Louise	Ellie May Gillespie
Rochelle Hudson	Virginia Maydew
Berton Churchill	Senator Horace K. Maydew
David Landau	Bob Gillis
Brenda Fowler	Mrs. Caroline Priest
Hattie McDaniel	Aunt Dilsey
Stepin' Fetchit	Jeff Poindexter
Frank Melton	Flem Tally

Roger Imhof . . . . Billy Gaynor
Charley Grapewin . . . . Sgt. Jimmy Bagby
Francis Ford . . . . Juror No. 12
Paul McAllister . . . . Doc Lake
Matt McHugh . . . . Gabby Rives
Hy Meyer . . . . Herman Feldsburg
Louis Mason . . . . Sheriff Birdsong
Robert Parrish

1935 *The Whole Town's Talking* (Columbia)

Director: John Ford
Producer: Lester Cowan
Scenarist: Jo Swerling, from novel by W. R.
                               Burnett
Dialogue: Robert Riskin
Photographer: Joseph H. August
Editor: Viola Lawrence
Assistant Director: Wilbur McGaugh
Edward G. Robinson . . . . *Arthur Ferguson Jones; "Killer" Mannion*
Jean Arthur . . . . Miss "Bill" Clark
Wallace Ford . . . . Mr. Healy
Arthur Byron . . . . Mr. Spencer
Arthur Hohl . . . . Det. Sgt. Michael Boyle
Donald Meek . . . . Mr. Hoyt
Paul Harvey . . . . J. G. Carpenter
Edward Brophy . . . . "Slugs" Martin
J. Farrell McDonald . . . . Warden
Etienne Girardot . . . . Mr. Seaver
James Donlan . . . . Howe
John Wray . . . . Henchman
Effie Ellsler . . . . Aunt Agatha
Robert Emmett O'Connor . . . . . . Police Lt.
Joseph Sawyer
Francis Ford
Robert Parrish

1935 *The Informer* (RKO Radio)

Director: John Ford
Associate Producer: Cliff Reid
Scenarist: Dudley Nichols, from novel by Liam
                               O'Flaherty
Photographer: Joseph H. August
Art Directors: Van Nest Polglase, Charles Kirk
Set Decorator: Julia Heron
Costumes: Walter Plunkett
Music: Max Steiner
Editor: George Hively
Victor McLaglen . . . . *Gypo Nolan*

(The Informer, cont.)

Heather Angel	Mary McPhillip
Preston Foster	Dan Gallagher
Margot Grahame	Katie Madden
Wallace Ford	Frankie McPhillip
Una O'Connor	Mrs. McPhillip
J. M. Kerrigan	Terry
Joseph Sawyer	Bartley Mulholland
Neil Fitzgerald	Tommy Conner
Donald Meek	Pat Mulligan
D'Arcy Corrigan	The blindman
Leo McCabe	Donahue
Gaylord Pendleton	Daley
Francis Ford	"Judge" Flynn
May Boley	Mrs. Betty
Grizelda Harvey	An obedient girl
Dennis O'Dea	Street singer
Jack Mulhall	Look-out
Robert Parrish	Soldier
Clyde Cook	
Barlowe Borland	
Frank Moran	
Arthur McLaglen	

1935   *Steamboat Round the Bend* (20th Century-Fox)

Director:	John Ford
Producer:	Sol M. Wurtzel
Scenarists:	Dudley Nichols, Lamar Trotti, from story by Ben Lucian Burman
Photographer:	George Schneiderman
Art Director:	William Darling
Set Decorator:	Albert Hogsett
Music Director:	Samuel Kaylin
Editor:	Alfred De Gaetano
Assistant Director:	Edward O'Fearna
Will Rogers	*Dr. John Pearly*
Anne Shirley	Fleety Belle
Eugene Pallette	Sheriff Rufe Jeffers
John McGuire	Duke
Berton Churchill	The New Moses
Stepin' Fetchit	George Lincoln Washington
Francis Ford	Efe
Irvin S. Cobb	Capt. Eli
Roger Imhof	Pappy
Raymond Hatton	Matt Abel
Hobart Bosworth	Chaplain
Louis Mason	Boat-race organizer
Charles B. Middleton	Fleety's father
Si Jenks	A drunk
Jack Pennick	Ringleader of boat attack

1936 *The Prisoner of Shark Island* (20th Century-Fox)

Director:	John Ford
Producer:	Darryl F. Zanuck
Associate Producer-Scenarist:	Nunnally Johnson, from life of Dr. Samuel A. Mudd
Photography:	Bert Glennon
Art Director:	William Darling
Set Decorator:	Thomas Little
Music Director:	Louis Silvers
Editor:	Jack Murray
Assistant Director:	Edward O'Fearna

Warner Baxter . . . . *Dr. Samuel A. Mudd*
Gloria Stuart . . . . Mrs. Peggy Mudd
Claude Gillingwater . . . . Col. Dyer
Arthur Byron . . . . Mr. Ericson
O.P. Heggie . . . . Dr. McIntyre
Harry Carey . . . . Commandant of Fort Jefferson, 'Shark Island'
Francis Ford . . . . Cpl. O'Toole
John Carradine . . . . Sgt. Rankin
Frank McGlynn, Sr. . . . . Abraham Lincoln
Douglas Wood . . . . Gen. Ewing
Joyce Kay . . . . Martha Mudd
Fred Kohler, Jr. . . . . Sgt. Cooper
Francis McDonald . . . . John Wilkes Booth
John McGuire . . . . Lt. Lovell
Ernest Whitman . . . . Buckland Montmorency "Buck" Tilford
Paul Fix . . . . David Herold
Frank Shannon . . . . Holt
Leila McIntyre . . . . Mrs. Lincoln
Etta McDaniel . . . . Rosabelle Tilford
Arthur Loft . . . . Carpetbagger
Paul McVey . . . . Gen. Hunter
Maurice Murphy . . . . Orderly
Jack Pennick . . . . Soldier who sends flag messages
J. M. Kerrigan . . . . Judge Maiben
Whitney Bourne
Robert Parrish

1936 *Mary of Scotland* (RKO Radio)

Director:	John Ford
Producer:	Pandro S. Berman
Scenarist:	Dudley Nichols, from play by Maxwell Anderson
Photography:	Joseph H. August
Art Directors:	Van Nest Polglase, Carroll Clark
Set Decorator:	Darrell Silvera
Costumes:	Walter Plunkett
Music:	Max Steiner

(Mary of Scotland, cont.)

Editor:	Jane Loring
Assistant Editor:	Robert Parrish
Special effects:	Vernon L. Walker
Katharine Hepburn	*Mary Stuart*
Fredric March	Bothwell
Florence Eldridge	Elizabeth
Douglas Walton	Darnley
John Carradine	David Rizzio
Monte Blue	Messager
Jean Fenwick	Mary Seton
Robert Barrat	Morton
Gavin Muir	Leicester
Ian Keith	James Stuart Moray
Moroni Olsen	John Knox
Donald Crisp	Huntley
William Stack	Ruthven
Molly Lamont	Mary Livingston
Walter Byron	Sir Francis Walsingham
Ralph Forbes	Randolph
Alan Mowbray	Throckmorton
Frieda Inescort	Mary Beaton
David Torrence	Lindsay
Anita Colby	Mary Fleming
Lionel Belmore	English fisherman
Doris Lloyd	His wife
Bobby Watson	His son
Lionel Pape	Burghley
Ivan Simpson, Murray Kinnell, Lawrence Grant, Nigel DeBrulier, Barlowe Borland	Judges
Alec Craig	Donal
Mary Gordon	Nurse
Wilfred Lucas	Lexington
Leonard Mudie	Maitland
Brandon Hurst	Arian
D'Arcy Corrigan	Kirkcaldy
Frank Baker	Douglas
Cyril McLaglen	Faudoncide
Robert Warwick	Sir Francis Knellys
Earle Foxe	Duke of Kent
Wyndham Standing	Sergeant
Gaston Glass	Chatelard
Neil Fitzgerald	Nobleman
Paul McAllister	Du Croche

1936   *The Plough and the Stars* (RKO Radio)

Director:	John Ford
Associate Producers:	Cliff Reid, Robert Sisk
Scenarist:	Dudley Nichols, from play by Sean O'Casey

Photography: Joseph H. August
Art Director: Van Nest Polglase
Music: Nathaniel Shilkret, Roy Webb
Editor: George Hively
Barbara Stanwyck . . . . *Mora Clitheroe*
Preston Foster . . . . Jack Clitheroe
Barry Fitzgerald . . . . Fluther Good
Dennis O'Dea . . . . The Young Covey
Eileen Crowe . . . . Bessie Burgess
Arthur Shields . . . . Padraic Pearse
Erin O'Brien Moore . . . . Rosie Redmond
Brandon Hurst . . . . Sgt. Tinley
F. J. McCormick . . . . Capt. Brennon
Una O'Conner . . . . Maggie Corgan
Moroni Olsen . . . . Gen. Connolly
J. M. Kerrigan . . . . Peter Flynn
Neil Fitzgerald . . . . Lt. Kangon
Bonita Granville . . . . Mollser Gogan
Cyril McLaglen . . . . Cpl. Stoddart
Robert Homans . . . . Barman
Mary Gordon . . . . First woman
Mary Quinn . . . . Second woman
Lionel Pape . . . . The Englishman
Michael Fitzmaurice . . . . ICA
Gaylord Pendleton . . . . ICA
Doris Lloyd
D'Arcy Corrigan
Wesley Barry

1937   *Wee Willie Winkie* (20th Century-Fox)

Director: John Ford
Producer: Darryl F. Zanuck
Associate Producer: Gene Markey
Scenarists: Ernest Pascal, Julian Josephson, from
                                              story by Rudyard Kipling
Photography: Arthur Miller
Set Decorator: Thomas Little
Music: Louis Silvers
Editor: Walter Thompson
Shirley Temple . . . . *Priscilla Williams*
Victor McLaglen . . . . Sgt. MacDuff
C. Aubrey Smith . . . . Col. Williams
June Lang . . . . Joyce Williams
Michael Whalen . . . . Lt. "Coppy" Brandes
Cesar Romero . . . . Khoda Khan
Constance Collier . . . . Mrs. Allardyce
Douglas Scott . . . . Mott
Gavin Muir . . . . Capt. Bibberbeigh
Willie Fung . . . . Mohammed Dihn
Brandon Hurst . . . . Bagby
Lionel Pape . . . . Maj. Allardyce

(Wee Willie Winkie, cont.)

Clyde Cook	Pipe Maj. Sneath
Lauri Beatty	Elsie Allardyce
Lionel Braham	Maj. Gen. Hammond
Mary Forbes	Mrs. MacMonachie
Cyril McLaglen	Cpl. Tummel
Pat Somerset	Officer
Hector Sarno	Conductor

1937   *The Hurricane* (Goldwyn-United Artists)

Director:	John Ford
Producer:	Samuel Goldwyn
Associate Producer:	Merrit Hulburd
Scenarist:	Dudley Nichols, from novel by Charles Nordhoff, James Norman Hall, adapted by Oliver H. P. Garrett
Associate Director:	Stuart Heisler
Hurricane sequence:	James Basevi
Photography:	Bert Glennon, Archie Stout (second-unit)
Art Directors:	Richard Day, Alex Golitzen
Set Decorator:	Julia Heron
Costumes:	Omar Kiam
Music:	Alfred Newman
Editor:	Lloyd Nosler
Sound recording:	Thomas Moulton
Assistant Director:	Wingate Smith
Dorothy Lamour	*Marama*
Jon Hall	Terangi
Mary Astor	Mrs. DeLaage
C. Aubrey Smith	Father Paul
Thomas Mitchell	Dr. Kersaint
Raymond Massey	Mr. DeLaage
John Carradine	Guard
Jerome Cowan	Capt. Nagle
Al Kikume	Chief Meheir
Kuulei DeClercq	Tita
Layne Tom, Jr.	Mako
Mamo Clark	Hitia
Movita Castenada	Arai
Reri	Reri
Francis Kaai	Tavi
Pauline Steele	Mata
Flora Hayes	Mama Rua
Mary Shaw	Marunga
Spencer Charters	Judge
Roger Drake	Captain of the guards
Inez Courtney	Girl on boat
Paul Stader	

1938   *Four Men and a Prayer* (20th Century-Fox)

Director:	John Ford
Producer:	Darryl F. Zanuck
Associate Producer:	Kenneth Macgowan
Scenarists:	Richard Sherman, Sonya Levien, Walter Ferris, from novel by David Garth
Photography:	Ernest Palmer
Art Directors:	Bernard Herzbrun, Rudolph Sternad
Set Decorator:	Thomas Little
Music:	Louis Silvers, Ernst Toch
Editor:	Louis R. Loeffler

Loretta Young . . . . *Lynn Cherrington*
Richard Greene . . . . Jeffrey Leigh
George Sanders . . . . Wyatt Leigh
David Niven . . . . Christopher Leigh
William Henry . . . . Rodney Leigh
C. Aubrey Smith . . . . Col. Loring Leigh
J. Edward Bromberg . . . . Gen. Torres
Alan Hale . . . . Farnoy
John Carradine . . . . Gen. Adolfo Arturo Sebastian
Reginald Denny . . . . Douglas Loveland
Berton Churchill . . . . Martin Cherrington
Claude King . . . . Gen. Bryce
John Sutton . . . . Capt. Drake
Barry Fitzgerald . . . . Mulcahy
Cecil Cunningham . . . . Pyer
Frank Baker . . . . Defense attorney
Frank Dawson . . . . Mullins
Lina Basquette . . . . Ah-Nee
William Stack . . . . Prosecuting attorney
Harry Hayden . . . . Cherrington's secretary
Winter Hall . . . . Judge
Will Stanton . . . . Cockney
John Spacey, C. Montague Shaw . . . Lawyers
Lionel Pape . . . . Coroner
Brandon Hurst . . . . Jury foreman

1938   *Submarine Patrol* (20th Century-Fox)

Director:	John Ford
Producer:	Darryl F. Zanuck
Associate Producer:	Gene Markey
Scenarists:	Rian James, Darrell Ware, Jack Yellen, from novel, *The Splinter Fleet,* by John Milholland
Photography:	Arthur Miller
Art Directors:	William Darling, Hans Peters
Set Decorator:	Thomas Little
Music Director:	Arthur Lange
Editor:	Robert Simpson

(*Submarine Patrol, cont.*)
Richard Greene . . . . *Perry Townsend, III*
Nancy Kelly . . . . Susan Leeds
Preston Foster . . . . Lt. John C. Drake
George Bancroft . . . . Capt. Leeds
Slim Summerville . . . . Ellsworth "Spotts" Ficketts
Joan Valerie . . . . Anne
John Carradine . . . . McAllison
Warren Hymer . . . . Rocky Haggerty
Henry Armetta . . . . Luigi
Douglas Fowley . . . . Brett
J. Farrell McDonald . . . . Quincannon
Dick Hogan . . . . Johnny
Maxie Rosenbloom . . . . Sgt. Joe Duffy
Ward Bond . . . . Olaf Swanson
Robert Lowery . . . . Sparks
Charles Tannen . . . . Kelly
George E. Stone . . . . Irving
Moroni Olsen . . . . Capt. Wilson
Jack Pennick . . . . Guns McPeck
Elisha Cook, Jr. . . . . "Professor" Pratt
Harry Strang . . . . Grainger
Charles Trowbridge . . . . Admiral Joseph Maitland
Victor Varconi . . . . Chaplain
Murry Alper . . . . Sailor
E. E. Clive

1939   *Stagecoach* (Wanger-United Artists)

Director-Producer: John Ford
Executive Producer: Walter Wanger
Scenarist: Dudley Nichols, from story, "Stage to
                                      Lordsburg," by Ernest Haycox
Photography: Bert Glennon
Art Director: Alexander Toluboff
Set Decorator: Wiard B. Ihnen
Costumes: Walter Plunkett
Music (adapted from 17 American
  folk tunes of early 1880's):   Richard Hageman, W. Franke
                                      Harling, John Leipold, Leo
                                      Shuken, Louis Gruenberg
Editorial Supervisor: Otho Lovering
Editors: Dorothy Spencer, Walter Reynolds
Second Unit Director: Yakima Canutt
Assistant Director: Wingate Smith
John Wayne . . . . *The Ringo Kid*
Claire Trevor . . . . Dallas
John Carradine . . . . Hatfield
Thomas Mitchell . . . . Dr. Josiah Boone
Andy Devine . . . . Buck
Donald Meek . . . . Samuel Peacock
Louise Platt . . . . Lucy Mallory

Tim Holt . . . . Lt. Blanchard
George Bancroft . . . . Sheriff Curly Wilcox
Berton Churchill . . . . Henry Gatewood
Tom Tyler . . . . Hank Plummer
Chris Pin Martin . . . . Chris
Elvira Rios . . . . Yakima, his wife
Francis Ford . . . . Billy Pickett
Marga Daighton . . . . Mrs. Pickett
Kent Odell . . . . Billy Pickett, Jr.
Yakima Canutt, Chief Big Tree . . . . Stuntmen
Harry Tenbrook . . . . Telegraph operator
Jack Pennick . . . . Jerry, barman
Paul McVey . . . . Express agent
Cornelius Keefe . . . . Capt. Whitney
Florence Lake . . . . Mrs. Nancy Whitney
Louis Mason . . . . Sheriff
Brenda Fowler . . . . Mrs. Gatewood
Walter McGrail . . . . Capt. Sickel
Joseph Rickson . . . . Luke Plummer
Vester Pegg . . . . Ike Plummer
William Hoffer . . . . Sergeant
Bryant Washburn . . . . Capt. Simmons
Nora Cecil . . . . Dr. Boone's housekeeper
Helen Gibson, Dorothy Annleby . . . Dancing girls
Buddy Roosevelt, Bill Cody . . . . . . Ranchers
Chief White Horse . . . . Indian chief
Duke Lee . . . . Sheriff of Lordsburg
Mary Kathleen Walker . . . . Lucy's baby
Ed Brady
Steve Clemente
Theodore Larch
Fritzi Brunette
Leonard Trainor
Chris Phillips
Tex Driscoll
Teddy Billings
John Eckert
Al Lee
Jack Mohr
Patsy Doyle
Wiggie Blowne
Margaret Smith

1939 *Young Mr. Lincoln* (Cosmopolitan-20th Century-Fox)

Director:	John Ford
Executive Producer:	Darryl F. Zanuck
Producer:	Kenneth Macgowan
Scenarist:	Lamar Trotti, based on life of Abraham Lincoln
Photography:	Bert Glennon
Art Directors:	Richard Day, Mark Lee Kirk

(*Young Mr. Lincoln, cont.*)

Set Decorator:	Thomas Little
Music:	Alfred Newman
Editor:	Walter Thompson
Sound-effects Editor:	Robert Parrish
Henry Fonda	*Abraham Lincoln*
Alice Brady	Abigail Clay
Marjorie Weaver	Mary Todd
Arleen Whelan	Hannah Clay
Eddie Collins	Efe Turner
Pauline Moore	Ann Rutledge
Richard Cromwell	Matt Clay
Ward Bond	John Palmer Cass
Donald Meek	John Felder
Spencer Charters	Judge Herbert A. Bell
Eddie Quillan	Adam Clay
Judith Dickens	Carrie Sue
Milburn Stone	Stephen A. Douglas
Cliff Clark	Sheriff Billings
Robert Lowery	Juror
Charles Tannen ·	Ninian Edwards
Francis Ford	Sam Boone
Fred Kohler, Jr.	Scrub White
Kay Linaker	Mrs. Edwards
Russell Simpson	Woolridge
Charles Halton	Hawthorne
Edwin Maxwell	John T. Stuart
Robert Homans	Mr. Clay
Jack Kelly	Matt Clay, as child
Dicky Jones	Adam Clay, as child
Harry Tyler	Hairdresser
Louis Mason	Court clerk
Jack Pennick	Big Buck
Steven Randall	Juror
Clarence Wilson	
Elizabeth Jones	

1939 *Drums Along the Mohawk* (20th Century-Fox)

Director:	John Ford
Executive producer:	Darryl F. Zanuck
Producer:	Raymond Griffith
Scenarists:	Lamar Trotti, Sonya Levien, from novel by Walter D. Edmonds
Photography (in color):	Bert Glennon, Ray Rennahan
Art Directors:	Richard Day, Mark Lee Kirk
Set Decorator:	Thomas Little
Music:	Alfred Newman
Editor:	Robert Simpson
Sound-effects Editor:	Robert Parrish
Claudette Colbert	*Lana Borst Martin*
Henry Fonda , ...	Gilbert Martin

Edna May Oliver	Mrs. McKlennan
Eddie Collins	Christian Reall
John Carradine	Caldwell
Dorris Bowdon	Mary Reall
Jessie Ralph	Mrs. Weaver
Arthur Shields	Father Rosenkranz
Robert Lowery	John Weaver
Roger Imhof	General Nicholas Herkimer
Francis Ford	Joe Boleo
Ward Bond	Adam Hartmann
Kay Linaker	Mrs. Demooth
Russell Simpson	Dr. Petry
Chief Big Tree	Blue Back
Spencer Charters	Fisk, innkeeper
Arthur Aysleworth	George
Si Jenks	Jacobs
Jack Pennick	Amos
Charles Tannen	Robert Johnson
Paul McVey	Capt. Mark Demooth
Elizabeth Jones	Mrs. Reall
Lionel Pape	General
Clarence Wilson	Paymaster
Edwin Maxwell	Pastor
Clara Blandick	Mrs. Borst
Beulah Hall Jones	Daisy
Robert Greig	Mr. Borst
Mae Marsh	

1940   *The Grapes of Wrath* (20th Century-Fox)

Director:	John Ford
Producer:	Darryl F. Zanuck
Associate Producer-Scenarist:	Nunnally Johnson, from novel by John Steinbeck
Photography:	Gregg Toland
Art Directors:	Richard Day, Mark Lee Kirk
Set Decorator:	Thomas Little
Music:	Alfred Newman
Song, "Red River Valley," played on accordion by:	Dan Borzage
Editor:	Robert Simpson
Sound:	George Leverett, Roger Heman
Sound-effects Editor:	Robert Parrish
Assistant Director:	Edward O'Fearna
Henry Fonda	*Tom Joad*
Jane Darwell	Ma Joad
John Carradine	Casey
Charley Grapewin	Grampa Joad
Dorris Bowdon	Rosasharn
Russell Simpson	Pa Joad
O. Z. Whitehead	Al
John Qualen	Muley

(The Grapes of Wrath, cont.)

Eddie Quillan	Connie
Zeffie Tilbury	Grandma Joad
Frank Sully	Noah
Frank Darien	Uncle John
Darryl Hickman	Winfield
Shirley Mills	Ruth Joad
Grant Mitchel	Guardian
Ward Bond	Policeman
Frank Faylen	Tim
Joe Sawyer	Accountant
Harry Tyler	Bert
Charles B. Middleton	Conductor
John Arledge	Davis
Hollis Jewell	Muley's son
Paul Guilfoyle	Floyd
Charles D. Brown	Wilkie
Roger Imhof	Thomas
William Pawley	Bill
Arthur Aysleworth	Father
Charles Tannen	Joe
Selmar Jackson	Inspector
Eddie C. Waller	Proprietor
David Hughes	Frank
Cliff Clark	Townsman
Adrian Morris	Agent
Robert Homans	Spencer
Irving Bacon	Conductor
Kitty McHugh	Mae
Mae Marsh	
Francis Ford	
Jack Pennick	

1940 *The Long Voyage Home* (Wanger-United Artists)

Director:	John Ford
Producer:	Walter Wanger
Scenarist:	Dudley Nichols, from one-act plays, "The Moon of the Caribbees," "In the Zone," "Bound East for Cardiff," "The Long Voyage Home," by Eugene O'Neill
Photography:	Gregg Toland
Art Director:	James Basevi
Set Decorator:	Julia Heron
Music:	Richard Hageman
Editor:	Sherman Todd
Sound Editor:	Robert Parrish
Special effects:	Ray Binger, R. T. Layton
Thomas Mitchell	*Aloysius Driscoll*
John Wayne	Ole Olsen
Ian Hunter	Thomas Fenwick, "Smitty"

Barry Fitzgerald . . . . Cocky
Wilfred Lawson . . . . Captain
Mildred Natwick . . . . Freda
John Qualen . . . . Axel Swanson
Ward Bond . . . . Yank
Joe Sawyer . . . . Davis
Arthur Shields . . . . Donkeyman
J. M. Kerrigan . . . . Crimp
David Hughes . . . . Scotty
Billy Bevan . . . . Joe
Cyril McLaglen . . . . Mate
Robert E. Perry . . . . Paddy
Jack Pennick . . . . Johnny Bergman
Constantin Frenke . . . . Narvey
Constantin Romanoff . . . . Big Frank
Dan Borzage . . . . Tim
Harry Tenbrook . . . . Max
Douglas Walton . . . . Second lieutenant
Raphaela Ottiano . . . . Daughter of the tropics
Carmen Morales, Carmen d'Antonio . Girls in canoe
Harry Woods . . . . The admiral's sailor
Edgar "Blue" Washington
Lionel Pape
Jane Crowley
Maureen Roden-Ryan

1941   *Tobacco Road* (20th Century-Fox)

Director: John Ford
Producer: Darryl F. Zanuck
Associate Producers: Jack Kirkland, Harry H. Oshrin
Scenarist: Nunnally Johnson, from play by
                                     Kirkland and novel by Erskine
                                     Caldwell
Photography: Arthur Miller
Art Directors: Richard Day, James Basevi
Set Decorator: Thomas Little
Music: David Buttolph
Editor: Barbara McLean
Sound-effects Editor: Robert Parrish
Charley Grapewin . . . . *Jeeter Lester*
Marjorie Rambeau . . . . Sister Bessie
Gene Tierney . . . . Ellie May Lester
William Tracy . . . . Dude Lester
Elizabeth Patterson . . . . Ada Lester
Dana Andrews . . . . Dr. Tim
Slim Summerville . . . . Henry Peabody
Ward Bond . . . . Lov Bensey
Grant Mitchell . . . . George Payne
Zeffie Tilbury . . . . Grandma Lester
Russell Simpson . . . . Sheriff
Spencer Charters . . . . Employee

(Tobacco Road, cont.)

Irving Bacon	Teller
Harry Tyler	Auto salesman
George Chandler	Employee
Charles Halton	Mayor
Jack Pennick	Deputy sheriff
Dorothy Adams	Payne's secretary
Francis Ford	Vagabond

1941 *Sex Hygiene* (Audio Productions-U.S. Army)

Director:	John Ford
Producer:	Darryl F. Zanuck
Photographer:	George Barnes
Editor:	Gene Fowler, Jr.

Charles Trowbridge

1941 *How Green Was My Valley* (20th Century-Fox)

Director:	John Ford
Producer:	Darryl F. Zanuck
Scenarist:	Philip Dunne, from novel by Richard Llewellyn
Photography:	Arthur Miller
Art Directors:	Richard Day, Nathan Juran
Set Decorator:	Thomas Little
Costumes:	Gwen Wakeling
Music:	Alfred Newman
Choral effects:	Eisteddfod Singers of Wales
Editor:	James B. Clark
Narrator:	Rhys Williams
Walter Pidgeon	*Mr. Gruffydd*
Maureen O'Hara	Angharad Morgan
Donald Crisp	Mr. Morgan
Anna Lee	Bronwen Morgan
Roddy McDowall	Huw Morgan
John Loder	Ianto Morgan
Sara Allgood	Mrs. Beth Morgan
Barry Fitzgerald	Cyfartha
Patrick Knowles	Ivor Morgan
The Welsh Singers	Singers
Morton Lowery	Mrs. Jonas
Arthur Shields	Mr. Parry
Ann Todd	Ceiwen
Frederick Worlock	Dr. Richards
Richard Fraser	Davy Morgan
Evan S. Evans	Gwinlyn
James Monks	Owen Morgan
Rhys Williams	Dai Bando
Lionel Pape	Old Evans
Ethel Griffies	Mrs. Nicholas
Marten Lamont	Jestyn Evans

Mae Marsh . . . . Miner's wife
Louis Jean Heydt . . . . Miner
Denis Hoey . . . . Motschell
Tudor Williams . . . . Singer
Clifford Severn
Eve March

1942 *The Battle of Midway* (U. S. Navy-20th Century-Fox)

Director-Photographer:	Lt. Comdr. John Ford, U.S.N.R.
Narration:	Ford, Dudley Nichols, James Kevin McGuinness
Additional photography:	Jack McKenzie
Music:	Alfred Newman
Editors:	Ford, Robert Parrish
Voices of:	Henry Fonda, Jane Darwell, Donald Crisp

1942 *Torpedo Squadron* (U.S. Navy)

Director:	Lt. Comdr. John Ford, U.S.N.R.

1943 *December 7th* (U. S. Navy)

Directors:	Lt. Gregg Toland, U.S.N.R., Lt. Comdr. John Ford, U.S.N.R.
Photography:	Toland
Second-unit director:	James C. Havens, U.S.M.C.
Music:	Alfred Newman
Editor:	Robert Parrish

1943 *We Sail at Midnight* (Crown Film Unit-U. S. Navy)

Director:	Lt. Comdr. John Ford, U.S.N.R.
Narration written by:	Clifford Odets
Music:	Richard Addinsell

1945 *They Were Expendable* (Metro-Goldwyn-Mayer)

Director-Producer:	John Ford
Associate Producer:	Cliff Reid
Scenarist:	Frank W. Wead, from book by William L. White
Photography:	Joseph H. August
Art Directors:	Cedric Gibbons, Malcolm F. Brown
Set Decorators:	Edwin B. Willis, Ralph S. Hurst
Music:	Herbert Stothart
Editors:	Frank E. Hull, Douglas Biggs
Second-unit Director:	James C. Havens (rear projection plates by Robert Montgomery)
Assistant Director:	Edward O'Fearna

Robert Montgomery . . . . *Lt. John Brickley*
John Wayne . . . . Lt. Rusty Ryan

(They Were Expendable, cont.)

Donna Reed	Lt. Sandy Davis
Jack Holt	Gen. Martin
Ward Bond	Boots Mulcahey
Louis Jean Heydt	Ohio, flyer in hospital
Marshall Thompson	Snake Gardner
Russell Simpson	Dad, chief of shipyard
Leon Ames	Maj. Morton
Paul Langton	Andy Andrews
Arthur Walsh	Jones
Donald Curtis	Shory
Cameron Mitchell	George Cross
Jeff York	Tony Aiken
Murray Alper	Slug Mahan
Harry Tenbrook	Larsen
Jack Pennick	Doc Charlie
Charles Trowbridge	Adm. Blackwell
Robert Barrat	General
Bruce Kellogg	Tomkins
Tim Murdock	Brant
Vernon Steele	Doctor
Alex Havler	Benny
Wallace Ford	
Tom Tyler	

1946 *My Darling Clementine* (20th Century-Fox)

Director:	John Ford
Producer:	Samuel G. Engel
Scenarists:	Engel, Winston Miller, from story by Sam Hellman, based on book, *Wyatt Earp, Frontier Marshal,* by Stuart N. Lake
Photography:	Joseph P. MacDonald
Art Directors:	James Basevi, Lyle R. Wheeler
Set Decorators:	Thomas Little, Fred J. Rode
Costumes:	Rene Hubert
Music:	Cyril J. Mockridge
Editor:	Dorothy Spencer
Assistant Director:	William Eckhardt
Henry Fonda	*Wyatt Earp*
Linda Darnell	Chihuahua
Victor Mature	Doc John Holliday
Walter Brennan	Old Man Clanton
Tim Holt	Virgil Earp
Ward Bond	Morgan Earp
Cathy Downs	Clementine Carter
Alan Mowbray	Granville Thorndyke
John Ireland	Billy Clanton
Grant Withers	Ike Clanton
Roy Roberts	Mayor
Jane Darwell	Kate Nelson
Russell Simpson	John Simpson

Francis Ford . . . . Dad, old soldier
J. Farrell McDonald . . . . Mac, barman
Don Garner . . . . James Earp
Ben Hall . . . . Barber
Arthur Walsh . . . . Hotel clerk
Jack Pennick . . . . Coach driver
Louis Mercier . . . . Francois
Micky Simpson . . . . Sam Clanton
Fred Libby . . . . Phin Clanton
Harry Woods . . . . Luke
Charles Stevens . . . . Indian Joe
Danny Borzage . . . . Accordion Player
Mae Marsh

1947 *The Fugitive* (Argosy Pictures-RKO Radio)

Director:	John Ford
Producers:	Ford, Merian C. Cooper
Associate Producer:	Emilio Fernandez
Scenarist:	Dudley Nichols, from novel, *The Labyrinthine Ways* (or *The Power and the Glory*), by Graham Greene
Photography:	Gabriel Figueroa
Art Director:	Alfred Ybarra
Set Decorator:	Manuel Parra
Music:	Richard Hageman
Editor:	Jack Murray
Executive Assistant:	Jack Pennick
Directorial Assistant:	Melchor Ferrer
Assistant Director:	Jesse Hibbs

Henry Fonda . . . . *The Fugitive*
Dolores Del Rio . . . . Mexican woman
Pedro Armendariz . . . . Police lieutenant
Ward Bond . . . . El Gringo
Leo Carrillo . . . . Chief of police
J. Carroll Naish . . . . Police spy
Robert Armstrong . . . . Police sergeant
John Qualen . . . . Doctor
Fortunio Bonanova . . . . Governor's cousin
Chris Pin Martin . . . . Organ player
Miguel Inclan . . . . Hostage
Fernando Fernandez . . . . Singer
Jose I. Torvay . . . . A Mexican
Melchor Ferrer

1948 *Fort Apache* (Argosy Pictures-RKO Radio)

Director:	John Ford
Producers:	Ford, Merian C. Cooper
Scenarist:	Frank S. Nugent, from story, "Massacre," by James Warner Bellah
Photography:	Archie Stout

(Fort Apache, cont.)

Art Director:	James Basevi
Set Decorator:	Joe Kish
Music:	Richard Hageman
Second-unit Director:	Cliff Lyons
Production Manager:	Bernard McEveety
Assistant Directors:	Lowell Farrell, Jack Pennick

John Wayne . . . . *Capt. Kirby York*
Henry Fonda . . . . Lt. Col. Owen Thursday
Shirley Temple . . . . Philadelphia Thursday
John Agar . . . . Lt. Michael O'Rourke
Ward Bond . . . . Sgt. Maj. O'Rourke
George O'Brien . . . . Capt. Sam Collingwood
Victor McLaglen . . . . Sgt. Mulcahy
Pedro Armendariz . . . . Sgt. Beaufort
Anna Lee . . . . Mrs. Collingwood
Irene Rich . . . . Mrs. O'Rourke
Guy Kibbee . . . . Dr. Wilkens
Grant Withers . . . . Silas Meacham
Miguel Inclan . . . . Cochise
Jack Pennick . . . , ... Sgt. Schattuck
Mae Marsh . . . . Mrs. Gates
Dick Foran . . . . Sgt. Quincannon
Frank Ferguson . . . . Newspaperman
Francis Ford . . . . Bartender
Ray Hyke
Movita Castenada
Mary Gordon

1948 *Three Godfathers* (Argosy Pictures-Metro-Goldwyn-Mayer)

Director:	John Ford
Producers:	Ford, Merian C. Cooper
Scenarists:	Laurence Stallings, Frank S. Nugent, from story by Peter B. Kyne
Photography (in color):	Winton C. Hoch, Charles P. Boyle (second unit)
Art Director:	James Basevi
Set Decorator:	Joe Kish
Music:	Richard Hageman
Editor:	Jack Murray
Production Manager:	Lowell Farrell
Assistant Directors:	Wingate Smith, Edward O'Fearna

John Wayne . . . . *Robert Marmaduke Sangster Hightower*
Pedro Armendariz . . . . Pedro Roca Fuerte
Harry Carey, Jr. . . . . William Kearney, "The Abilene Kid"
Ward Bond . . . . Perley "Buck" Sweet
Mildred Natwick . . . . Mother
Charles Halton . . . . Mr. Latham
Jane Darwell . . . . Miss Florie
Mae Marsh . . . . Mrs. Perley Sweet
Guy Kibbee . . . . , ... , , Judge

Dorothy Ford   . . . . Ruby Latham
Ben Johnson, Michael Dugan, Don
    Summers . . . . Patrolmen
Fred Libby   . . . . Deputy sheriff
Hank Worden   . . . . Deputy sheriff
Jack Pennick   . . . . Luke, train conductor
Francis Ford   . . . . Drunk

1949 *She Wore A Yellow Ribbon* (Argosy Pictures-RKO Radio)

Director:	John Ford
Producers:	Ford, Merian C. Cooper
Associate Producer:	Lowell Farrell
Scenarists:	Frank S. Nugent, Laurence Stallings, from story, "War Party," by James Warner Bellah
Photography (in color):	Winton C. Hoch, Charles P. Boyle (second-unit)
Art Director:	James Basevi
Set Decorator:	Joe Kish
Music:	Richard Hageman
Editor:	Jack Murray
Assistant Editor:	Barbara Ford
Second-unit Director:	Cliff Lyons
Assistant Directors:	Wingate Smith, Edward O'Fearna

John Wayne   . . . . *Capt. Nathan Brittles*
Joanne Dru . . . . Olivia
John Agar   . . . . Lt. Flint Cohill
Ben Johnson   . . . . Sgt. Tyree
Harry Carey, Jr.   . . . . Lt. Pennell
Victor McLaglen   . . . . Sgt. Quincannon
Mildred Natwick   . . . . Mrs. Allshard
George O'Brien   . . . . Maj. MacAllshard
Arthur Shields   . . . . Dr. O'Laughlin
Francis Ford   . . . . Barman
Harry Woods   . . . . Karl Rynders
Chief Big Tree   . . . . Pony-That-Walks
Noble Johnson   . . . . Red Shirt
Cliff Lyons   . . . . Trooper Cliff
Tom Tyler   . . . . Quayne
Michael Dugan   . . . . Hochbauer
Mickey Simpson   . . . . Wagner
Fred Graham   . . . . Hench
Frank McGrath   . . . . Trumpeter
Don Summers   . . . . Jenkins
Fred Libby   . . . . Col. Krumrein
Jack Pennick   . . . . Sergeant major
Billy Jones   . . . . Courier
Bill Gettinger   . . . . Officer
Fred Kennedy   . . . . Badger
Rudy Bowman   . . . . Pvt. Smith
Post Park   . . . . Officer

(She Wore A Yellow Ribbon, cont.)
Ray Hyke . . . . McCarthy
Lee Bradley . . . . Interpreter
Chief Sky Eagle
Dan White

1950   ***When Willie Comes Marching Home*** (20th Century-Fox)
Director: John Ford
Producer: Fred Kohlmar
Scenarists: Mary Loos, Richard Sale, from
                                 story, "When Leo Comes
                                 Marching Home," by Sy Gom-
                                 berg
Photography: Leo Tover
Art Directors: Lyle R. Wheeler, Chester Gore
Set Decorators: Thomas Little, Bruce MacDonald
Music: Alfred Newman
Editor: James B. Clark
Assistant Director: Wingate Smith
Dan Dailey . . . . *Bill Kluggs*
Corinne Calvet . . . . Yvonne
Colleen Townsend . . . . Marge Fettles
William Demarest . . . . Herman Kluggs
James Lydon . . . . Charles Fettles
Lloyd Corrigan . . . . Mayor Adams
Evelyn Varden . . . . Gertrude Kluggs
Kenny Williams . . . . Musician
Lee Clark . . . . Musician
Charles Halton . . . . Mr. Fettles
Mae Marsh . . . . Mrs. Fettles
Jack Pennick . . . . Sergeant-instructor
Mickey Simpson . . . . M. P. Kerrigan
Frank Pershing . . . . Maj. Bickford
Don Summers . . . . M. P. Sherve
Gil Herman . . . . Lt. Comdr. Crown
Peter Ortiz . . . . Pierre
Luis Alberni . . . . Barman
John Shulick . . . . Pilot
Clarke Gordon, Robin Hughes   . . . . Marine officers
Cecil Weston . . . . Mrs. Barnes
Harry Tenbrook . . . . Joe, taxi driver
Russ Clark . . . . Sgt. Wilson
George Spaulding . . . . Judge Tate
James Eagle . . . . Reporter
Harry Strang . . . . Sergeant
George Magrill . . . . Chief petty officer
Hank Worden . . . . Choir leader
John McKee . . . . Pilot
Larry Keating . . . . Gen. G. Reeding
Dan Riss . . . . Gen. Adams
Robert Einer . . . . Lt. Bagley

Russ Conway . . . . Maj. J. A. White
Whit Bissell . . . . Lt. Handley
Ann Codee . . . . French instructor
Ray Hyke . . . . Maj. Crawford
Gene Collins . . . . Andy
James Flavin . . . . Gen. Brevort
David McMahon . . . . Col. Ainsley
Charles Trowbridge . . . . Gen. Merrill
Kenneth Tobey . . . . Lt. K. Geiger
Maj. Sam Harris . . . . Hospital patient
Alberto Morin, Louis Mercier . . . . . Resistance fighters
Paul Harvey . . . . Officer
James Waters
Ken Lynch

1950   *Wagonmaster* (Argosy Pictures-RKO Radio)

Director: John Ford
Producers: Ford, Merian C. Cooper
Associate Producer: Lowell Farrell
Writers: Frank S. Nugent, Patrick Ford from
                                   an original story by John Ford.
Photography: Bert Glennon, Archie Stout (second
                                   unit)
Art Director: James Basevi
Set Decorator: Joe Kish
Music: Richard Hageman
Songs: "Wagons West," "Rollin' Shadows in
                                   the Dust," "Song of the Wagon
                                   Master," "Chuck-A-Walla-Swing,"
                                   by Stan Jones, sung by The Sons
                                   of the Pioneers
Editor: Jack Murray
Assistant Editor: Barbara Ford
Second-unit Director: Cliff Lyons
Assistant Director: Wingate Smith
Ben Johnson . . . . *Travis Blue*
Harry Carey, Jr. . . . . Sandy Owens
Joanne Dru . . . . Denver
Ward Bond . . . . Elder Wiggs
Charles Kemper . . . . Uncle Shiloh Clegg
Alan Mowbray . . . . Dr. A. Locksley Hall
Jane Darwell . . . . Sister Ledeyard
Ruth Clifford . . . . Fleuretty Phyffe
Russell Simpson . . . . Adam Perkins
Kathleen O'Malley . . . . Prudence Perkins
James Arness . . . . Floyd Clegg
Fred Libby . . . . Reese Clegg
Hank Worden . . . . Luke Clegg
Mickey Simpson . . . . Jesse Clegg
Francis Ford . . . . Mr. Peachtree
Cliff Lyons , , ... Sheriff of Crystal City

(Wagonmaster, cont.)

Don Summers	Sam Jenkins
Movita Castenada	Young Navajo girl
Jim Thorpe	Navajo
Chuck Hayward	

1950 *Rio Grande* (Argosy Pictures-Republic)

Director:	John Ford
Producers:	Ford, Merian C. Cooper
Scenarist:	James Kevin McGuinness, from story, "Mission with No Record," by James Warner Bellah
Photography:	Bert Glennon, Archie Stout (second-unit)
Art Director:	Frank Hotaling
Set Decorators:	John McCarthy, Jr., Charles Thompson
Music:	Victor Young
Songs:	"My Gal Is Purple," "Footsore Cavalry," "Yellow Stripes," by Stan Jones; "Aha, San Antone," by Dale Evans; "Cattle Call," by Tex Owens; and "Erie Canal," "I'll Take You Home Again, Kathleen," "Down by the Glen Side," "You're in the Army Now," sung by The Sons of the Pioneers
Editor:	Jack Murray
Assistant Editor:	Barbara Ford
Second-unit Director:	Cliff Lyons
John Wayne	*Lt. Col. Kirby Yorke*
Maureen O'Hara	Mrs. Yorke
Ben Johnson	Trooper Tyree
Claude Jarman, Jr.	Trooper Jeff Yorke
Harry Carey, Jr.	Trooper Daniel Boone
Chill Wills	Dr. Wilkins
J. Carroll Naish	Gen. Philip Sheridan
Victor McLaglen	Sgt. Quincannon
Grant Withers	Deputy marshal
Peter Ortiz	Capt. St. Jacques
Steve Pendleton	Capt. Prescott
Karolyn Grimes	Margaret Mary
Alberto Morin	Lieutenant
Stan Jones	Sergeant
Fred Kennedy	Heinze
Jack Pennick, Pat Wayne, Chuck Roberson, The Sons of the Pioneers (Ken Curtis, Hugh Farr, Karl Farr, Lloyd Perryman, Shug Fisher, Tommy Doss)	Regimental singers

1951 *This Is Korea!* (U.S. Navy-Republic)

Director:	Rear Adm. John Ford, U.S.N.R.
Voices of:	John Ireland, others

1952 *What Price Glory* (20th Century-Fox)

Director:	John Ford
Producer:	Sol C. Siegel
Scenarists:	Phoebe and Henry Ephron, from play by Maxwell Anderson, Laurence Stallings
Photography (in color):	Joseph MacDonald
Art Directors:	Lyle R. Wheeler, George W. Davis
Set Decorators:	Thomas Little, Stuart A. Reiss
Music:	Alfred Newman
Song, "My Love, My Life," by	Jay Livingston, Roy Evans
Editor:	Dorothy Spencer

James Cagney . . . . *Capt. Flagg*
Corinne Calvet . . . . Charmaine
Dan Dailey . . . . Sgt. Quirt
William Demarest . . . . Cpl. Kiper
Craig Hill . . . . Lt. Aldrich
Robert Wagner . . . . Lewisohn
Marisa Pavan . . . . Nicole Bouchard
Casey Adams . . . . Lt. Moore
James Gleason . . . . Gen. Cokely
Wally Vernon . . . . Lipinsky
Henry Letondal . . . . Cognac Pete
Fred Libby . . . . Lt. Schmidt
Ray Hyke . . . . Mulcahy
Paul Fix . . . . Gowdy
James Lilburn . . . . Young soldier
Henry Morgan . . . . Morgan
Dan Borzage . . . . Gilbert
Bill Henry . . . . Holsen
Henry "Bomber" Kulkovich . . . . . . Company cook
Jack Pennick . . . . Ferguson
Ann Codee . . . . Nun
Stanley Johnson . . . . Lt. Cunningham
Tom Tyler . . . . Capt. Davis
Olga Andre . . . . Sister Clotilde
Barry Norton . . . . Priest
Luis Alberni . . . . The great uncle
Torben Meyer . . . . Mayor
Alfred Zeisler . . . . English colonel
George Bruggeman . . . . English lieutenant
Scott Forbes . . . . Lt. Bennett
Sean McClory . . . . Lt. Austin
Charles FitzSimmons . . . . Capt. Wickham
Lewis Mercier . . . . Bouchard

(*What Price Glory, cont.*)
Mickey Simpson . . . . M.P.
Peter Oriz
Paul Guilfoyle

                  1952   *The Quiet Man* (Argosy Pictures-Republic)
Director: John Ford
Producers: Ford, Merian C. Cooper
Scenarist: Frank S. Nugent, from story by
                                          Maurice Walsh
Photography (in color):   Winton C. Hoch, Archie Stout
                                          (second-unit)
Art Director: Frank Hotaling
Set Decorators: John McCarthy, Jr., Charles
                                          Thompson
Music: Victor Young
Songs: "The Isle of Innisfree," by Richard
                                          Farrelly; "Galway Bay," by Dr.
                                          Arthur Colahan, Michael Donovan;
                                          "The Humour Is on Me Now," by
                                          Richard Hayward; "The Young
                                          May Moon," by Thomas Moore;
                                          and "The Wild Colonial Boy,"
                                          "Mush-Mush-Mush"
Editor: Jack Murray
Assistant Editor: Barbara Ford
Second-unit Directors (uncredited):   John Wayne, Patrick Ford
Assistant Director: Andrew McLaglen
John Wayne . . . . *Sean Thornton*
Maureen O'Hara . . . . Mary Kate Danaher
Barry Fitzgerald . . . . Michaeleen Oge Flynn
Ward Bond . . . . Father Peter Lonergan
Victor McLaglen . . . . Red Will Danaher
Mildred Natwick . . . . Mrs. Sarah Tillane
Francis Ford . . . . Dan Tobin
Eileen Crowe . . . . Mrs. Elizabeth Playfair
May Craig . . . . Woman at railroad station
Arthur Shields . . . . Reverend Cyril Playfair
Charles FitzSimmons . . . . Forbes
Sean McClory . . . . Owen Glynn
James Lilburn . . . . Father Paul
Jack MacGowran . . . . Feeney
Ken Curtis . . . . Dermot Fahy
Mae Marsh . . . . Father Paul's mother
Harry Tenbrook . . . . Policeman
Maj. Sam Harris . . . . General
Joseph O'Dea . . . . Guard
Eric Gorman . . . . Railroad conductor
Kevin Lawless . . . . Fireman
Paddy O'Donnell . . . . Porter
Webb Overlander . . . . Railroad station chief
Hank Worden . . . . Trainer in flashback

Patrick Wayne
Elizabeth Jones
Antonia Wayne
Melinda Wayne

1953   *The Sun Shines Bright* (Republic)

Director:	John Ford
Producers:	Ford, Merian C. Cooper
Scenarist:	Laurence Stallings, from stories, "The Sun Shines Bright," "The Mob from Massac," "The Lord Provides," by Irvin S. Cobb
Photography:	Archie Stout
Art Director:	Frank Hotaling
Set Decorators:	John McCarthy, George Milo
Music:	Victor Young
Editor:	Jack Murray
Assistant Editor:	Barbara Ford
Assistant Director:	Wingate Smith

Charles Winninger . . . . *Judge William Pittman Priest*
Arleen Whelan . . . . Lucy Lee Lake
John Russell . . . . Ashby Corwin
Stepin' Fetchit . . . . Jeff Poindexter
Russell Simpson . . . . Dr. Lewt Lake
Ludwig Stossel . . . . Herman Felsburg
Francis Ford . . . . Feeney
Paul Hurst . . . . Sgt. Jimmy Bagby
Mitchell Lewis . . . . Andy Redcliffe
Grant Withers . . . . Buck Ramsey
Milburn Stone . . . . Horace K. Maydew
Dorothy Jordan . . . . Lucy's mother
Elzie Emanuel . . . . U.S. Grant Woodford
Henry O'Neil . . . . Jody Habersham
Slim Pickens . . . . Sterling
James Kirkwood . . . . Gen. Fairfield
Mae Marsh . . . . Old lady at ball
Jane Darwell . . . . Amora Ratchitt
Ernest Whitman . . . . Uncle Pleasant Woodford
Trevor Bardette . . . . Rufe, leader of lynch mob
Hal Baylor . . . . His son
Eve March . . . . Mallie Cramp
Clarence Muse . . . . Uncle Zach
Jack Pennick . . . . Beaker
Ken Williams
Patrick Wayne

1953   *Mogambo* (Metro-Goldwyn-Mayer)

Director:	John Ford
Producer:	Sam Zimbalist
Scenarist:	John Lee Mahin, from play, *Red Dust*, by Wilson Collison

(Mogambo, cont.)
Photography (in color):   Robert Surtees, Fredrick A. Young
Art Director: Alfred Junge
Costumes: Helen Rose
Editor: Frank Clarke
Second-unit Directors: Richard Rosson, Yakima Canutt,
                          James C. Havens

Assistant Directors: Wingate Smith, Cecil Ford
Clark Gable . . . . *Victor Marswell*
Ava Gardner . . . . Eloise Y. Kelly
Grace Kelly . . . . Linda Nordley
Donald Sinden . . . . Donald Nordley
Philip Stainton . . . . John Brown Pryce
Eric Pohlmann . . . . Leon Boltchak
Laurence Naismith . . . . Skipper
Dennis O'Dea . . . . Father Joseph
Asa Etula . . . . Young native girl
Wagenia Tribe
Samburu Tribe
Bahaya Tribe
M'Beti Tribe

1955 *The Long Gray Line* (Rota Productions-Columbia)
Director: John Ford
Producer: Robert Arthur
Scenarist: Edward Hope, from autobiography,
                        Bringing Up the Brass, by Marty
                        Maher with Nardi Reeder Campion

Photography (in color and
  CinemaScope):   Charles Lawton, Jr.
Art Director: Robert Peterson
Set Decorator: Frank Tuttle
Music adaptation: George Duning
Editor: William Lyon
Assistant Directors: Wingate Smith, Jack Corrick
Tyrone Power . . . . *Martin Maher*
Maureen O'Hara . . . . Mary O'Donnell
Robert Francis . . . . James Sundstrom, Jr.
Donald Crisp . . . . Old Martin
Ward Bond . . . . Capt. Herman J. Koehler
Betsy Palmer . . . . Kitty Carter
Phil Carey . . . . Charles Dotson
William Leslie . . . . Red Sundstrom
Harry Carey, Jr. . . . . Dwight Eisenhower
Patrick Wayne . . . . Cherub Overton
Sean McClory . . . . Dinny Maher
Peter Graves . . . . Capt. Rudolph Heinz
Milburn Stone . . . . Capt. John Pershing
Erin O'Brien-Moore . . . . Mrs. Koehler

Walter D. Ehlers . . . . Mike Shannon
Don Barclay   . . . . Maj. Thomas
Martin Milner   . . . . Jim O'Carberry
Chuck Courtney   . . . . Whitey Larson
Willis Bouchey . . . . Doctor
Jack Pennick   . . . . Sergeant

1955   *Mister Roberts* (Orange Productions-Warner Bros.)

Directors: John Ford, Mervyn LeRoy
Producer: Leland Hayward
Scenarists: Frank S. Nugent, Joshua Logan, from
                                    play by Logan, Thomas Heggen,
                                    and novel by Heggen

Photography (in color and
  CinemaScope):   Winton C. Hoch
Art Director: Art Loel
Set Decorator: William L. Kuehl
Music: Franz Waxman
Editor: Jack Murray
Assistant Director: Wingate Smith
Henry Fonda . . . . *Lt. Roberts*
James Cagney   . . . . Captain
Jack Lemmon   . . . . Ens. Frank Thurlowe Pulver
William Powell . . . . Doc
Ward Bond . . . . C. P. O. Dowdy
Betsy Palmer . . . . Lt. Ann Girard
Phil Carey   . . . . Mannion
Nick Adams   . . . . Reber
Harry Carey, Jr.   . . . . Stefanowski
Ken Curtis   . . . . Dolan
Frank Aletter . . . . Gerhart
Fritz Ford . . . . Lidstrom
Buck Kartalian   . . . . Mason
William Henry   . . . . Lt. Billings
William Hudson   . . . . Olson
Stubby Kruger   . . . . Schlemmer
Harry Tenbrook   . . . . Cookie
Perry Lopez   . . . . Rodrigues
Robert Roark . . . . Insigna
Pat Wayne   . . . . Bookser
Tige Andrews   . . . . Wiley
Jim Moloney   . . . . Kennedy
Denny Niles   . . . . Gilbert
Francis Conner   . . . . Johnson
Shug Fisher   . . . . Cochran
Danny Borzage   . . . . Jonesey
Jim Murphy   . . . . Taylor
Kathleen O'Malley, Maura Murphy,
  Mimi Doyle, Jeanne
  Murray-Vanderbilt, Lonnie Pierce   . Nurses
Martin Milner   . . . . Shore patrol officer

(Mister Roberts, cont.)
Gregory Walcott . . . . Shore Patrolman
James Flavin   . . . . M.P.
Jack Pennick   . . . . Marine sergeant
Duke Kahanamoko   . . . . Native chief

1955   ***Rookie of the Year*** (Hal Roach Studios; episode for the *Screen Directors Playhouse* television series)

Director: John Ford
Scenarist: Frank S. Nugent
Pat Wayne   . . . . *Lyn Goodhue*
Vera Miles   . . . . Rose Goodhue
Ward Bond   . . . . Larry Goodhue, alias Buck Garrison
James Gleason   . . . . Ed
Willis Bouchey   . . . . Newspaper editor
John Wayne   . . . . Mike, a reporter

1955   ***The Bamboo Cross*** (Lewman Ltd.-Revue; episode for the *Fireside Theater* television series)

Director: John Ford
Producer: William Asher
Scenarist: Laurence Stallings, from play by
                                 Theophane Lee
Photographer: John MacBurnie
Art Director: Martin Obzina
Set Decorator: James S. Redd
Music Supervisor: Stanley Wilson
Supervising Editor: Richard G. Wray
Assistant Director: Wingate Smith
Jane Wyman   . . . . *Sister Regina*
Betty Lynn   . . . . Sister Anne
Soo Yong . . . . Sichi Sao
Jim Hong . . . . Mark Chu
Judy Wong . . . . Tanya
Don Summers   . . . . Ho Kwong
Kurt Katch   . . . . King Fat
Pat O'Malley   . . . . Priest
Frank Baker   . . . . Bit man

1956   ***The Searchers*** (C. V. Whitney Pictures-Warner Bros.)

Director: John Ford
Producers: Merian C. Cooper, C. V. Whitney
Associate Producer: Patrick Ford
Scenarist: Frank S. Nugent from the novel by
                                 Alan LeMay.
Photography (in color and
  VistaVision):   Winton C. Hoch, Alfred Gilks
                                 (second-unit)
Art Directors: Frank Hotaling, James Basevi

Set Decorator: Victor Gangelin
Music: Max Steiner
Title song: Stan Jones
Editor: Jack Murray
Production Supervisor: Lowell Farrell
Assistant Director: Wingate Smith
John Wayne . . . . *Ethan Edwards*
Jeffrey Hunter . . . . Martin Pawley
Vera Miles . . . . Laurie Jorgensen
Ward Bond . . . . Capt. Rev. Samuel Clayton
Natalie Wood . . . . Debbie Edwards
John Qualen . . . . Lars Jorgensen
Olive Carey . . . . Mrs. Jorgensen
Henry Brandon . . . . Chief Scar
Ken Curtis . . . . Charlie McCorry
Harry Carey, Jr. . . . . Brad Jorgensen
Antonio Moreno . . . . Emilio Figueroa
Hank Worden . . . . Mose Harper
Lana Wood . . . . Debbie as a child
Walter Coy . . . . Aaron Edwards
Dorothy Jordan . . . . Martha Edwards
Pippa Scott . . . . Lucy Edwards
Pat Wayne . . . . Lt. Greenhill
Beulah Archuletta . . . . Look
Jack Pennick . . . . Private
Peter Mamakos . . . . Futterman
Cliff Lyons, Billy Cartledge, Chuck
   Hayward, Slim Hightower, Fred
   Kennedy, Frank McGrath, Chuck
   Roberson, Dale van Sickle, Henry
   Wills, Terry Wilson . . . . Stunt men
Away Luna, Billy Yellow, Bob Many
   Mules, Exactly Sonnie Betsuie,
   Feather Hat, Jr., Harry Black
   Horse, Jack Tin Horn, Many Mules
   Son, Percy Shooting Star, Pete
   Grey Eyes, Pipe Line Begishe,
   Smile White Sheep . . . . Comanches
Mae Marsh
Dan Borzage

1957   *The Wings of Eagles* (Metro-Goldwyn-Mayer)

Director: John Ford
Producer: Charles Schnee
Associate Producer: James E. Newcom
Scenarists: Frank Fenton, William Wister
                                        Haines, based on life and writings
                                        of Commander Frank W. Wead,
                                        USN.
Art Directors: William A. Horning, Malcolm Brown
Set Decorators: Edwin B. Willis, Keogh Gleason

(The Wings of Eagles, cont.)

Costumes:	Walter Plunkett
Music:	Jeff Alexander
Editor:	Gene Ruggiero
Aerial stunts:	Paul Mantz
Assistant Director:	Wingate Smith

John Wayne . . . . *Frank W. "Spig" Wead*
Maureen O'Hara . . . . Minnie Wead
Dan Dailey . . . . Carson
Ward Bond . . . . John Dodge
Ken Curtis . . . . John Dale Price
Edmund Lowe . . . . Adm. Moffett
Kenneth Tobey . . . . Herbert Allen Hazard
James Todd . . . . Jack Travis
Barry Kelley . . . . Capt. Jock Clark
Sig Ruman . . . . Manager
Henry O'Neill . . . . Capt. Spear
Willis Bouchey . . . . Barton
Dorothy Jordan . . . . Rose Brentmann
Peter Ortiz . . . . Lt. Charles Dexter
Louis Jean Heydt . . . . Dr. John Keye
Tige Andrews . . . . "Arizona" Pincus
Dan Borzage . . . . Pete
William Tracy . . . . Air Force officer
Harlan Warde . . . . Executive officer
Jack Pennick . . . . Joe
Bill Henry . . . . Naval aide
Alberto Morin . . . . Second manager
Mimi Gibson . . . . Lila Wead
Evelyn Rudie . . . . Doris Wead
Charles Trowbridge . . . . Adm. Crown
Mae Marsh . . . . Nurse Crumley
Janet Lake . . . . Nurse
Fred Graham . . . . Officer in brawl
Stuart Holmes . . . . Producer
Olive Carey . . . . Bridy O'Faolain
Maj. Sam Harris . . . . Patient
May McEvoy . . . . Nurse
William Paul Lowery . . . . Wead's baby, "Commodore"
Chuck Roberson . . . . Officer
Cliff Lyons
Veda Ann Borg
Christopher James

1957 *The Rising of the Moon* (Four Provinces Productions-Warner Bros.)

Director:	John Ford
Producer:	Michael Killanin
Scenarist:	Frank S. Nugent, from story "The Majesty of the Law," by Frank O'Connor, and plays, *A Minute's Wait,* by Michael J. McHugh, *The Rising of the Moon,* by Lady Gregory

Photography: Robert Krasker
Art Director: Ray Simm
Costumes: Jimmy Bourke
Music: Eamonn O'Gallagher
Editor: Michael Gordon
Introduction: *Tyrone Power*
The Majesty of the Law
Noel Purcell . . . . *Dan O'Flaherty*
Cyril Cusack . . . . Inspector Michael Dillon
Jack MacGowran . . . . Mickey J.
Eric Gorman . . . . Neighbor
Paul Farrell . . . . Neighbor
John Cowley . . . . The Gombeen Man
A Minute's Wait
Jimmy O'Dea . . . . Porter
Tony Quinn . . . . Railroad station chief
Paul Farrell . . . . Chauffeur
J. G. Devlin . . . . Guard
Michael Trubshawe . . . . Col. Frobisher
Anita Sharp Bolster . . . . Mrs. Frobisher
Maureen Potter . . . . Barmaid
Godfrey Quigley . . . . Christy
Harold Goldblatt . . . . Christy's father
Maureen O'Connell . . . . May Ann McMahon
May Craig . . . . May's aunt
Michael O'Duffy . . . . Singer
Ann Dalton . . . . Fisherman's wife
1921
Dennis O'Dea . . . . Police sergeant
Eileen Crowe . . . . His wife
Maurice Good . . . . P. C. O'Grady
Frank Lawton . . . . Major
Edward Lexy . . . . R.Q.M.S.
Donal Donnelly . . . . Sean Curran
Joseph O'Dea . . . . Chief of guards
Dennis Brennan, David Marlow . . . English officers
Doreen Madden, Maureen Cusack . . False nuns
Maureen Delaney . . . . Old woman
Members of the Abbey Theater
   Company

1958 *So Alone* (Free Cinema-British Film Institute)

Director: John Ford
Photography: Winton Hoch, Walter Lassally
Music: Malcolm Arnold
John Qualen, James Hayter . . . . . . *Two minstrels*

1958 *The Last Hurrah* (Columbia)

Director-Producer: John Ford
Scenarist: Frank S. Nugent, from novel by
                                 Edwin O'Conner

(The Last Hurrah, cont.)

Photography:	Charles Lawton, Jr.
Art Director:	Robert Peterson
Set Decorator:	William Kiernan
Editor:	Jack Murray
Assistant Directors:	Wingate Smith, Sam Nelson
Spencer Tracy	*Frank Skeffington*
Jeffrey Hunter	Adam Caulfield
Dianne Foster	Maeve Caulfield
Pat O'Brien	John Gorman
Basil Rathbone	Norman Cass, Sr.
Donald Crisp	The cardinal
James Gleason	Cuke Gillen
Edward Brophy	Ditto Boland
John Carradine	Amos Force
Willis Bouchey	Roger Sugrue
Basil Ruysdael	Bishop Gardner
Ricardo Cortez	Sam Weinberg
Wallace Force	Charles J. Hennessey
Frank McHugh	Festus Garvey
Anna Lee	Gert Minihan
Jane Darwell	Delia Boylan
Frank Albertson	Jack Mangan
Charles FitzSimmons	Kevin McCluskey
Carleton Young	Mr. Winslow
Bob Sweeney	Johnny Degnan
Edmund Lowe	Johnny Byrne
William Leslie	Dan Herlihy
Ken Curtis	Monseigneur Killian
O. Z. Whitehead	Norman Cass, Jr.
Arthur Walsh	Frank Skeffington, Jr.
Helen Westcott	Mrs. McCluskey
Ruth Warren	Ellen Davin
Mimi Doyle	Mamie Burns
Dan Borzage	Pete
James Flavin	Police captain
William Forrest	Doctor
Frank Sully	Fire chief
Charlie Sullivan	Chauffeur
Ruth Clifford	Nurse
Jack Pennick	Policeman
Richard Deacon	Plymouth Club Director
Harry Tenbrook	
Eve March	
Bill Henry	
James Waters	

1959 *Gideon of Scotland Yard (Gideon's Day)* (Columbia British Productions-Columbia)

Director:	John Ford
Producer:	Michael Killanin

Associate Producer: Wingate Smith
Scenarist: T. E. B. Clarke, from novel *Gideon's Day,* by J. J. Marric (pseudonym for John Creasey)

Photography (in color but released in
  black and white):   Frederick A. Young
Art Director: Ken Adam
Music: Douglas Gamley
Editor: Raymond Poulton
Assistant Director: Tom Pevsner
Jack Hawkins . . . . *Inspector George Gideon*
Dianne Foster . . . . Joanna Delafield
Anna Massey . . . . Sally Gideon
Cyril Cusack . . . . Herbert "Birdie" Sparrow
Andrew Ray . . . . P.C. Simon Farnaby-Green
James Hayter . . . . Mason
Ronald Howard . . . . Paul Delafield
Howard Marion-Crawford . . . . Chief of Scotland Yard
Laurence Naismith . . . . Arthur Sayer
Derek Bond . . . . Det. Sgt. Eric Kirby
Griselda Harvey . . . . Mrs. Kirby
Frank Lawton . . . . Det. Sgt. Liggott
Anna Lee . . . . Mrs. Kate Gideon
John Loder . . . . Ponsford, "The Duke"
Doreen Madden . . . . Miss Courtney
Miles Malleson . . . . Judge at Old Bailey
Marjorie Rhodes . . . . Mrs. Saparelli
Michael Shelpley . . . . Sir Rupert Bellamy
Michael Trubshawe . . . . Sgt. Golightly
Jack Watling . . . . Rev. Julian Small
Hermione Bell . . . . Dolly Saparelli
Donal Donnelly . . . . Feeney
Billie Whitelaw . . . . Christine
Malcolm Ranson . . . . Ronnie Gideon
Mavis Ranson . . . . Jane Gideon
Francis Crowdy . . . . Fitzhubert
David Aylmer . . . . Manners
Brian Smith . . . . White-Douglas
Barry Keegan . . . . Riley, chauffeur
Maureen Potter . . . . Ethel Sparrow
Henry Longhurst . . . . Rev. Mr. Courtney
Charles Maunsell . . . . Walker
Stuart Saunders . . . . Chancery Lane policeman
Dervis Ward . . . . Simmo
Joan Ingram . . . . Lady Bellamy
Nigel Fitzgerald . . . . Insp. Cameron
Robert Raglan . . . . Dawson
John Warwick . . . . Insp. Gillick
John Le Mesurier . . . . Prosecuting attorney
Peter Godsell . . . . Jimmy
Robert Bruce . . . . Defending attorney

(Gideon of Scotland Yard (Gideon's Day), cont.)

Alan Rolfe	C.I.D. man at hospital
Derek Prentice	First employer
Alastair Hunter	Second employer
Helen Goss	Woman employer
Susan Richmond	Aunt May
Raymond Rollett	Uncle Dick
Lucy Griffiths	Cashier
Mary Donevan	Usherette
O'Donovan Shiell, Bart Allison, Michael O'Duffy	Policemen
Diana Chesney	Barmaid
David Storm	Court Clerk
Gordon Harris	C.I.D. man

1959 *Korea* (U. S. Department of Defense)

Director:	Rear Adm. John Ford, U.S.N.R.
Producers:	Ford, Capt. George O'Brien, U.S.N. (retd.)
O'Brien	*Narration*

1959 *The Horse Soldiers* (Mirisch Company-United Artists)

Director:	John Ford
Producers-Scenarists:	John Lee Mahin, Martin Rackin, from novel by Harold Sinclair
Photography (in color):	William H. Clothier
Art Director:	Frank Hotaling
Set Decorator:	Victor Gangelin
Music:	David Buttolph
Song:	"I Left My Love," by Stan Jones
Editor:	Jack Murray
Assistant Directors:	Wingate Smith, Ray Gosnell, Jr.
John Wayne	*Col. John Marlowe*
William Holden	Maj. Hank Kendall
Constance Towers	Hannah Hunter
Althea Gibson	Lukey
Hoot Gibson	Brown
Anna Lee	Mrs. Buford
Russell Simpson	Sheriff Capt. Henry Goodboy
Stan Jones	Gen. U.S. Grant
Carleton Young	Col. Jonathan Miles
Basil Ruysdael	Commandant, Jefferson Military Academy
Willis Bouchey	Col. Phil Secord
Ken Curtis	Wilkie
O. Z. Whitehead	"Hoppy" Hopkins
Judson Pratt	Sgt. Maj. Kirby
Denver Pyle	Jagger Jo
Strother Martin	Virgil
Hank Worden	Deacon

Walter Reed .... Union officer
Jack Pennick .... Sgt. Maj. Mitchell
Fred Graham .... Union soldier
Chuck Hayward .... Union captain
Charles Seel .... Newton Station bartender
Stuart Holmes, Maj. Sam Harris .... Passengers to Newton Station
Richard Cutting .... Gen. Sherman
Bing Russell
William Forrest
William Leslie
Bill Henry
Ron Hagherty
Dan Borzage
Fred Kennedy

1960   *The Colter Craven Story* (Revue Productions; episode from the *Wagon Train* television series)

Director:	John Ford
Producer:	Howard Christie
Writer:	Tony Paulson
Photography:	Benjamin N. Kline
Art Director:	Martin Obzina
Set Decorator:	Ralph Sylos
Editors:	Marston Fay, David O'Connell

Ward Bond .... *Maj. Seth Adams*
Carleton Young .... Colter Craven
Frank McGrath .... Chuck Wooster
Terry Wilson .... Bill Hawks
John Carradine .... Park
Chuck Hayward .... Quentin
Ken Curtis .... Kyle
Anna Lee .... Alarice Craven
Cliff Lyons .... Creel
Paul Birch .... Sam Grant
Annelle Hayes .... Mrs. Grant
Willis Bouchey .... Jesse Grant
Mae Marsh .... Mrs. Jesse Grant
Jack Pennick .... Drill sergeant
Hank Worden .... Shelley
Charles Seel .... Mort
Bill Henry .... Krindle
Chuck Roberson .... Junior
Dennis Rush .... Jamie
Harry Tenbrook .... Shelley's friend
Beulah Blaze
Lon Chaney, Jr.
John Wayne (under pseudonym
    Michael Morris) .... Gen. Sherman

1960 *Sergeant Rutledge* (Ford Productions-Warner Bros.)

Director:	John Ford
Producers:	Patrick Ford, Willis Goldbeck
Writers:	Goldbeck, James Warner Bellah
Photography (in color):	Bert Glennon
Art Director:	Eddie Imazu
Set Decorator:	Frank M. Miller
Music:	Howard Jackson
Song:	"Captain Buffalo," by Mack David, Jerry Livingston
Editor:	Jack Murray
Assistant Directors:	Russ Saunders, Wingate Smith
Jeffrey Hunter	*Lt. Tom Cantrell*
Constance Towers	Mary Beecher
Woody Strode	Sgt. Braxton Rutledge
Billie Burke	Mrs. Cordelia Fosgate
Juano Hernandez	Sgt. Matthew Luke Skidmore
Willis Bouchey	Col. Otis Fosgate
Carleton Young	Capt. Shattuck
Judson Pratt	Lt. Mulqueen
Bill Henry	Capt. Dwyer
Walter Reed	Capt. MacAfee
Chuck Hayward	Capt. Dickinson
Mae Marsh	Nellie
Fred Libby	Chandler Hubble
Toby Richards	Lucy Dabney
Jan Styne	Chris Hubble
Cliff Lyons	Sam Beecher
Charles Seel	Dr. Eckner
Jack Pennick	Sergeant
Hank Worden	Laredo
Chuck Roberson	Juror
Eva Novak, Estelle Winwood	Spectators
Shug Fisher	Mr. Owens

1961 *Two Rode Together* (Ford-Shpetner Productions-Columbia)

Director:	John Ford
Producer:	Stan Shpetner
Scenarist:	Frank Nugent, from novel, *Comanche Captives*, by Will Cook
Photography (in color):	Charles Lawton, Jr.
Art Director:	Robert Peterson
Set Decorator:	James M. Crowe
Music:	George Duning
Editor:	Jack Murray
Assistant Director:	Wingate Smith
James Stewart	*Guthrie McCabe*
Richard Widmark	Lt. Jim Gary
Shirley Jones	Marty Purcell
Linda Cristal	Elena de la Madriaga

Andy Devine . . . . Sgt. Darius P. Posey
John McIntire . . . . Maj. Frazer
Paul Birch . . . . Edward Purcell
Willis Bouchey . . . . Harry J. Wringle
Henry Brandon . . . . Quanah Parker
Harry Carey, Jr. . . . . Ortho Clegg
Ken Curtis . . . . Greely Clegg
Olive Carey . . . . Abby Frazer
Chet Douglas . . . . Ward Corbey
Annelle Hayes . . . . Belle Aragon
David Kent . . . . Running Wolf
Anna Lee . . . . Mrs. Malaprop
Jeanette Nolan . . . . Mrs. McCandless
John Qualen . . . . Ole Knudsen
Ford Rainey . . . . Henry Clegg
Woody Strode . . . . Stone Calf
O. Z. Whitehead . . . . Lt. Chase
Cliff Lyons . . . . William McCandless
Mae Marsh . . . . Hannah Clegg
Frank Baker . . . . Capt. Malaprop
Ruth Clifford . . . . Woman
Ted Knight . . . . Lt. Upton
Maj. Sam Harris . . . . Post doctor
Jack Pennick . . . . Sergeant
Chuck Roberson . . . . Comanche
Dan Borzage
Bill Henry
Chuck Hayward
Edward Brophy

1962 *The Man Who Shot Liberty Valance* (Ford Productions-Paramount)

Director:	John Ford
Producer:	Willis Goldbeck
Scenarists:	Goldbeck, James Warner Bellah, from story by Dorothy M. Johnson
Photography:	William H. Clothier
Art Directors:	Hal Pereira, Eddie Imazu
Set Decorators:	Sam Comer, Darrell Silvera
Costumes:	Edith Head
Music:	Cyril J. Mockridge; theme from *Young Mr. Lincoln,* by Alfred Newman
Editor:	Otho Lovering
Assistant Director:	Wingate Smith

James Stewart . . . . *Ransom Stoddard*
John Wayne . . . . Tom Doniphon
Vera Miles . . . . Hallie Stoddard
Lee Marvin . . . . Liberty Valance
Edmond O'Brien . . . . Dutton Peabody
Andy Devine . . . . Link Appleyard
Ken Murray . . . . Doc Willoughby
John Carradine . . . . Starbuckle

(The Man Who Shot Liberty Valance, cont.)

Jeanette Nolan	Nora Ericson
John Qualen	Peter Ericson
Willis Bouchey	Jason Tully
Carleton Young	Maxwell Scott
Woody Strode	Pompey
Denver Pyle	Amos Carruthers
Strother Martin	Floyd
Lee Van Cleef	Reese
Robert F. Simon	Handy Strong
O. Z. Whitehead	Ben Carruthers
Paul Birch	Mayor Winder
Joseph Hoover	Hasbrouck
Jack Pennick	Barman
Anna Lee	Passenger
Charles Seel	President, Election Council
Shug Fisher	Drunk

Earle Hodgins
Stuart Holmes
Dorothy Phillips
Buddy Roosevelt
Gertrude Astor
Eva Novak
Slim Talbot
Monty Montana
Bill Henry
John B. Whiteford
Helen Gibson
Maj. Sam Harris

1962   *Flashing Spikes* (Avista Productions-Revue; episode for the *Alcoa Premiere* television series)

Director:	John Ford
Associate Producer:	Frank Baur
Scenarist:	Jameson Brewer, from novel by Frank O'Rourke
Photography:	William H. Clothier
Art Director:	Martin Obzina
Set Decorators:	John McCarthy, Martin C. Bradfield
Music:	Johnny Williams
Editors:	Richard Belding, Tony Martinelli
Titles:	Saul Bass
Series host:	Fred Astaire
James Stewart	*Slim Conway*
Jack Warden	Commissioner
Pat Wayne	Bill Riley
Edgar Buchanan	Crab Holcomb
Tige Andrews	Gaby Lasalle
Carleton Young	Rex Short
Willis Bouchey	Mayor
Don Drysdale	Gomer

Stephanie Hill . . . . Mary Riley
Charles Seel . . . . Judge
Bing Russell . . . . Hogan
Harry Carey, Jr. . . . . Man in dugout
Vin Scully . . . . Announcer
Walter Reed . . . . Second reporter
Sally Hughes . . . . Nurse
Larry Blake . . . . First reporter
Charles Morton . . . . Umpire
Cy Malis . . . . The bit man
Bill Henry . . . . Commissioner's assistant
John Wayne . . . . Drill sergeant in Korea
Art Passarella . . . . Umpire
Vern Stephens, Ralph Volkie, Earl
  Gilpin, Bud Harden, Whitey
  Campbell . . . . Baseball players

1962 *How the West Was Won* (Cinerama-Metro-Goldwyn-Mayer)

Directors: John Ford *(The Civil War)*, George
                                    Marshall *(The Railroad)*, Henry
                                    Hathaway *(The Rivers, The Plains,
                                    The Outlaws)*
Producer: Bernard Smith
Scenarist: James R. Webb, suggested by series
                                    in *Life*
Art Directors: George W. Davis, William Ferrari,
                                    Addison Hehr
Set Decorators: Henry Grace, Don Greenwood, Jr.,
                                    Jack Mills
Music: Alfred Newman, Ken Darby
Editor: Harold F. Kress
Narrator: Spencer Tracy
For the Ford sequence:
Photography (in color Cinerama and
  Ultra Panavision):   Joseph La Shelle
Assistant Director: Wingate Smith
John Wayne . . . . *Gen. William T. Sherman*
George Peppard . . . . Zeb Rawlings
Carroll Baker . . . . Eve Prescott
Henry (Harry) Morgan . . . . Gen. U.S. Grant
Andy Devine . . . . Cpl. Peterson
Russ Tamblyn . . . . Deserter
Willis Bouchey . . . . Surgeon
Claude Johnson . . . . Jeremiah Rawlings

1963 *Donovan's Reef* (Ford Productions-Paramount)

Director-producer: John Ford
Scenarists: Frank S. Nugent, James Edward
                                    Grant
Photography (in color):   William H. Clothier

(Donovan's Reef, cont.)

Art Directors:	Hal Pereira, Eddie Imazu
Set Decorators:	Sam Comer, Darrell Silvera
Costumes:	Edith Head
Music:	Cyril J. Mockridge
Editor:	Otho Lovering
Assistant Director:	Wingate Smith
John Wayne	*Michael Patrick "Guns" Donovan*
Lee Marvin	Thomas Aloysius "Boats" Gilhooley
Elizabeth Allen	Amelia Sarah Dedham
Jack Warden	Dr. William Dedham
Cesar Romero	Marquis Andre De Lage
Dorothy Lamour	Miss Lafleur
Jacqueline Malouf	Lelani Dedham
Mike Mazurki	Sgt. Menkowicz
Marcel Dalio	Father Cluzeot
Jon Fong	Mister Eu
Cheryline Lee	Sally Dedham
Tim Stafford	Luki Dedham
Carmen Estrabeau	Sister Gabrielle
Yvonne Peattie	Sister Matthew
Frank Baker	Capt. Martin
Edgar Buchanan	Boston notary
Pat Wayne	Navy lieutenant
Charles Seel	Grand Uncle Sedley Atterbury
Chuck Roberson	Festus
Mae Marsh, Maj. Sam Harris	Members of the family counsel
Dick Foran, Cliff Lyons	Officers

1964   *Cheyenne Autumn* (Ford-Smith Productions-Warner Bros.)

Director:	John Ford
Producer:	Bernard Smith
Scenarist:	James R. Webb, from book by Mari Sandoz
Photography (in color and Panavision):	William H. Clothier
Art Director:	Richard Day
Set Decorator:	Darrell Silvera
Associate Director:	Ray Kellogg
Music:	Alex North
Editor:	Otho Lovering
Sound Editor:	Francis E. Stahl
Assistant Directors:	Wingate Smith, Russ Saunders
Richard Widmark	*Capt. Thomas Archer*
Carroll Baker	Deborah Wright
James Stewart	Wyatt Earp
Edward G. Robinson	Secretary of the Interior Carl Schurz
Karl Malden	Capt. Wessels
Sal Mineo	Red Shirt
Dolores Del Rio	Spanish woman
Ricardo Montalban	Little Wolf

Gilbert Roland . . . . Dull Knife
Arthur Kennedy . . . . Doc Holliday
Patrick Wayne . . . . Second Lt. Scott
Elizabeth Allen . . . . Guinevere Plantagenet
John Carradine . . . . Maj. Jeff Blair
Victor Jory . . . . Tall Tree
Mike Mazurki . . . . Top Sgt. Stanislas Wichowsky
George O'Brien . . . . Maj. Braden
Sean McClory . . . . Dr. O'Carberry
Judson Pratt . . . . Mayor "Dog" Kelly
Carmen D'Antonio . . . . Pawnee woman
Ken Curtis . . . . Joe
Walter Baldwin . . . . Jeremy Wright
Shug Fisher . . . . Skinny
Nancy Hsueh . . . . Little Bird
Chuck Roberson . . . . Platoon sergeant
Harry Carey, Jr. . . . . Trooper Smith
Ben Johnson . . . . Trooper Plumtree
Jimmy O'Hara . . . . Trooper
Chuck Hayward . . . . Trooper
Lee Bradley . . . . Cheyenne
Frank Bradley . . . . Cheyenne
Walter Reed . . . . Lt. Peterson
Willis Bouchey . . . . Colonel
Carleton Young . . . . Aide to Carl Schurz
Denver Pyle . . . . Senator Henry
John Qualen . . . . Svenson
Nanomba "Moonbeam" Morton . . . . Running Deer
Dan Borzage, Dean Smith, David H.
   Miller, Bing Russell . . . . Troopers

1965 *Young Cassidy* (Sextant Films-Metro-Goldwyn-Mayer)
Directors: Jack Cardiff, John Ford (official
                                    credit: 'A John Ford Film')
Producers: Robert D. Graff, Robert Emmett
                                    Ginna, Jr.
Associate Producer: Michael Killanin
Scenarist: John Whiting, from autobiography,
                                    Mirror in My House, by Sean
                                    O'Casey
Photography (in color):   Ted Scaife
Art Director: Michael Stringer
Costumes: Margaret Furse
Music: Sean O'Riada
Editor: Anne V. Coates
Rod Taylor . . . . *Sean Cassidy*
Maggie Smith . . . . Nora
Julie Christie . . . . Daisy Battles
Flora Robson . . . . Mrs. Cassidy
Sian Phillips . . . . Ella
Michael Redgrave . . . . William Butler Yeats

(Young Cassidy, cont.)

Dame Edith Evans . . . . Lady Gregory
Jack MacGowran . . . . Archie
T. P. McKenna . . . . Tom
Julie Ross . . . . Sara
Robin Sumner . . . . Michael
Philip O'Flynn . . . . Mick Mullen
Pauline Delaney . . . . Bessie Ballynoy
Arthur O'Sullivan . . . . Foreman
Tom Irwin . . . . Constable
John Cowley . . . . Barman
William Foley . . . . Publisher's clerk
John Franklyn . . . . Bank teller
Harry Brogan . . . . Murphy
James Fitzgerald . . . . Charlie Ballynoy
Donal Donnelly . . . . Undertaker's man
Harold Goldblatt . . . . Director of Abbey Theatre
Ronald Ibbs . . . . Theatre employee
May Craig, May Cluskey . . . . Women in the hall
Tom Irwin
Shivaun O'Casey
Members of the Abbey Theatre

1966 *Seven Women* (Ford-Smith Productions-Metro-Goldwyn-Mayer)

Director: John Ford
Producer: Bernard Smith
Scenarist: Janet Green, John McCormick, from
                                   story, "Chinese Finale," by Norah
                                   Lofts

Photography (in color and
  Panavision):   Joseph La Shelle
Art Directors: George W. Davis, Eddie Imazu
Set Decorators: Henry Grace, Jack Mills
Costumes: Walter Plunkett
Music: Elmer Bernstein
Editor: Otho Lovering
Assistant Director: Wingate Smith
Anne Bancroft . . . . *Dr. D.R. Cartwright*
Sue Lyon . . . . Emma Clark
Margaret Leighton . . . . Agatha Andrews
Flora Robson . . . . Miss Binns
Mildred Dunnock . . . . Jane Argent
Betty Field . . . . Florrie Pether
Anna Lee . . . . Mrs. Russell
Eddie Albert . . . . Charles Pether
Mike Mazurki . . . . Tunga Khan
Woody Strode . . . . Lean Warrior
Jane Chang . . . . Miss Ling
Hans William Lee . . . . Kim
H.W. Gim . . . . Coolie
Irene Tsu . . . . Chinese girl

1970   *Chesty: A Tribute To a Legend*

Director: John Ford
Producer: James Ellsworth
Photography: Brick Marquard
John Wayne

1971   *Vietnam! Vietnam!* (U.S.I.A.)

Director: Sherman Beck
Executive Producer: John Ford

Without credit, Ford directed sequences in *Silver Wings* (1922), *The Adventures of Marco Polo* (1938), *Pinky* (1949), *Hondo* (1953), and *The Alamo* (1960). He has a co-producer's credit on *Mighty Joe Young* (1949) and he helped edit *The Bullfighter and the Lady* (1951). He also acted himself three times at the end of his life in Mark Haggard's *John Ford: Memorial Day 1970*, Peter Bogdanovich's *Directed By John Ford* (1971), and Denis Sanders's *The American West of John Ford* (1971).

Index